to: Rose,

Thank you for kindness & support.

The Keepers and The Caged

Heroes and Necromancers in the Prison System Today

Blessings,

Jean Marie Christenson
P.O. Box 5451
Wenatchee, WA 98807-5451

Jean Marie Christenson
8.9.00

KENDALL/HUNT PUBLISHING COMPANY
4050 Westmark Drive Dubuque, Iowa 52002

This edition has been printed directly from camera-ready copy.

ISBN 0-7872-2066-3

Library of Congress Catalog Card Number: 96-75380

Printed in the United States of America
10 9 8 7 6 5 4 3 2 1

Dedicated to My Son,
My Wise Counsel

William Hamilton Christenson

What is happening in the prison system in the state of Washington is happening in every state in the country.

The public does not know the truth.

After reading THE KEEPERS AND THE CAGED, they will.

Must the hunger
become anger
and the anger
become fury
before anything will be done?

John Steinbeck

Contents

SECTION FOUR:
What About God?

SECTION FIVE:
Are There Solutions to the Problems We Are Facing Today?

Introduction

Dear Friends,

When I first walked into Washington State Reformatory, I came as a volunteer counselor and personal growth teacher. I was completely ignorant about what went on inside the adult prison system. One of the first questions I asked a prisoner was, "Where did you get those clothes, and why aren't you wearing a striped uniform?" I am the perfect person to write a book of questions on the topic of adult corrections because I clearly did not know. What I have come to realize is most of the American public is in the same boat as I was.

I was curious and fascinated by what I saw and heard. I wondered what causes a criminal to think the way he does, or why one human being would kill, rob or rape another. I wondered why it seems the tougher we get on crime, the more crime we have. And I was curious to find out if the people we have locked up in our prison system are really human at all.

As time passed, I began to realize that what I was learning was important and needed to be made available to others. It is my hope that reading this book will help the public understand both how those who commit the crimes and those who are affected by them reason and make decisions.

THE KEEPERS AND THE CAGED is one step in a journey of huge proportion to create an understanding between all people.

> "This is our town, but it is like any town filled with voices crying out to be heard though a cloud of fear and confusion, attempting to bring clarity to a volatile subject. Each voice adds a sound that screams, 'We are all human.' And leaves the conclusion to the reader."
>
> Jean Marie Christenson

I acknowledge the courage it took for the people I have interviewed to come forth with their truth. I spoke to those willing to speak, those whose message was considered more important to them then any selfish interest. It is from their courage I gathered the strength to see this project through. For those who could not be interviewed for this book, I am sure they too will be inspired to come forth the next time, and together we will take incremental steps to help dissipate strong holds of fear, hate, and ignorance.

The subject matter covered in THE KEEPERS AND THE CAGED relates to life in the prison system, but that is just a microcosm of a world in which we all live. If we think we are safe because there is a wall around what we do not want to look at, then we have fallen into the Darkest Angel's trap and will suffer the consequences of our own ignorance.

THE KEEPERS AND THE CAGED holds a hopeful message: It is not too late to wake up; there are solutions to our most nagging dilemmas; and, in spite of any evidence to the contrary, it is within the very problem that we will find these solutions. "We" hold the keys to our tomorrow. "We" are THE KEEPERS AND THE CAGED.

Freedom,

Jean Marie Christenson

Section One

What About the System? How Is It? How Was It?

Chase Riveland

My name is Jean Marie Christenson, and I'm in the office of Chase Riveland. I'm going to be interviewing you today, Mr. Riveland, for a book. Perhaps you can just tell us who you are, in connection with the Department of Corrections, and speak a little bit about yourself.

I'm the Secretary of the Department of Corrections, and I have held that position a little over eight years, having come here from Colorado, where I had a similar position; and prior to that, from Wisconsin, where I had been in the correctional system for about 19 years.

The head of the Department of Corrections. Can you give me an overview of what that means? What do you direct?

Well, the Secretary of the Department of Corrections is appointed by, and serves at the pleasure of, the governor and is responsible for the administration of the agency as well as directing the policies in the criminal justice area on behalf of the governor. In terms of the department, that includes the administration of six divisions: Division of Prisons, the Division of Community Corrections, the Division of Correctional Industries, the Division of Management and Budget, the Division of Human Resources, and the Division of Offender Programs. Directors of those divisions, as well as several other people, form the executive staff of the Department and are responsible for the day-to-day operations of the Department of Corrections, predominantly found in the two major field organizations: Prisons, which has 13 facilities, and Community Corrections, which has 17 facilities, including work release and pre-release, as well as 66 offices around the state.

And you supervise all of that?

Well, in effect. I supervise the people that supervise all of that, yes.

I see. And then you report directly to the governor?

I report to the governor; that's correct.

You hold a significant position. Perhaps you can share with us your philosophy in regard to corrections?

I think corrections is a business of challenges. It's a business of challenges provided by all of our customers, whether they're residents in our institutions or staff that we work with, communities that we serve, the court system that we serve, and the responsibilities we have to the people of the state of Washington.

Challenges, I think, also present themselves because of the legal pressures that are placed on corrections. It doesn't get to choose its clientele; it takes whoever comes through its gates or doors and yet has a responsibility to try to deal with a population of people who have been through some very difficult times themselves and frequently not had opportunities that many people in this country have had; or have frequently presented themselves as persons who have been abused, or chronically addictive, or have deficits in their skills or education. In many instances, they are mentally ill and present a whole host of problems that present real challenges for people who run unnatural places. Certainly in the domains of our institutions, it is a very unnatural place. We have a responsibility for large numbers of people, for their daily care and feeding, as well as trying to prepare them for a better life, whether that life is going to be in the institution forever or a long time, or whether that life is going to be back in the community.

Frequently, a major challenge in the institutional setting is trying to do that with a population that frequently doesn't want that done for, or to, or with them. It further exaggerates challenges because the community itself frequently has few advocates for the benefit of the people who are incarcerated.

On the flip side, an important part of my philosophy is the system. It's a continuum. It's a continuum of supervision in the community; it's a continuum of pre-sentence investigation; it's a continuum of trying to keep people out of institutions rather than getting them in, and then, with having to deal with them in an incarcerated setting. So, one of the challenges that frequently is less seen is the involvement that many of us have in the policies of the state regarding incarceration, as to who should be there and how long and why, and who should not. And that presents probably one of the biggest challenges these days.

How much influence do you have in those decisions--you, personally, in your role as the head of the department?

Well, it varies from time to time. Certainly I have my own agendas that I try to run, and I have to be consistent with whoever the governor is at the time. I certainly work closely with the legislature, trying to influence either an opposition to some policy issues as well as to support some. And I think that varies. At times we're very successful in influencing a policy, and sometimes we're absolutely failures.

You mentioned that we have incarcerated a really wide variety of people and great numbers of people. About how many people are incarcerated in this state, would you say?

At the moment, we have about---almost 11,000.

Eleven thousand people incarcerated. And some percentage of those people are separated from various stages of mental illness?
We would make an estimate that at any given point in time, we have somewhere between 10 and 15% of the population that would present themselves as being clinically mentally ill. It's very difficult because some came to us mentally ill, and some have become mentally ill since they've been with us.
You said people come to you with mental illness, and some become mentally ill once incarcerated. Can you just expand on that, "becoming mentally ill once incarcerated"?
Well, I suspect in many instances it's people that have had predispositions. And again, mental illness covers a wide range of things. But, for example, depression. I have little doubt that if I were to be locked up in a small cell most of my life, with little hope, that I would suffer from depression. And that, of course, depending on its severity, can qualify somebody for that. And so people who may not have had clinical diagnoses of mental illness prior to incarceration certainly can suffer from depression and other kinds of illness after their arrival. And there are instances, of course, where people have traumatic things happen. They're incarcerated and their loved ones die; or they're divorced, one of the challenges that is difficult for them to deal with because they are so powerless when they're in a prison, powerless to deal with being able to be helpful. And I think there are many folks who, since the de-institutionalization of mental hospitals, are thrust into the criminal justice system simply because the communities don't know what to do with them otherwise. And one of the faster ways is to find them guilty of criminal behavior even though they're presenting problems that may actually be underlying mental illness.
In that regard, do you believe in treatment?
Well, I think it's not even a matter solely of belief, although I do. It's a matter that we have a responsibility to deal with people as best we can. Obviously we have limited resources to do that.... Treatment in a prison setting is a very difficult thing to do sometimes because the pressures and the characteristics that may contribute to that mental illness may be exaggerated in the prison setting, rather than having a normative setting where you can try to deal with those characteristics or symptoms, as the case may be. So yeah, we do our best.
I've read some things that you've written, and one that stands out in my mind is describing "Three Strikes You're Out" as "drive-by legislation." I thought that was a creative thing for you to say.
Or stupid, as the case may be.
I don't know. I thought it was courageous.
Regarding "Three Strikes and You're Out", I was asked by an editorial writer, "What do you think about that?" The law prohibited appointed people from talking about it, so I said, "We're neither for nor against that stupid legislation."

And, to some degree, I guess, the problem is not that some people that support things like that may not be well-intended, but the reality of the political rhetoric in recent years, both as exemplified in "Three Strikes and You're Out" laws, the Federal Crime Bill, things like boot camps, is that there are a lot of promises being made that if we do those kinds of things, crime will go down, or be solved, or fixed, or whatever. And the reality is we know that that's not accurate. We know that those symbolic kinds of things don't get the job done, that they don't make people safer, and that, in fact, it may give them a false sense of security. What we'll end up with with "Three Strikes and You're Out" is a number of people who will reach an age at which they probably no longer would have criminal behavior anyway but will still continue to pay for it.

But of even more concern to me is that we'll give this false sense of security that something has been done to make our communities and our people safe. And at great cost, we'll find out that's not true. In my opinion, the entire Federal Crime Bill fits that same mold. It's a bunch of rhetoric from a bunch of people wanting to be elected, or re-elected, who are trying to play to the media to give the impression that they were doing something meaningful. And I can see very little--very, very little--in the entire crime bill that's going to really make a difference in terms of making our communities safer.

It does seem like we are building prisons as fast as we can and then filling them as fast as we build them. What is your insight into the future of this situation?

Well, I think there will be a point in time, maybe for the wrong reason, that will come to a halt. We're going to be up against the wall. We have a cap on resources--financial resources--but a continuing major growth in correctional needs. And what will happen is if we don't deal with that whole issue from a policy perspective, we'll start eroding the resources of every other need the government provides, whether it's the environment, K through 12, higher education, health needs and others. Hopefully, if for no other reason, lawmakers eventually will get to the point that they'll say enough is enough, and I think that's going to happen at the federal level also at some point in time. I say that's for the wrong reason because it would be delightful if people could have a rational debate about crime and could sit at the table with an environment that allows them to look at the valid facts of what it is we're doing, who it is we need to incarcerate, and what we need to do for those that we don't.

And I think that one of the problems we have is we incarcerate two kinds of people now. We incarcerate those that we're physically afraid of and then we incarcerate those we're just mad at.

What category of crimes would that be--"mad at"?

Drugs--drug dealers, drug addicts, non-violent property crimes, and there's a whole series of things like that. Sometimes they're even victimless, and those are people we get kind of mad at. They don't behave like we do, and the image they present on television or in the newspapers is so different from what we want the world to be that we say, "We'll get them out of here and lock them up."

What is your suggestion to do with those people? If we don't lock them up, what are we going to do?

Well, I think what we don't want to get ourselves into is to think that there's categorical responses that are going to cure things. That's the mistake we made under the Medical Rehabilitation Law, that we're going to provide treatment to everybody and then many will get cured, and we found that fell apart. What we need to be is selective in our response to individuals. We do know some things work.

We do know that persons who have addictions to drug and alcohol--if they're provided with treatment and monitoring, both in-patient and out-patient ... it may not make them wonderful people, it may not make them happy people, but it reduces significantly their involvement in criminal behavior, including drug dealing. And I don't think the corrections system need be responsible for happiness. It does need to be responsible for assisting in reducing criminal behavior, and that we can do with drug treatment and do it best in the community. The pressures that get people into addictions are greatest in their neighborhood, or their home, or their community, and that's where it needs to be dealt with, not in some cell that is 300 miles away, where the pressures are not the same that they're going to have to face on a daily basis.

We do know that there are other kinds of things, that there are some people involved in crime because they are--they're illiterate, they're unskilled, and we can identify them, and we can provide those kinds of opportunities for them. There are some people we can't deal with. There are some people we need to incarcerate because they're dangerous and predatory, and we do that very well.

Thank you. So that covers the people we're angry at. Now, the people we need to incarcerate?

Well, we have folks who are redundantly predatory, both sex offenders as well as violent offenders, and clearly I have no qualms that the community needs to be protected from some people like that. We're casting nets today, saying we're going to take huge numbers of people, hoping that we're catching the few that we're afraid of, and we're not sure if we're doing that. What we do know is that incarceration rates and crime rates have very little relevance together, and if we really want to reduce crime, other than the people we're afraid of, we need to re-think that on a rational basis.

If we really want to reduce crime, what are we going to think? What are some solutions to this?

I'm not sure the solutions can be mine. I think they have to be community solutions, and that people have to figure out the tolerance levels of given communities, and some are not going to be the same as others.

It's ironic, when we look back to colonial times, what people did for punishment when there was a sense of community. The worst punishments included things that embarrassed you in front of your community. They put you in stocks, or they dump you in a pool, or they tie something around your neck or around your head, or they stitch a letter on your clothing. And embarrassment was a major punishment because people thought they were part of communities, and one of the worst things that could happen to you was that you be banished from your community and not allowed to return to it.

Today we use the out-of-sight, out-of-mind method. We send you off somewhere where you, quite honestly, don't have to face the admonishment that your own community or neighborhood may give you. In fact, we almost make it, for many inner city neighborhoods, a graduate school for people, and there's no embarrassment at all in being sent to prison.

I think we have to figure out ways to reshuffle those values. Obviously, one of the big drivers that we have to deal with is the whole drug issue. But again, communities have to make choices. Is their goal decriminalization or treatment, incarceration for some, or what is the mix of all that? At the moment we aren't really looking at much of that at all. We're simply saying incarceration is the solution.

Can you talk to me a little bit about the costs involved in incarcerating people?

Incarcerating people is expensive.

And that's...?

Oh, you wanted more?

Well, I don't know. Can you talk to me more about it?

We know that we build one cell today, and that cell costs on an average of $45,000. Then we look out 30 years for that one cell or one bed, and we take into consideration the debt service, and the operating costs of the staffing and programming, and everything else; that's a million-dollar cell at the end of 30 years. People sort of hone in on what they would like to see out of that.

But if we look at simply the constitutional requirements that we have to meet, such as medical services, adequate food, recreation, access to law libraries, or legal access, and a range of other kinds of minimal legal requirements, there probably is no way to get a cost below $20,000 to $22,000 a year in the state of Washington, on the average. Obviously, in some instances, the people in units for mentally ill ranges up to maybe $90,000 a year.

But the reality is, we're running little cities now. Some of our prisons are 2,000 and more inmates, several hundred staff, several hundred visitors and volunteers coming in on a daily basis, and so our communities, if you call them that, are exceeding, on some days, 3,000 to 4,000 people, and we have to provide 24-hour-a-day, 7-day care for all of those people that we touch in those days. So it's no wonder that it's a very expensive proposition.

What we're seeing now is the rhetoric that, well, the way to deal with all this cost is we'll nibble at the fringes. We'll get rid of televisions; we'll get rid of weight rooms; we'll get rid of whatever. The reality is that 85% of our costs are staff or contractual responsibilities, and a good 12 or 13% of the remaining cost is constitutionally demanded by any federal court.

So what people are really doing is politically nibbling at the fringes; they're not talking about saving any real money at all. The real money to be saved is by changing the law. The way to save money is not put so many people in prison.

Talk to me a little bit about boot camp; what that is, and how you feel about that?

I guess, in the short form, I think boot camps are one of those fluffy, stupid things that people came up with because they were politically attractive, and despite the fact we now have pretty good research that most, if not all, of them have little impact; that in some cases they simply incarcerate more people and have higher recidivism rates, and they're continuing to proliferate throughout the country. And I think the belief that one can use the military model to change behavior in 90 days is rather naive in some cases, in the best cases of its supporters, and stupid in the incidence of many others.

Even if one takes the military model and looks at it extensively, we find that people going into military boot camps, and I was one of those, go through a period of time when you are indeed sort of reduced to the norm and made to feel that you're not a unique individual. But the other thing that the military did is they then followed that short period of time of discipline, both physical and mental discipline, with vocational training. That could be to be a jet fighter pilot, to be a soldier, to be a truck driver, to be whatever it was, but a skill was imparted to people. And then people for two or three, or sometimes 20 or 30 years, were placed in an environment where they used that skill. They were given a job, they were rewarded, both through financial rewards, through medals, through promotions, through all kinds of things, to put those things into place. And the whole thing is an environment that reinforced those things.

Most boot camps around the country simply do the part of discipline and harassment and then think, "Boy, that's cheap and that's a nice way, and maybe Johnny will be different in ninety days." Then they put Johnny or Judy back on the block with the same influences and nothing has changed--no skill development, no job offers, no rewards for good behavior, just simply more of the same.

I think it is extremely naive of us to believe that we can be successful in any sense and, in my opinion, that's one of those things that politically has put the public to sleep, believing that something positive is happening, and the reality is almost nothing is.

In this state, we did something a little bit different. The legislature wanted a boot camp. We basically said, "No, we're not going to do anything military." We created a work ethic camp. We do put people through work training and skill training in a brief period of time. There is no harassment, and a little piece of the law that was passed said that the Secretary of Corrections may consider a military overlay. I called the sponsor probably one day after the bill was passed and said, "I have considered that, and we're not going to do it."

We're taking a much different approach to that kind of concept, and we hope we can have some impact on work skills, on confidence, on self-esteem, but don't have to gain that through harassment.

It seems like these days there's more of a tendency to be trying youth as adults and then placing the convicted youth in adult facilities. Can you speak to that issue?

Well, I like to say that we've already locked up all the people between 18 and 26, and now we have to get down further to find eligible candidates for incarceration. And, in fact, the next phase we're going to try is we're going to grow our own. We're going to just have babies in prisons and grow them up as inmates. Then we don't have to go through the arrest, and the conviction, and the trial, and all that stuff. We'll just have nicely trained designer inmates.

But the reality is, I think, it's just a continuation of this rhetoric that's existed around "We'll solve all the problems, and drugs, and crime, and violence, and fear, homelessness, and mental illness, with incarceration." And what we've really run into now is the baby boom echo. It's no surprise that when we get large piles of kids that are from 15 to 22, your crime rate's going to go up.... Every time the country has had the demographics for that age group, the adverse age group has increased, our crime rate goes up and, "Voila," what a surprise that some people are active in that kind of thing. And that's a big piece of what's happening to us right now, along with the drug phenomena. If we wanted to do absolutely nothing, except wait until the baby boom echo was gone, we'd see our crime rate go down.

But, in the meantime, it's politically correct to say, "We've been locking all these people up; we're afraid of something; we're afraid of youth violence. So, let's move it down a little bit and we'll lock them up, too." And it's a sad commentary, because you hear other rhetoric that people say, for example, "Let's throw this generation away, and start thinking about the new one." That's unfortunate. That's an unfortunate attitude for people in this country to have.

How do you feel about the conditions in our state's prisons?

In general, I think they're good, considering the fact that we're overcrowded and congested in every facility that we have. I think they're safe; I think we're in control of them; I think we have a very professional staff that are consistent, which is a big part of what we do. I think that, for the most part, our staff are very sensitive, both to the needs of inmates as well as the community, and to the needs of other staff. I think the services we provide, in general, although we'd like to have more, are pretty well provided, and there are some excellent educational programs throughout the system that are equal to those provided in the community. We could always use more of each of those kinds of things, but, for the most part, I think Washington has been a bit blessed, creating pretty good environments and solid programs as well as solid security, which is critical.

Having said that, one of the problems that we've gone through for a number of years is overcrowding. We can't get new facilities on-line fast enough to relieve the overcrowding. And the overcrowding itself hasn't presented us with major problems, but it does for individual inmates. What it does mean is that there's not enough legitimate work assignments, industry assignments particularly. We frequently run short on availability of academic and vocational educational spaces, and I think it creates a stressful situation for both staff and inmates. Having said that, we're probably better off than much of the country, and there are many systems across the country that suffer both from more overcrowding, or the same or less overcrowding, but with less resources than we have. So, at this point in time, the important thing is that we control the institutions, which is an absolute first step. Then you can do more. It's important we also have a very strong community correction system that both helps keep some people from coming in, as well as provides good supervision and assistance on the way out.

Did you say community corrections?

Yes. We probably put a higher percentage of our population in work release and pre-release than any system. 10% of our population on any given day (10,000 or 11,000 people) are in community corrections on their way out, either in pre-release facilities or work-release facilities. Another 3,000 are in minimum security camps. If you pile that together, I doubt if there's any system in the country that has that percentage of the population in lower security facilities.

Last week I read an article, "Must Our Prisons be Resorts?" I think that there is sort of a feeling by some that inmates may be living a better life than a lot of the population is. Will you speak to that?

The first part is if any part of the population is living at a lower level than inmates do, then we should bring them up. That would be the first part of my reaction to that, which, I think, is not the solution that normally is presented. It's "Let's bring the level of inmates down." First of all, the purpose for being in prison, the punishment statement, is that incarceration or imprisonment in and of itself is the punishment. We're not supposed to find additional punishment to throw on them. First of all, most of our physical facilities, much of the staffing for our recreation programs, are paid for, not out of taxpayers' funds, but out of the inmate welfare fund, which is gathered both from our vending machines, as well as our telephone system.

The other part is, many of those things are good security. In a situation where there is overcrowding--there are not enough jobs, or not adequate education sign-ups for people--there still is the ability for people to use recreation. Like all of us, if you get people tired, they're less likely to be troublesome; and it's one of the few things we have available to occupy the time of people until we can get them into either educational or other assignments. And the third part is there's a certain level of all of that that would be required by the courts. Any system that tries to lock large numbers of populations down, without programming, would be in federal court really quickly.

Could you tell me about extended family visits?

Yeah. I think it's probably one of the best behavior controls that there is in the system. We do have family visiting at all of our facilities. I think people frequently think only spouses participate in family visiting, but it very frequently involves the children of families as well; and sometimes it's not a spouse at all, but grandpa and grandma, and aunts and uncles, and anybody that's a relative either through blood or marriage that is approved. It's not infrequent that grandpa and grandma come from many miles, stay for the weekend with Johnny or Judy. And the important thing of that is, I think, really two-fold. One, it retains a connection that the inmate has with the outside world, and that's important, so that they aren't over-affected by unnaturalness of the inside world. But secondly, one thing we know is inmates being released that have strong family ties, either through marriage or through relationships with their own relatives and their support system, are much more likely to be influenced to make it than those that do not.

On a security perspective, one thing we find is that people who are eligible for, and participate in, family visiting have much fewer infractions or disciplinary problems while they're in the institution because they know if they get into disciplinary trouble, they lose their rights to that program. And seldom do we have people getting infractions who are participating in that program. So we see it is a major security boost also.

How do you perceive the role of women interacting within the system?

Well, in male institutions, it's not that long ago that women's staff presence was recognized. One doesn't have to go back 12, 14 years, and you find few, if any, women working in male institutions, at least as custody people or in direct contact with inmates. That's radically changed over the years, and for the most part, that's been healthy in several ways. One, I think that we notice that when women are in direct contact with inmates (custody staff, particularly), behavior changes for the better. It creates a more natural setting to have women in the environment, and we generally see a behavior change. The language is cleaner for the most part.

In terms of wives, again, I think that wives are normally a stabilizing influence, assuming that they're staying in contact with the male inmate, both while the individual is in the institution, as well as when a person leaves.

Can you give me an idea of what the difference is in dealing with administrating an

adult male institution versus a female institution? Are there differences, or are they basically the same?

Yes, I think there are differences. Actually, we've had three versions. We've had male institutions, female institutions, and coed institutions, and there are, obviously, differences between them all. At least in my experience, some of the differences in women's institutions are that normally the custody needs aren't as great for two reasons. One, most women come to us not because of violent and predatory behavior. They come to us frequently for drug behavior and other kinds of behavior that may be self-destructive behavior, but not necessarily violent against other people. The custody needs or the security needs are normally not as great in women's facilities as in male facilities. The other part is that, whether real or not, the community doesn't envision them as being as dangerous as the male offenders. If I filled an institution up with a hundred female murderers, and they had another institution of a hundred male burglars, the fears in the neighborhood would probably be greater around the male institution than the female. So there's generally a bit more flexibility.

The difficult factor is that women's populations traditionally have been much smaller; and therefore, trying to replicate the same degree of programming for women's institutions is difficult just from a research perspective. That's traditionally true, I think, and women have frequently been short-changed because of that. There are a lot of different kinds of needs around self-esteem, around medical procedures, around parenting programs, and other kinds of things that non-traditional vocational programming can prepare them differently than they traditionally have been. So the challenges are always kind of interesting between the two. From my perspective, what is not very healthy are coed institutions, and we've run several. For the most part, I don't want to be stereotypical, but to some degree, it's pretty true: There's a lot of co-dependency issues that exist in women's populations, and male inmates frequently hit upon people who have those co-dependency needs and aren't necessarily healthy role models. So, what we hoped might be a healthy environment, I'm afraid, too frequently, we found to be not too healthy an environment, particularly for the women inmates in a coed situation.

Have you been involved in any history of riots? Why do they occur, and how can we prevent them?

Well, they occur for just all kinds of reasons. It can be something that's endemic or conditions have been such for a long period of time that inmates respond to that. Normally, when that happens, there are typically some strong leaders who are able to influence a large part of an inmate population in a given facility to react to something. It can happen over a situational thing, instances where a rumor starts that something happened to an inmate and that a certain staff member may have been involved. It may be completely conjecture, but it spreads very quickly and people react. And the same kind of thing happens in our communities--that there's something over a long period of time forcing people to react, or a crisis situation that gets people hot and uncontrollable with the leadership in front of them.

We haven't had a major "riot" in the state in quite some period of time. We've had some incidents within yards. We've had some shots fired. We've had smaller incidents, but nothing major, and again, I attribute that to the sensitivity that our staff has. I think our staff spend a lot of their time when potential situations do start brewing. People from the administrative level in institutions on down know that their job is to get out and talk, find out what the problem is, and try to find legitimate solutions to that problem. So when we hear that there's a problem, we just move staff out into the population quickly or into the program areas, and people start talking. Typically we find that allows us to deal with whatever the perception of the issue is or to figure out, in some cases, how we're going to forcefully control it.

Is there anything that you would like to cover that I have not asked you about?

I think one of the things that's sometimes harmful when we talk about corrections is we think of prisons, and one of the important things in correctional systems is to get balanced systems where the field part of what we do, the community corrections part of what do, is considered as important, if not more important, than what happens in prisons. We probably don't have enough public education about the community corrections part of what we do, and any correctional system that's going to be worth its salt needs both parts of those and some sense of equilibrium and balance, both for the safety of the community, as well as for the best interests of those who are convicted of crimes in our criminal justice system.

I want to thank you very much for your time today.

Well, it's a fun state to work in, a good place to be.

Bob

Bob, are you aware that this conversation is being tape-recorded?
Yes, ma'am.
Bob, what is your association with the Department of Corrections?
I'm a prisoner.
And how did you earn that title?
I committed second degree murder.
Can you tell me what that is?
Second degree murder is a murder that may not have been premeditated or planned. It just happened.
And how long have you been incarcerated?
Six years.
Six years?
Six years.
And where have you done most of your time?
Walla Walla, Washington.
Can you talk to me a little bit about Walla Walla and your time there?
Yeah, it sucks, to put it bluntly. It's oppressive; it's degrading; the cops have total control over there now. There's no programming; there's no clubs or self-help programs, like go on here at Washington State Reformatory in Monroe.
You're locked down most of the time. There's very little work. Your yard is scheduled for you and preplanned. Everything's done on a quadrant system, so if somebody else was on, let's say Six Wing side, and I'm on Eight Wing side, you never really have a chance to see anybody or interact. They basically have total control of the joint.
Why did that happen? It didn't always used to be that way.
No, that came about because of, I think, the '79 riots and then the riot in '81, where

the inmates had control of the prison, and through the riots, and different violent situations that happened over there, you got three or four guys getting stabbed a week to dying and all kinds of assaults going on. It led up to these riots, and then the cops got total control.

Now that they are in total control, the pendulum's swung back the other way, and it's the cops' turn to be brutal and oppressive and violent. And that went on for a period of time, and now it's just kind of at a state where it's just controlled.

You were saying how many people got stabbed every week?

Oh, I'd venture to say three or four guys a week got stabbed.

Okay, now you're talking about other prisoners?

Right. Other prisoners.

How could this go on? Why wasn't it stopped?

They couldn't stop it. There was no way to stop it. In fact, the prosecutor downtown said, "Don't send any more of these murder suspects down here, or assault suspects, unless one of your guards have actually witnessed the stabbing, because I'm not going to hear any more of them. They're not going to come before me." It was that prevalent.

Okay. You used some terminology here, Bob, and I'd like to just ask you to define it if you would.

Sure.

You used the term "locked down." Then you discussed there's no work over there, or very little work over there. And maybe you could talk about the work that happens inside prisons for prisoners.

Okay.

And then you talked about a yard. What's a yard?

Okay, lock-down is if you're at Walla Walla doing time, you're locked in your cell probably an average of 20 hours a day, total lock-down, with anywhere from three to four men in a cell. The only time you'll get out is for meals, or if you have a medical call-out, or an appointment to see somebody, or if you have your yard time. And that's when you go to recreation. That's what I meant by "yard." That could be either going to the library, or going to the gym, or going to yard. The times switch every other day. So if you have afternoon yard one day, you may go out to yard from 12:30 to 3:30. Well, that's the only time you're going to get out of your house that day, besides your meals. And when they're running Eight Wing side for afternoon yard, they're running Six Wing side for evening yard. And that's from 6:30 to 8:20.

Okay. When you say you're locked down, you're in your cell 20 hours a day with maybe four people?

Absolutely.

How large are those cells? What are the conditions?
Ten by fourteen, double bunk beds and real crowded. Real crowded. If you're in with two or three people you know, or you're in with some partners, that's fine. But coming into the joint and not knowing anybody or being a youngster, and them putting you in a house with maybe two or three guys that are doing life without, and then if you're young, you may run the risk of getting put in a house with a predator. And you're basically on your own.
And what would happen to that youngster?
Well, he might get extorted for money. He might get his property taken. He might get threatened with bodily harm, and he might get broke down and punked out. He might be pressured into sexual favors.
I see. And that's what you mean by broke down and---?
Punked out.
Punked out?
Right.
I see. Okay. So what can he do about that? Let's say that a young man does come into the institution, and he doesn't want to get punked out?
Well, if a young kid comes in the institution and he carries himself well, and I believe he's got an honorable crime, so he doesn't already have some type of sex beef or molestation charge, and people are trying to prey on him, or the predators are on him, if he stands up for himself and says, "No!" and sticks to his guns and fights back, win or lose, people that are about something are going to take notice of that and maybe take him under his wing or stand up for him because they seen that he had some heart and stood up for himself. They might go as far as going to the people and telling them to back off or whatever.
But if the kid doesn't stand up for himself and show some heart, he's probably going to be left on his own, however he can deal with it. And he can deal with it by breaking down, or wait until they go to sleep and dealing with it whichever way he can.
Okay. When you used the phrase "people who are about something," are you talking about convicts?
Yes, ma'am. Yes, ma'am.
Talk to me about convicts.
Convicts. Convicts are people that do their own time, that mind their own business, that don't rat or inform. Convicts are people that will stand together for a common cause. And a convict is somebody who, in my opinion, has an honorable beef.
Okay. And what's an "honorable beef"?
Oh, I don't want to sound like murder's honorable, but it's kind of looked at that way in the system. You have a pecking order. And I'd say your honorable beefs could be

bank robberies or robberies--I don't have too much respect for burglars or thieves, even though that's their own thing--assaults of some sort. But the bottom of your pecking order is going to be your snitches, your informants, your child molesters and your rapists.

And those people do not have honorable beefs?

Oh, absolutely not.

Okay. So they're going to have a harder time in prison, maybe?

Well, every prison but here at Monroe. At Walla Walla, they have a protective custody unit, and when you come up to Walla Walla, they'll ask you if you desire protective custody. And, that'll--maybe your crime dictates you've raped or molested a bunch of women or kids or whatever, you got some real sick -- sick, senseless murders, well, chances are you may check into PC.

If you have informed on somebody or ratted on somebody for violence of drugs or extortion, you'll probably check into PC. If you have trouble paying a gambling debt, if you get into the card tables or the gambling, and you've run up a bill and you can't pay, you may check into PC.

Monroe doesn't have a PC, as such, like Walla Walla.

Now at Walla Walla, the protective custody unit, is that a whole wing?

It's a whole wing.

Oh.

It's a whole wing to itself. Five Wing.

I see. And so are these people let out to yard at different times?

Oh, absolutely.

They're kept separately?

Yeah, they're totally kept separate from population. Anytime there's a Five Wing movement, and if we were out and about moving somewhere, we'd be locked up or told to go behind a fence while they escorted PC to the yard, or to the gym, or to the library. So, you have no access to PC.

The only time you have access to somebody out of protective custody is if they have a trailer visit the same time you do. Then whoever is in protective custody has to sign a waiver saying if anything happens to him while he is out in the trailers, the state or the prison is not liable if he should have a problem.

And what sort of things could happen to him?

Well, for instance, if some guy informed on another guy or, or perpetrated a sick crime, and somebody else was foolish enough to want to do something to him while he was out in a trailer, he would have an opportunity if they should both show up outside to smoke a cigarette at the same time. But that's never happened.

And I don't think it ever will happen because the people that are in protective custody, signing that waiver, they certainly don't want no trouble. They just want to be with their families. After all, their families can't help who they are or what they've done. And anybody else that goes out there leaves all that inside the prison when they go out there because they don't want to jeopardize the program or involve their family. So I want to stress that's never happened.

Okay.

But the potential is there, in the minds of D.O.C., so that's why they usually have them sign a waiver, just as a precaution.

I see. Let's say someone who did not have an honorable beef was just wandering through the yard one day with general population. Is that person in danger?

Maybe in the old days, or maybe anywhere from five years ago back. But now, the way the prison system's set up, he probably wouldn't be in any danger unless one of his victims or a friend of the victim, or he had such an outrageous crime, or such a scandalous, sick crime, and people knew about it. Then somebody might make a move on him to peel his head, or to run him off the yard, or to PC him up, or something like that.

But Walla Walla's so large, there's guys there that you may see every day but you don't get close to them. And if you're not close to them, you're not going to know their crime. And the way the systems are now, there's so many of those type of people throughout the whole system that if you were going to beat up every informant or sex offender that was in the system, it would be a 24-hour job. And probably the minute you did, you'd be put in IMU and shipped out anyway. So it would have to be a drastic situation.

So, here at Washington State Reformatory, there are a lot of people who have dishonorable beefs wandering around in general population?

Yes.

Is that true?

Yes.

You consider yourself a convict, is that true?

Yes.

So how does that make you feel?

Well, when I first got here, it bothered the hell out of me because I wasn't used to being around those type of people. You kind of have to weigh the good and the bad at this place. The good thing is I can come up here and talk to you. I can have 46-hour trailer visits. I can program and go to self-help programs. The joint's wide open, where I don't have to be locked in all day. The guards and the staff over here are fairly respectful. There's a different breed of staff over here than are at the other joints.

Mr. DuCharme runs this place, and feels that rehabilitation and self-help is important. There's jobs. There's school opportunities.

So, a fella has to weigh that in one hand, against weighing the scum in the other hand. It balanced out for me.

So I just put on a pair of blinders. I'm not going to associate with these people; they're not my friends; they're not my brothers. I'm not going to talk with them. But, then again, I'm not going to go around peeling their head or looking for trouble either, because that's going to--that's the quickest way out of here.

What does "peeling your head" mean?

Just probably--just beat them up.

Beat them up?

Beat them up.

I see. I'm just not familiar with that term.

That's okay. That's okay. Hit them in the head with a weight, whatever it takes.

Oh, I see.

This is a retirement home. That's how I like to look at it.

Washington State Reformatory?

Washington State Reformatory is a retirement home for a lot of people that's been in the system for a while, or been in the system at other joints. And once they come here, you pretty well just want to finish out your time and leave.

Of course, there's always the possibility a situation may come up, and you could be transferred, or you could get more time. That's prison. But I think once you make it to Monroe, you've settled down and you've matured a little bit, and you want to start looking at yourself and what you can do to help and rehabilitate yourself. Because this is the only place you're going to get that chance. So you got to take advantage of it while you're here.

But still, there's certain principles and lines someone can't step over, and boundaries. And then, if that happens, you got to deal with it.

You said that the officers and staff here are a little more respectful than they are maybe at Walla Walla or other institutions. Can you tell me how they are at Walla Walla, for instance?

Well, they run in cliques. And you gotta realize a lot of those guards over there took a lot of abuse from prisoners before they took control back of the joint. And they're real pieces of shit. They got certain cliques and family groups they run in, and they're just as brutal or just as violent and oppressive than any prisoner ever thought of being. They're a different breed of people.

Over here, you're close to Seattle and metropolitan areas, and I think you have a different mentality with somebody that's grown up in a city and been around different things. Where, over at Walla Walla, you have a bunch of inbred farm hicks is how I'd consider them. And mom and dad have worked there, and grandpa and grandma worked there, and sister and brother and cousin and wife, and they're just a bunch of ignorant assholes. And that's how I look at almost every guard at Walla Walla. And that's exactly how they come across.

And they got a image to protect. The Penitentiary. The last stop. The end of the road. Only the worst go there. They think only the toughest guards can get on at Walla Walla, and that's the image they try to project.

The guards cause a lot of the problems over there now, these days, because they'll try to incite a problem. They know if the population's divided, and you have the Black gangs fighting each other, and you got the White guys fighting against the Blacks, and the Mexicans don't like the Indians, and there's always that constant problem, and they have total control with a lock-down possibility, then you're not going to have any united front or can't stand together against all the shit they're pulling on you. And that's how they like it, and that's how they'd like to see it continue to run.

When you say these people are violent or brutal --

Mm-hmm.

Could you give me an example of what, what are you talking about? What's violent mean?

I've had personal friends hand-cuffed and had nightsticks rammed up their ass while they were in the hole. I've had personal friends that the goon squad run in and gooned them four or five deep.

What does that mean?

Ran in and beat them up. I've had personal friends, and myself included, in IMU, where you're fire-hosed or you're beat. It's just real repressive. They used to have the finger waves over at Walla Walla.

What's that?

That's where they do a digital rectum check for contraband. That was no more than humiliation because they never did find any contraband drugs or weapons in a man's rectum when he went to the hole.

But no matter what your infraction was, or no matter what reason you were going to the hole for, they would do a digital probe. It was humiliating, and that's exactly what it was meant to be. They'd videotape it. You were shackled. They'd pull down your overalls, stand on your ankle chains, bend you over a bed and give you a digital probe. Then they'd wipe their finger on the back of your leg, pull your pants up, and you wouldn't be able to shower for 24 hours.

It was nothing more than a humiliation. And it was taken to court, and the prisoners won on it, and now it's outlawed in the state of Washington.

So let's say there are several officers, and they have taken it upon themselves to approach a man who is incarcerated and abuse him. Is there nothing that person, that prisoner, can do?

Well, if there's other witnesses, he can get affidavits. He could probably file suit on them. He could file a staff misconduct.

But a lot of times, it boils down to the "man's" word against the "convict's" word. Before things even get to a court situation, it's got to go through the little kangaroo court, and infraction and grievance hearing, and everything that D.O.C.'s got set up. And nine times out of ten they will side with the officer. So that would be a hard situation to really fight.

Does it ever happen that a prisoner will fight back? I mean physically fight back?

Oh, absolutely. Sometimes they do; sometimes they don't.

What happens to him if he does?

Well, it used to be if the goon squad run in our house for any particular reason, and we had contraband or something illegal in the house and they're coming in, you may try to stop them, and give our cellies, or our partners, or brothers time to get rid of whatever evidence. And if a fight ensued, the fight would last until you were hand-cuffed.

So, if I bust the first guard in the nose coming through the house and then he gets a few hits in on me, I'm handcuffed; everything's fine. I go to the hole, I do two or three days in the hole, and they let me out. We may even joke with the cops about it back and forth.

Nowadays, if the situation arises where the pigs feel that they have to use force or have to run in on somebody, and you strike an officer, chances are you're going to be taken downtown and charged with custodial assault, possibly second degree assault. You're probably going to go to the hole, and you're probably going to go to IMU.

Can you tell me what IMU is?

IMU is an intensive management unit that they've had in this state for about ten years. It's a total control unit where you're locked in a cell with the lights on 23 hours a day. You have nothing in your house but a sink and a bed. You're not allowed personal clothing or anything like that. You're allowed one hour out at their choice for phone privileges or exercise. It could be 4:00 in the morning; it could be 6:00 in the morning; it could be 1:00 in the afternoon. Sometimes they won't give it to you at all. You're always handcuffed when you leave the cell. You never leave your cell uncuffed. And a lot of times you may have two officers with you. In extreme situations, they'll put the dog collar on you. That's where they have a collar around your neck with a chain, and they hang onto that chain, and you're also handcuffed behind your back.

This is how you take a shower, also. They'll lock you in the shower; you'll stick your hands through the port; they'll undo your handcuffs. Then you'll shower; then they'll rehandcuff you and take you back to your house. You're not allowed any human contact.

Does this still exist?

Oh, absolutely. There's a IMU at Shelton, there's a IMU at Clallam Bay, and there's a IMU at Walla Walla. And they can give you up to two years at a time in IMU. They're real big on sensory deprivation where the lights are on all the time. It's real loud and noisy. It's oppressive. They usually got the assholes of the assholes working those units. A lot of times the punks that can't walk mainline--either they're too scared or too much of an asshole to be a mainline bull--they'll go ahead and put them in a control unit.

How does that affect a man's mind?

Well, it's all meant to break you down mentally and physically to begin with. So if a person's already weak or not too sound, it could really fuck a guy's head up. So you have to really be strong mentally to put up with all the bullshit they're giving you, plus just the conditions you have to live in.

Those sort of conditions sound to me like you could drive somebody insane?

Yeah, you could.

And I suppose some people do go insane?

Sure. I want to stress you don't have to be given an infraction, per se, a drug infraction, or an escape infraction, or an assault infraction, or anything else that goes on in prison, to go to IMU.

You may be the type of individual that files paperwork, that does a lot of legal work against the system. You might be real handy with helping other inmates at their legal work. Well, if that gets underneath the administration's skin, they can lock you up for investigation and put you in IMU.

I've known people personally that have done six months to a year in IMU at a time and were released and never given an infraction, never given a write-up, and were just held in there indefinitely pending investigation. So you're really at the whims of the belly of the beast when these situations come up.

It would seem that living in the sort of environment you're describing at Walla Walla could create a lot of animosity between the prisoner and the officers. Is that true?

Absolutely. Absolutely. There is such a level of tension, but there's even as much, if not more, tension at Clallam Bay because it runs along the same philosophy as Walla Walla, and in a lot of ways, worse.

How could it be worse?

Well, when I was at Clallam Bay, before I got shipped out to Walla Walla, they informed us there was D.O.C. rules, department rules and Clallam rules.

They're really unprofessional up there. If you thought Walla Walla's guards were bad, imagine a bunch of farmers and a bunch of loggers that are out of work, have no experience working with people, and all of a sudden they're thrown into a position of authority.

Guards are no better than a prisoner, other than the fact that when they put that uniform on, they have control.

They did a study at Stanford University one year. They took half the class and made guards, and the other half they made prisoners. This was supposed to go on for a month or so. Well, after a week they had to discontinue the program because the people that were playing the guards' roles were abusing the inmates. They asked them why, and they said, "Well, because they let us. Because we were in power." Well, that's how it goes. And that's how it is.

You spoke about self-help programs and rehabilitation. Do you believe in rehabilitation?

The only way a person's going to rehabilitate himself is to have programs available that offer him the opportunity.

If you're a dope fiend or if you're a criminal, or no matter what you are, you have to want to change yourself before anything will work. So that's the most important. A person's going to have to want to do it himself.

But if a person decides he wants to change, he wants to learn a new trade or he wants to rehabilitate himself, the only place he can really get that opportunity is at Monroe. D.O.C. doesn't believe in rehabilitation. That's why no other joint has any of these programs. And any program you take, even here at Monroe, even though they're afforded to you, it's got to be despite D.O.C.

The Department of Corrections is a business, and their business is bodies and bed space. There is so much money involved in this "new economy." It's a growing business across the whole United States, and Washington jumped on the bandwagon. And while the public screams about turnstiles and people getting right back out of prison and not holding them long enough, and all this, well, that's exactly what D.O.C. wants because they can't make money, and this thing can't grow to what it is today without bodies.

If you rehabilitate somebody or give them the opportunity or make all joints the way Monroe is, you might actually have some success. And that means you're not going to have somebody coming back in that's still fucked up.

When you talk about Ken DuCharme at Washington State Reformatory, you're talking about the Superintendent? Another term would be, Warden?

Right.

And yet, I hear respect in your voice. Am I hearing that correctly?
Yeah, I got respect for the man because he hasn't buckled under to pressure by D.O.C. and other wardens around the state to fall in line with their policy and procedures. I don't know how long this will last. I don't know how long this will keep up, but I feel fortunate enough to have gotten the opportunity to come over here and participate.

It will be a real sad thing when this place, if it ever does, conforms with the other institutions. I would rather see the other institutions modify and conform to here. But with this "Get tough on crime," and the "Three Strikes You're Out," and "The dirty bastards are in prison; they ain't got nothing coming and they don't deserve anything," I don't really think the prison system's going to change to Monroe's way of running things. I think, if anything, over the next five or ten years, it could get worse.

When you talk about a philosophy of running a prison, are you saying that you think what happens here at Washington State Reformatory is a viable solution to crime problems, or a beginning of that? Maybe you can talk to me about what your philosophy is, of what would work?
I think what would work is where a human being is treated like a human being and can still be a prisoner. He's treated with a little respect and a little dignity, but he's still a prisoner.

I realize you have to have security. I realize you have to have control. And I realize a person has to go to prison to serve his time to pay for whatever he done. But the public has to get it through their head that being separated from family and loved ones, not being able to go where you want, do what you want, and taking the simple things out of someone's life, is punishment enough.

We were sent to prison as punishment. We weren't sent to prison to be punished.

If you got somebody and you don't give them any opportunity to change.... If a 19-year-old comes in, and he's kind of wild, and he's had a juvenile record, and he's committed a crime, and he's got to do 20 years--if that man is afforded the opportunity to change and be treated like a human being, by the time he's 40, he's a different person than what he was at 19. And if he's got a little education, if he's learned some type of job skill, even if it is a little bit behind what's really happening on the streets, that's going to give him the possibility when he gets out to become a productive member of society.

But if you take that same person, and you take their TVs away, you take the weights away, you take conjugal visits away, you take education away, and you take most jobs away, and you keep him in a cage, he's like an animal. That person's going to come out worse and have more animosity and bitterness and a lot of fear than he would if you gave him the other opportunities.

What the public has to remember is about 98% of everybody in the system gets out someday. So who do they want living next door to them: somebody that has family ties; somebody that's changed; somebody that's got off drugs; somebody that's went to a vocational school, got a little education; somebody that's matured, and got some self worth, and wants to make an honest attempt, and knows where he went wrong?

Or do you want somebody that's came out worse than when he went in, and all fucked up, and he is. Do you want that individual living next door to you? Because we're all going to get out someday. The public's got to make a choice. They ought to take some of this money they're spending on prisons and use it to stop juveniles from getting to where I am today, whether it be through drug treatment, or job training or whatever.

I don't want you to answer any question that would incriminate you, okay?

Sure.

But can you tell me in your crime, what instigated it? What was the issue?

The issue? The issue was probably brought on through the drug trade even though it wasn't drug-motivated or drug-oriented.

I was involved with individuals in the drug trade, and one of the individuals was a real piece of shit. He was suspected of killing as many as 40 women in Seattle and 40 to 45 women in San Diego, California. And it's not the type of person I want to be around. And through different situations and some things that happened, he raped a girlfriend of mine, and I killed him.

I see.

Yeah.

Just as an aside, it's very interesting to me, when I talk to convicts versus talking to an inmate or a resident, there's almost a sense of nobility. It's as if you fellas see yourselves as Knights of the Round Table.

We are.

Are you?

Sure we are because we have codes we live by and we stand by them. And no one's going to change our mind on that. We've set guidelines up, and we've set a line in the sand, let's say, and we won't let anybody step over that line, whether it be in prison or out on the streets.

There's just a certain code you live by. I'm not saying if somebody crosses that line, you go out and kill them. But you do what you think the right thing to do would be. You do what you feel is right no matter who likes it, right or wrong.

Now the problem I see is that doesn't always fall within accepted bounds in society.

Yeah.

So, sometimes, living by a code of the Round Table, you're not living within the law.

Well, even if you adjusted it to live within the law, and you get out and you're a success and you're law-abiding, I believe those lines can still be drawn. They could be like a rubber band and be stretched because you would have to use control.

This is a different society inside, even though we're a reflection of society on the outside. There's different rules that dictate and govern our behavior in here than would be on the streets.

If you're on the streets, of course, you got to use anger management, self-control. You have to learn to recognize a situation or a problem, or a potential problem, before it even gets your way. And you gotta learn to sidestep it. You gotta learn to deal with it. You may have to learn to swallow your pride and walk away. But that's all the price you have to pay, if you want to stay out.

And do you think that's possible? Can you do that? Do you think you'd be able to do that?

Absolutely. I don't want to come back.

So what made you come to that conclusion? Was it the hard time at the Walls, just the length of time you spent in prison, or maybe the programs?

I think it was a combination of everything. I think it was separation from family and loved ones. I think it was my own maturity and my own self-evolving. I'm not the same guy I was at 30 years old.

How old are you now?

Almost 40. So a lot of things have changed in my mind, and I think a big part of me is finally deciding I don't want to come back. It's been a change that's came from within, from me. And I don't want to spend the rest of my life in these shit holes, to put it bluntly.

Yes, and being separated from people you love?

Yeah, being separated. That's--that's the biggest thing. People don't realize that. They see the visiting room here, and it's fairly nice. They see different programs we have going, how we can interact with the public. Or they see us lifting weights or playing softball or going to our job or whatever. And even though we can basically be out of our cell, except for counts, all day long, when that cell door closes at 9:00 o'clock, in a one-man house, you're all alone, and then reality sets in.

And when reality sets in, you start to realize things, like--my mom and dad are approaching 70. Are they going to be alive when I get out? Look at all the things I've missed. Look at all the opportunities I've lost. The family and loved ones, how are they? I can't be there when so-and-so is sick. I can't be there when Mom and Dad are having problems. I can't be there to help my brother and sister.

Whatever the case may be, you're away from all that; and to me, that's punishment enough.

I'd like to talk to you a little bit about your personal experience with life inside. You were in a riot at Clallam Bay? Tell me about that.

Okay. Clallam Bay. They got the unique habit up there of just randomly beating up prisoners.

And there was a friend of mind whose wife had died on her way to a trailer visit when he was at McNeil Island, and they transferred him to Clallam Bay. Well, he wasn't doing too well.

And, at the time, at Clallam Bay they had a rule that if you did not work or you did not program, you were locked in your house all day. Even though we were the first closed custody inmates up there, we were told, "If you don't program or work, you're locked up." The next thing out of their mouth was, "But there's no jobs, and you guys can't go to school." So this was real hard to swallow.

That, and you have a fairly new prison at the time. With any new prison, a lot of people that can't cut the mustard, or are troublemakers at other joints, get shipped out with the promotion to the new prison.

And with any new prison, they always have a tough time deciding what rules they want, implementing the rules; everyone's got a different reason or version for that rule or infraction. And it's usually a real headache. I would never want to go to a brand new prison when it just opens up. So all of this was going on.

Plus they're rather oppressive and real mean. I would say Clallam Bay's guards and staff are probably the most ignorant in the state. They might send them to Crown Academy for 30 days. It would be nothing to see a tour coming through of new prospective COs, and one minute you look at them and they have black camp-bustin' jeans on and a plaid work shirt and suspenders, and two weeks later they're in a uniform.

Well, half of them are alcoholics, and half of them got just as many problems as the people locked up, except now they're in power.

And they would just arbitrarily beat somebody up?

On occasion I'd witness that, yes. For small infractions. Instead of--they weren't people-oriented. They didn't know how to communicate. If you were doing something, a minor infraction, instead of pulling you aside and telling you, "Hey, don't do that" or "Hey, come here, let's talk" they would want to get tough or get rough or get disrespectful. And some guys fight back, which is natural.

So, they told this individual to lock up, and he refused. Well, the intelligent thing for staff to do would have been waited until the mainline movement, which is when everybody goes to chow, was over, then lock everybody up for their evening count at 4:00 o'clock. The individual is in his cell. Then you can go with two or three guards, arrest him if that's what it takes, and take him to the hole. But no, this officer deemed it necessary to call for the goon squad and call for assistance during a mainline movement.

So you have all kinds of inmates coming and going to their pods and to their cells, while Dudley Do-Right, with a blocking mattress and video camera, tries to come and arrest this guy. Well, a fight ensued. And a few more officers were called, and the fight escalated. They yelled for everyone to lock up, but they didn't open the cells so people could get in--those who wanted to--and inadvertently opened the pod door.

So now you have a full-blown escalation and a situation. So now there's four or five cops, and they're out there battling with eight or nine inmates, and you have about 60 to 70 inmates who either can't lock up or are now refusing to lock up. And it's full bedlam. It's out of hand, and they don't know how to control it.

So this fight ensued. But it didn't end there. Now you have 60 guys that are in a frenzy. Bulletin boards were broken; chairs and property were destroyed; the units were tore apart; weapons were made because we know it's not to end with just them going to the hole. Because now they've called the Emergency Response Team, which is their riot control team.

A lot of guys got all happy when the six guards left the area, claiming victory. Well, victory was short-lived because within an hour they probably had 60 to 70 helmeted, shield-toting, concussion grenades, pepper gas, billy clubs, and they marched into the unit and took back control. And they did that within an hour. By 5:00 o'clock--this happened around noon--by 5:00 o'clock we were taken out into a open area exercise yard and stripped. Our clothing, and what-have-you, was thrown into boxes. We were stripped down and verbally abused and threatened. Then we were shackled and chained and coveralls were given to us, and we were put on a chain bus and taken directly to Shelton IMU. And that's the last I saw of Clallam Bay.

I was called to testify in court for an individual who got a custodial assault charge. I spent 21 days in IMU awaiting that trial but was never called.

So then you were shipped to Walla Walla?

Then I was shipped back to Walla Walla.

Tell me about life at Walla Walla.

Life at Walla Walla. Your first impression is it looks like an old, medieval castle. And you pull up on the chain bus, and there's a small ramp just wide enough for two people, and you go up a ramp and then into the intake, or administration building. And on each side of this ramp they get all the biggest guards, and they line that ramp, and you got to walk down this gauntlet, and they're trying to intimidate you, either by their mere presence and size, or verbally. And outside of this line of cops you'll have a couple cops standing there with shotguns, and you have the guard in the tower with his M-14. They want you to know from the minute you get there that they're in control.

Now, if it's your first time in prison, this can be intimidating, or if you're a youngster. Because they're yelling at you when you're stripping, and they want you to go through the body search. And it can intimidate a youngster.

From there they take you to a chain tier, which is called a duck tier for new people that come in or people that have already been there, but they're coming back in the system. And they house there for up to a week until you get assigned a living unit. And until you're assigned a living unit or the property room has time to process you some state clothes, you run around in a orange jump suit.

Once you're in a living unit, you're given your state-issue clothes. You're assigned a counselor. I don't know why they call them counselors. All they are is a glorified pencil-pusher. They're kind of like a go-between, between administration and yourself. Overpaid and underworked.

After this you can sign up for work in the kitchen or the laundry, or some type of a unit job as a tier porter. But usually all those jobs are filled, and the best you can do is get on a waiting list.

There's really no education programs over there. There is a metal plant where they make license plates and some metal fabrication. If Monroe, for instance, wanted to buy a hundred chairs, the chairs would be made at Walla Walla.

They do have one outside industry, and that employs about 40 people. But other than that, there's no jobs, very little money, very little education. You could probably get an AA degree. The credits probably won't be transferred anywhere to any other college or major university. Probably the best thing they got there is a GED program.

There's no computers. There's no in-house curios anymore. So there's a lot of dead time, a lot of wasted time.

What you're telling me, Bob, is actually surprising me. Because I hear that people inside prisons have more benefits and more opportunities than people in the public.

All I can say is if people in the public aren't eating as well as I am, if they can't find a job that pays them better than $50 a month or 38 cents an hour, with DOC taking a cut for cost of corrections, you got a lot of lame people out there in the public.

Now, I know economics are hard, and times are hard; jobs are hard to come by. But I find it real hard to believe that I have it better than anybody on the streets.

How is the food here?

Well, I'm a vegetarian, so the food's not too awful bad. It's real small portions, and it gets real boring, because it's the same thing. You have beans and rice, eggs, peanut butter and jelly, or cheese.

Have you ever taken any of the opportunities made available to you here, the programming or the schools?

Yes, absolutely. I'm in the computer information class, a class out at the college. I'm a member of Prisoner Awareness Program. I'm a member of the Lifer's Club. I've been through Alternatives to Violence.

I had signed up for the drug treatment program my first year at Walla Walla. They told me I had too much time left to get into a program like that. Well, that kind of confused me because I thought, "If I have a drug problem, and if I continue to have a drug problem in prison, why wait to address or get any help on that problem?" It made no sense to me.

That just goes to show you that they don't want to fix anything. It's a Band-Aid on a fatal wound if it doesn't suit their purpose.

Can you get drugs inside the prison?

Sure.

How? How do you get drugs inside of a prison?

Well, the best way to get drugs into a prison, and the most commonly used way to get drugs in a prison, is through staff.

Staff?

Staff.

Why would staff bring drugs inside of a prison?

Money. They're human like anybody else. A lot of them are drug users themselves.

Are you talking about the officers?

Right, officers. I will have to say, though, there's very little drug use at Monroe. And I don't believe any staff is involved, that I know of, and I don't want to know.

But at other major institutions it's happened. They just had a guy that was teaching a class at McNeil Island last year got busted buying two ounces of coke that he was bringing in through the school program. He was an employee of D.O.C.

So, one way or another, staff's going to bring in any large amounts because they're the ones that most easily can bring large amounts in.

What kind of drugs are you talking about?

Cocaine, marijuana, heroin.

Just about anything, then?

Just about.

When you talk about doing the right thing, and the convict code and all of that ... let's say you were on the streets again, and somebody put their hands on your child or your wife. Would you think to call the police?

Absolutely. Now if a person's on the streets doing crime, or he has partners, and you're all doing crime and you get busted, or the police became involved, or you go to court or trial, if you become an informant or rat, then you're a snitch.

But anybody, whether it be somebody who's got out and living a straight life, or the public, if they see a crime, they should call the police. That's what they're there for. I don't consider that informing or snitching. That's just doing what you gotta do.

That's being a good citizen.

That's being a good citizen. I just wish the police had a better handle on their people, and there was a better system set up where innocent people weren't taken advantage of.

What do you mean by that?

Well, the cops shot that lady in Lynnwood when they thought she was involved with the armored car holdup. It was on bogus information. They ran in; she went to pick up her child, and the cop shot her and killed her. There was a big money settlement with Snohomish County, King County, and Lynnwood police about a year ago.

And there's all kinds of incidents like that that the public probably doesn't know about. The public should know. The more repression and more power the police get in the name of crime and in the name of this monster called a convict, the more of your constitutional rights are being taken away. And if your constitutional rights are being taken away in the name of "let's fight crime," and the public says, "Well, that's good," they should realize that means constitutional rights, and our liberties and freedoms are being taken away from everybody across the board.

They have the "no knock" rule. Cops used to have to come announce themselves, knock at your door, have a warrant, and then they can come in your house. Well, now they have a "no knock" rule. If they have probable cause, they don't need a warrant. So if they don't really follow up on their information, whether it's their own investigation or their reliable informants or their paid rats, a lot of innocent people can have their houses busted into. They can be arrested and manhandled.

And I think some police--not all police, some police--are just as violent and get off on that adrenaline rush of the heat of the moment just like a criminal would when he's creating a crime.

It's interesting. In Canada you have less handguns and you have less police brutality. If you happen to catch a show from Canada now and then on how they do their police work, they always seem to be very professional and courteous and kind to whoever they're talking to. And they usually diffuse the situation.

Where if you watch any of these gung-ho, John Wayne cop shows here in America, they're ready to bust in the door, throw you down, put a gun in your ear, jump on your back, handcuff you, throw you around and my God Almighty, you might not even be guilty. And a lot of it's done for petty drugs. I find it really ironic that the government wants to get tough and lock so many people away for crimes of drugs, when the government's the biggest supporter of drugs in this nation.

What do you mean by that?

The government brings in most of the cocaine, and I don't see any reason why the government is going to quit. It's fast, easy money, and it gives their cops something to do and gives the public something to be in a uproar about, and they make all the money off of it.

We just have a few minutes left, Bob. Is there anything that you would like to say?

I'd just like the public to know that we're human beings. And we hate a lot of the crime and senseless violence that's going on out there.

When I was on the streets, you didn't have this type of crime. But every time you turn on the TV, there's people running around, killing people senselessly, raping women and children. I just want the public to know that we hate that. Most convicts hate that and despise that just as much as they do. But the answer is not getting tough on us that are already locked up. The public has to do something out there. We shouldn't be the scapegoat for society's inability to raise their own children, put their own people to work, and not to control the streets. You need do it someway other than fighting back with brute force, or you're going to have a police state.

It's going to take education; it's going to take putting people to work and paying people decent wages, where both parents don't have to be out there working all the time. It's going to take an alcohol and drug program that really addresses the problem, not just throwing somebody in a 30-day program and then kicking them back loose on the streets. Because when you change your lifestyle, you have to change everything about you, who you associate with, your whole way of thinking.

And you need to give them a job. If there's no jobs out there, then the person's more likely going to turn back to crime.

It's going to take education, and it's going to take some money. I know the public's not scared of spending money, because they want to build more prisons. And the politicians want more money. They're the ones that ought to be locked up.

What is your position on gun control?

I believe every American has the right to own and bear arms. I shudder to think what'll happen when the day comes when the governments come to a law-abiding citizen's house, and telling them they gotta give up their guns in the name of gun control.

I think big money and big business, with the government knowing it, has caused this thing with the gun problem. They've allowed semi-automatic and attack weapons to flood our streets. They know it's happening because big business is buying them from other countries and bringing them in here, and the government didn't give a shit. They only give a shit because the people that are voting for them are causing a stink over it because too many children and innocent people are getting killed. But it's big business, it's big brother, and it's the rich, ruling class that's behind all this.

We're all expendable. Convicts are expendable; citizens are expendable because we don't mean anything to this country. The only thing that this country understands is money and power.

If they outlaw guns, the only people that'll have guns are criminals and the government. So gun control's not going to work. If you take guns away from people, then you're just inches away from a dictatorship and a police state. Because then they have total control.

Gordon Graham

One request is that I look at things before they're published.

Granted.

And that they are agreed on before they're published.

We can do that. And if we agree to do that and if that happens, then it's all right?

Sure.

Good. First of all, Mr. Graham, we can start by you telling me who you are, and I'd just like to hear your story.

Well, I'm Gordon Graham, and I have a small training company called Gordon Graham and Company, and we work with business and industry and corrections across the United States.

I grew up in the Washington Correctional System. I started out in Monroe in 1952, was transferred to Walla Walla in 1958, and during the course of a 20-year time frame, I did about 17 years inside of the joint. So I think I did about 14 in Walla Walla but started out in Monroe. And I've been associated with the corrections system in the state of Washington for probably--since 1952, so that's been a number of years, a number of years. I go back to Monroe occasionally. I don't get a chance to go back to Walla Walla that often, and I assume that I have a certain attitude about the state of Washington's correctional system. I'm not that impressed by their commitment to opportunities for inmates. And that's not a negative statement. It's just my perception, and it could well be based on my background.

Mr. Graham, may I ask you what you did time for?

Well, I went into the joint in 1952 for forgery. At that time, forgery carried a 20-year max, and so you went to the joint, and the parole board set your time, and then you did the balance on parole.

I went to the joint, first time I'd ever been in prison, and I was young, and I got 15 months from the parole board. But I think I wound up doing about five years for violations of rule infractions and fighting, and then I was involved in a riot in 1953 and did a year in the hole after that. So the time that I spent wasn't necessarily as a result of the crime that I committed on the streets. It was really as a result of not being able to adjust to the prison environment.

And that first stint in the joint, from the time I was probably 19 or so, I changed an awful lot of the way that I thought in regards to myself. I went in as a person who was convicted of forgery, and I came out as a convict. I thought like a convict, and I had taken on a lot of attitudes and characteristics that are picked up inside of a correctional setting and inside of a prison.

At that time, Monroe was ran by the convicts inside the joint, and it was a real cliquish kind of an institution. The administration ran it by letting the convicts run it. And so it was a tough place to do time for those people who were not connected with the cliques. If you were not a strong convict, if you didn't know anybody--those kinds of things were negative because you had to either know somebody or belong to a clique to have access to any of the real decent opportunities or jobs.

Monroe, at that time, didn't have hot water in the cells. They still had people who carried water on a tier, and convicts were charged for almost everything. You'd pay to get hot water; you had to pay to get any kind of things that were available in the joint. Some convict controlled that. I didn't adjust well to that. I didn't know anybody in the joint, and I wound up in a lot of conflict with both the inmates and with the staff.

So, that first experience in the joints changed my perceptions an awful lot. I got paroled, and I was out. At that time, I think you got $10 gate money and a bus ticket to Seattle.

Mr. Graham, may I interrupt you because I want to ask you a couple of things on what you've said so far?

Sure.

You just very casually said, "I did a year in the hole." A year is a long time, Mr. Graham. First of all, can you tell me what the hole is?

Well, the hole at that time was 12 cells, two tiers of six cells on the bottom and six cells on the top, behind the kitchen in Monroe. And they served fritters, which was a vegetable patty that was between two slices of bread. They served it twice a day and then every third day you got a meal. It seems to me like we showered every week; I can't recall for sure. You had a wooden plank for a bed--it was about six inches off the floor--and a blanket and coveralls. And that's what the hole consisted of, and you'd find ways to keep from going crazy.

Are you isolated?

They can black the door out, or put the blackout door on, but you can still holler, and you can still hear, and you can disrupt the cellblock outside. They used to give you metal cups, and you could rattle the bars with metal cups at midnight and wake up the cellblock and disturb the inmate population, which wasn't a nice thing to do. But it was kind of nice to let people know you were still back there, you know?

And it was a different world at that time. There wasn't any ACLU, or inmate rights, or any of that kind of stuff. And the convict thought different. At that time, when you got busted for something, you just did your time and you got out, and you did what you did....

I got put in the hole for being a ringleader in a riot, even though I wasn't a ringleader. I had knocked a guard down in the yard, I think, or something. I didn't feel that angry about the year in the hole. I felt that it just seemed like it was part of the punishment of being in prison, part of the consequences of getting busted doing something.

People didn't file suits at that time.

So when you were taken to isolation, were you told at that time, "It's been decided you're going to do a year in the hole," or did you just get thrown in there, and they arbitrarily decided they'd let you out a year later?

They let you out when they chose to. There was no control at that time. There was no court. At that time, if you got a write-up, infraction, we had a captain who would hold court. He would stand at the top of the stairs, and the inmates would stand down below, and the sergeant would call your name, or somebody would call you name, and you walked up the stairs. Captain would sentence you to whatever he wanted to sentence you to. You'd go to the hole. And that was kind of the formal court at that time for inmates. It was just a matter of if he decided you were guilty, you were guilty.

So when you were sent in there you didn't know if you were coming out in three months, six months, a year?

No.

For all you knew, you were going to spend the rest of your time in there? You just didn't know?

Yeah. Well, I knew I'd get out sometime.

Sometime?

I didn't know when, but I knew I'd get out sometime.

At that time, it was a totally different world. And yet, I don't know that it wasn't easier to do time at that time than it is now. You know, there was a clear, understood convict code that people lived by inside the joint. If you didn't do certain things, if you did them, there was consequences. Like, you didn't snitch on your fellow inmates. A snitch couldn't survive.

People who ran for sexual crimes--child molesting, rape, those kinds of things--were isolated from the population. They couldn't survive in the population for very long.

You didn't talk to the man, and the man didn't talk to you. You supported whatever the inmate activity was. If you were going to go on a hunger strike, you went on a hunger strike. There was just a clear-cut convict set of basic guidelines that people would come into the joint, and they learned it, and they operated under that.

And there was cliques. There were small cliques that formed that ran certain kinds of things. At that time there wasn't a lot of racial issues in Monroe. At that time, there wasn't that much awareness on racial discrimination, you know? Guards could be racist, and it was an acceptable practice at that time. It seems to me that was the way it was, and it probably still is to a degree. We need to go a long distance before equality is there.

You also made a comment, "I thought like a convict." What do you mean by thinking like a convict?

Well, today there's a real focus on cognitive restructuring. And what that means is people have suggested that there's a process of thinking that encompasses criminal thinking. I disagree with that. I think that there's people who think like a criminal, but a convict is different. "Convict thinking" is totally different than "criminal thinking."

You've got a lot of people who go into the joint who aren't criminals. They go in for a crime, but they don't think like a criminal. Could be someone that's in for a murder--emotional murder, emotional crime, someone who commits a crime one time and they don't think like a criminal. But they might think like a convict. A convict thinks different than a criminal. A convict thinks about beating "the man"; he thinks about the convict kind of code. See, to a convict, beating the system isn't criminal. You know, getting a little extra food isn't criminal. And maybe smuggling something in or out of the prison isn't criminal. That's convict thinking.

You have the same kind of thinking in a large industrial plant. Unions think different than management. But it's not criminal thinking.

So when I say I went in as a young man who had committed a crime, I came out thinking like a convict, I learned in those years what convicts do to survive in that environment--what's good, what's bad, what's right, what's wrong. And so, some of the convict thinking is if somebody gets in your face, you've got to react. You've got to do something about that, whether it's the man or another convict. If you don't, you begin to get misused by the people that you live around.

And so there are certain things that convicts learn that allow them to survive in an abnormal environment. See, when you're dealing with a prison, you're dealing with abnormal behavior and abnormal environment. So you learn to adjust to that abnormal environment.

You know, I have a friend who is a psychologist in a prison in Texas, and she had an inmate coming into the institution, a federal prison, and someone had sent her some information on this inmate, his characteristics, and they said, "This guy is a manipulator. He always likes to work in the psychology area, and he likes to work around women." And her reaction was, "That is normal. That's normal, in a normal environment, that someone would want to work inside, out of the cold, have a decent job around women." I mean, that's not abnormal thinking. It's abnormal in a prison because a prison is an abnormal environment. You see, that would be normal thinking in any other environment. But in a prison, it's perceived as being not acceptable.

So what happens, an inmate learns how to think so that he or she can survive in that abnormal environment. And so that criminal-thinking philosophy, or that approach, really doesn't include the fact you may come in thinking normal, like a normal human being who committed a crime, but gradually you think like a convict. And that's totally different than criminal thinking.

When you're speaking about convict thinking, I think what I'm hearing you say is it's almost a code of morality. It may not be society's code of morality, but it's a code of morality. And also it's survival tools.

Sure. There's a bond that develops in a joint between convicts, very similar to the bond that develops in a Vietnam, or any environment like that. I've got numbers of friends that are guys who have done a lot of time in the joints. There's a bond between us that nobody else understands. Nobody else understands it. They can't understand why I would do these things for these guys that come out of the joint because they don't understand what that bond is that develops when you go through certain things together that are sometimes life-threatening ... and someone supports you or backs you up in situations where your life is on the line ... and that begins to translate into a code of morality that's distorted from normal society's point of view. But, it's reality, regardless, in terms of how people think inside of a joint.

It seems to me one of the problems we're up against is we're attempting to change appropriate thinking for the environment. We're trying to change that into something that maybe isn't appropriate thinking for that environment, maybe even dangerous thinking for that environment?

Sure.

How do you get around that, or deal with that?

It's very difficult. You see, this is my statement: the culture that you live in or work in drives performance. And so if you're in a culture that's convict-oriented, and you try to change in that environment, you're at risk. You get all kinds of negative feedback.

It's like somebody who, for some reason, they have a religious experience, and they begin to start to go to church, where they've never went to church before, or they start reading the Bible. They're immediately labeled by their peers as a Bible-pusher, as a phony, as a fake, as a fraud. So, even though he or she may be very serious about it, that feedback makes it almost impossible for them to continue it.

And so the culture is not conducive to change. It's not conducive to any positive change. And it's very difficult to change that because you've got a population of people that are going to be there for a long time, and that's a survival process.

Then you've got a group of people that are on the verge of getting out, and yet to get out, you've got to change. And it's difficult for that process to work. Transitional programs help a little bit--halfway houses, living environments that are structured around a certain program or method of change, substance abuse programs. Some of those things are very positive, in terms of allowing people an opportunity to change. Sometimes it works.

But I think most changes that occur in individuals take place after they get out of the joint. You know, it's a conscious decision to change while they're in the joint, but they still have to function and operate in that environment for survival. They got all the tools and everything, and when they come out of the joint, then they can begin to really put it to use and make the changes real.

You mentioned that things have changed a lot, and one of those things is the mix of people who are now inside prisons, including a mix of different crimes.

There's a number of words for people who do time. There's inmates; there's residents; there's convicts. A convict thinks different than an inmate. A convict still operates under the old convict code. There aren't very many convicts doing time any more.

Rapists? A rapist who goes in somebody's window, swings out of a tree; that's not understandable to a convict. You can understand why a person cracks a safe, steals if they don't have money, uses drugs if they're in a hopeless situation. I can understand those motivations. The sexual things are much, much more difficult for me to comprehend.

And yet I believe in change, and I believe in people being treated decently. I don't want to see nobody afraid to come out of their cell, or misused or abused in an institution. That's not my way of seeing things. So, there's got to be some mechanism set up so that those people can get the treatment that they need, and a safe environment to express those things that are their ghosts, and devils, and things that live in them. And there's some things starting to happen like that.

In Oregon, they've got a sexual offender prison where just sexual offenders are there. And so it's a safe environment for someone to talk about why they do those things. Because I don't know that and I don't want to talk about it with them. I don't want to get that close to someone like that. I will teach what I teach to anybody; I will help support the process for anybody. But it's a tough area for me.

I think that the major changes that have taken place in the institutions are the things that have happened in society. We have a society at large that is more violent, with more and more youthful offenders that don't have much control. We have more and more people in our society that are living in prisons on the streets, which are worse than the prisons that they put them in when they incarcerate them. You go into certain inner cities--that's a prison in itself. People are trapped in that prison. And it's a hopeless kind of feeling to be in that kind of a prison, even though you're not inside of walls and bars. So you take a person out of that kind of a prison, and put them in a prison that has bars, and walls, and three square meals a day, and a certain amount of brotherhood or sisterhood, and it's not

that bad, you know?
And drugs have become a real monster, in terms of managing any population of people who live together. If you have a drug addict, young or old, they lose their value systems. Their value systems get distorted; they will do things that are incomprehensible to anybody else. They'll steal from their mother, steal from their friends. Force their mother or girlfriend or brother, or whatever, to bring drugs into them, in the prison. That drug thing is just a killer in terms of trying to create an environment that has any sanity to it.
The racial mix in prisons--the Latino, the African-American--is disconnected from the American dream. They have very little opportunity to access even the middle class area. If you grow up in an environment where there's drugs, and hustling, and prostitution, and drive-by shootings; and that's the life that you live when you're two, three, four, five, six, seven, eight, nine--you get to be 13 or 14 years old you've got a real different paradigm that you operate from.
But you look at that, and it's pretty easy to understand why that person might wind up in trouble with the law. And so what we're doing is we're filling our prisons up with a large portion of Latino and African-American young men and women who, instead of working on the cause and dealing with the problem where it's at, we try to lock the problem up in a prison. And you can't do that. It gradually will bankrupt society, and it will also--it will gradually create a system of haves and have-nots, and the haves will become more and more protective of what they've got, and the have-nots are going to become more and more angry. And gradually you'll have revolution, and it may take different forms; but, you'll have a revolution. I mean, you just can't continue to do that.
And there are just an awful lot of people in this country right now that are disconnected, that don't feel that they're a part of what America is supposed to be a part of. And that's disturbing to me.
I think that we have got to put resources into the communities that help change the environment that people come out of that. That doesn't justify crime, it doesn't justify drugs, or any of that kind of stuff--that's not it. I'm not soft on crime, but I am concerned about the direction that this country is going, and the state of Washington is right in the middle of it. There's no distinct difference between the state of Washington and any other state in the country.
The one exception is Oregon. I see Oregon as being one of the most progressive in the country in terms of corrections. I think they are trying different things. They've got a real strong visionary that's the Director of Corrections who doesn't fit the mold. I see Oregon as being a light in a real dark correctional world.
But, you know, inmates in the joints, when you get them one on one, most of them are the same. They want the same things. They want to be a part of something positive; they want to be treated with dignity; they want to be loved; they want to love; they want to

have material things that make life more comfortable. And they don't know how to get it legally, so they turn to the only means that they know, and that's illegal.

There are some very, very, very strong and good leaders in the correctional system. There are some good people, and they don't do things to consciously make life difficult for people that are in prison. But the systems that we set up, politically and economically, make it almost impossible for them to do anything but continue to build prisons. The "Three Strikes, You're Out," the "tough on crime" gets people elected, and it doesn't do anything to solve the problem. It just continues to increase the problem. It doesn't create safe societies, safe environments, safe communities. What it does is it creates a tremendous burden on the taxpayer, and they aren't getting any positive reward from that investment.

I think that the changes that are going to take place in the inner cities, and I use the term "inner cities" as being the ghettos that we've developed. An inner city could be a small rural community where there's no opportunities. It doesn't have to be in South Central Los Angeles, or anyplace like that.

But the answers are going to probably come out of prisons. The answers are going to come out of prisons because we're going to lock up all the young leaders; and the young leaders are going to gradually find their way to change inside a prison, where they're stopped. And they will come back and become the catalyst for positive change. That's probably a distorted view from any politician's perspective, but that's what I believe. That's the hope that I've got. I see it happening in certain environments already, and I think that will continue.

Perhaps this is a good place, Mr. Graham, for me to ask you to define three terms that you've used. The terms are "convict," "resident," and "inmate."

Well, when I started doing time it was convicts. Then the convict seemed to be a harsher term, for some reason, and we changed to inmates. Inmate then becomes a patient. An inmate is a patient. An inmate is generally somebody who is mentally deranged; an inmate is not necessarily a whole being.

That inmate mentality carried through the '70's, and then people started saying, "Well, these are residents." And that was to try to take away the stigma of being an inmate. And a resident then becomes an individual who wants to be there; that's a resident. The resident is someone who chooses to live in that environment.

And each name was used to try to change the way that inmates, residents or convicts looked at each other. And so the convict was an antisocial, who lived by a particular code. Alcatraz, or Walla Walla, or Leavenworth, or San Quentin, or Folsom was convicts. Then we changed. We started creating a different kind of an institution, a prison society, or a correctional environment. It turned from prison, changed to corrections.

In the correctional facility, they didn't want convicts because a convict was the kind of a guy that wasn't necessarily conducive to change. They were convicts. So then, we've changed the name, and people started being inmates. So, they functioned better in this new correctional environment, the inmate did.

After a period of time, we went a step further and said, "We're going to have residents, these are residents now." And each one was designed to make it easier for administration to manage a population of men and women who are in prisons. It wasn't designed to change the person in prison. It was designed to make it an easier management tool for the administration to break down the convict code.

And so gradually you've got a group of people who are in institutions. There is no moral code; there's no values; there's nothing that brings them together as a group, and so they're much easier to manage. Convicts were harder to manage because convicts lived by a particular code. Like if you had a hunger strike in a joint where you had convicts, nobody would eat. Nobody ate.

I don't think you could start a hunger strike today in the joint. There is nothing for people to rally around. There's so many people in there that are just manipulated by the systems. They have no loyalty and no real interest in their brothers or sisters. So you can't start anything in a joint where you've got inmates and residents.

That's one of the differences between the African-American, or even the Latino, and the white convict. The African-American, the black, has something to rally around. So they can pull their group together pretty well around their blackness, around their African-Americanness. The Latino can around their heritage. The white has nothing to rally around. So you have small gangs forming of whites--bikers, Aryan Brotherhood--because there's nothing for the white to come around. It takes some real leader, some real strong focal point to bring whites together on anything ... whites have no loyalty to anything.

And so sometimes you feel a certain amount of resentment or jealousy because the black convict has the blackness to pull himself together around. All of them know being black puts you in a one-down position. No more matter what people say, an African-American in our society does not have equal opportunity. Every black knows that. There isn't any black in this country that doesn't know that. The Latino has the same thing.

But the poor white, who really is in the same situation as the African-American except they're white, doesn't have anything to pull that group together around. So it takes a real strong, charismatic leader to pull whites together in a joint around anything.

Given what you've just said, would you prefer that persons incarcerated in institutions be referred to as convicts?

No, I don't think that's the answer. I think the answer is to change the way that we deal with men and women who are in prisons. People in prisons are prisoners. They're prisoners. They are not there not by choice. They're not there to be a convict. They're there as prisoners. They're prisoners. And that's what you should call them. They're prisoners.

We don't call a guy who's out of the joint an ex-inmate. We don't call him an ex-resident. They're an ex-convict. It's okay to be an ex-convict, but it ain't okay to be a convict. We label them as a convict when they get out, but when they're in, we don't want them to be a convict. We want them to be a resident or an inmate, something that's easier to manage. And so I think that when you're in prison, you're a prisoner. You're not there by choice; you're there because you've committed a crime, generally. Sometimes you're in there for other things, but most times, the guy's guilty of a crime. They're in there as a prisoner. When they get out, then you allow them to become a whole citizen again, not an ex-convict anymore, just a whole citizen.

Because what happens to a guy coming out of the joint is they're never whole again. They're never whole. I've been out of the joints 23 years. I'm still an ex-convict. People say, "Oh, he's an ex-convict." That's 23 years ago! If I walk off this earth plane when I'm a hundred, "Well, he was an ex-convict, you know." And so, you never get rid of that. But I think at some point we need to try to help people come back to the whole, full, potentially good life, as a human being.

You should look at institutions, and put a name on the institution. You shouldn't call them a correctional institution because they don't correct nothing. And if there are going to be correctional institutions then that should be the focus of the institution, correcting the behavior of the people that are in there.

And if you're going to have a prison, then it should be a prison. But don't try to punish them and change them at the same time. It's incongruous. It doesn't work like that.

The punishment takes place in the first six months of the first year, when people lost everything they had. They lose their credibility, their family, their job, their freedom. If you survive the first six months of punishment, then you can make it through your sentence.

You could get the same results in six months that you get in ten years. Because in 10 or 12 years, you've developed so many habits, and so many attitudes, and so much anger, and all of the stuff that an institution lays on a person. That's tough for somebody to get out of there and make it happen. It's not very realistic, in terms of corrections.

You spoke earlier about people feeling disenfranchised, not part of America. How could we help correct that?

We have to provide equal access to opportunities: equal access to education, equal access to good family structures, and equal access to the things that develop inside of that person who comes into this world as an infant. People need the ability to see that they are part of something, that they're not just a 13-year-old who was left on their own most of the day and night with no value system, with no sense of love, no sense of belonging to anything.

And then winding up in an institutional environment, where you're with another 200 or 300 little kids just like you, that come from the same environment. And you begin to think that's what the world is. And then you look at the TV, and you see all this stuff that's America, and you don't feel connected to that. You know that if you're an African-American, the way you get connected to that is by becoming an athlete, or a musician, or a drug dealer. That's the models that are portrayed on television. You don't see the truck driver, the carpenter, the farmer. The average African-American who is out there in the world--that's not the model that these kids look at.

And the same thing is true with whites who grow up in an environment where there's no education, no family structure; gradually, you get a distorted value of how you achieve things, and you don't feel connected to the American dream. Like when I was a thief, I didn't feel guilty about stealing. I felt guilty about getting caught, or if I didn't get enough money. I didn't lose sleep at night because I stole.

I don't think that you can change the things that are going on in society unless you address those issues that are in the communities, where these young people are winding up in prisons at 13 or 14 for shooting each other, for robbing and stealing, and doing crack and selling crack. I mean, it just doesn't make sense to me.

A friend of mine in D.C. told me that "if we continue locking people up the same rate we're locking them up today, by the year 2020, we'll have 20 million people incarcerated." Now, nobody in their right mind can see that as a solution to the crime problems. It's going down a road towards bankruptcy and fascism.

I'm going to take you back right now to where we started at the beginning of the interview, when you were talking about yourself going through the system. You were just leaving the institution. Can you tell me what happened then? You were out on the streets now. How was that for you?

It's not always that easy to remember; but, I remember at that time you got $10 gate money and a bus ticket to Seattle. I hit Seattle and got involved with some other guys that had just hit Seattle. I went up on Pike Street where everybody hung out and connected with a couple people, and 30 days later, I was back in the joint for parole violation.

Back in the joint. I think we had a hunger strike, or some damn thing, in Monroe, and I went to the hole again and was transferred from the hole to Walla Walla. And at that time, Walla Walla was the fish tank. The fish tank was bucket cells. They didn't have any toilets. They had lime water in buckets. There were two-man cells, and it was August, and it was some really hot metal cells. But I went over with a couple of guys that were friends of mine and fell into the routines in Walla Walla. By that time, I had gotten a reputation of being a tough guy, and all that kind of junk. Did about 14 years. Wound up being one of the convict leaders and an advocate for convicts in the joint and learned how to make the system work, to manipulate the system. I escaped out of Walla Walla and did a lot of different things that you do in the joint.

You know, a convict's always trying to get "even." If you do five years, you've got to make enough money to make it worthwhile; and so, you're always trying to get even with the system. You're always too broke to go straight. "I want to make one good score, and then I'm going to go straight": that's the convict mentality.

Mr. Graham, you run a company called "Gordon Graham and Company," which teaches a program, "Breaking Barriers." Maybe you could speak to me of your vision? The vision for Gordon Graham Company is we are committed to constructive, positive change. Committed to trying to bridge the gap between people who have and the people who have not, from management to labor, from inmate to correctional staff, from society to the inmate; to try to build a framework of awareness that lets people see through another set of eyes, that people are pretty much the same, incarcerated or on the streets. Inside, we are pretty much the same.

I have a vision of a country that provides equal access to opportunity and to health care, whether you're black, white, brown or rich, a society that is a land of opportunity.

The way that people think controls the way they act. If you think from a scarcity mentality, then you're always trying to protect what you've got. And you're always afraid of somebody else getting it. In a scarcity way of thinking, there's only so much of things, only so many opportunities, only so many jobs, only so much money, only so much.

I don't think like that. I believe there's an abundance. And if you think from an abundance mentality, then you're not threatened by other people, you're not trying to keep someone else down, you're not trying to keep information from people. And a person who thinks from an abundance mentality is constantly just sharing what they've got because they know that there's an abundance. And I think that we need to get back to that way of thinking. And so, you know, my vision is to try to help spread that kind of thinking philosophy around so that people are more into abundance and sharing what they've got: knowledge, and love, and material things. So that's basically what my vision is. It's not that profound, really.

Mr. Graham, I want to thank you very much for your time today.

My pleasure.

I also want to thank you for all the wonderful work that you have done and the influence you've been on so many people. So it's not just a thank-you from me, but from an awful lot of people.

Well, I appreciate your interest. You take good care, and give my best to those guys up there when you see them.

Johnny Fox

Everybody calls me Johnny Fox, and I prefer to be called Johnny Fox.
Okay, I'll call you Johnny Fox then.
Tell me about Johnny Fox. You spent some time at Washington State Reformatory?
Yes, I did.
How much time?
All told, about eleven and a half years.
Did you spend time anyplace else?
Yeah, in Joliet. Joliet, Illinois.
How much time did you spent there?
Seven and a half years.
So, all told, you've put in quite a few years?
Been around the block a couple times.
How old are you now, Johnny Fox?
Forty-eight. Just turned 48.
The first time you went to prison, what did you go for?
Armed robbery, assault. They dropped first degree assault with intent to kill, to assault and a burglary.
What was your beef here in Washington originally?
It was first--a first degree assault.
Oh, assault again?
While armed with a deadly weapon.
Sounds like you have a temper, Johnny Fox?
Yeah, I used to.
You're not in prison right now?
Nope. I got my discharge papers. And the government sent me a piece of paper saying that ATF (Alcohol, Tobacco and Firearms) gave me back my rights to carry a gun.

They did?

Yeah, they did. They asked me why I wanted to carry a gun or why I wanted a gun in my home. I said, "For home protection, and I am an avid hunter."

They gave you your right to bear arms?

Yeah. It's like putting an escalator in an outhouse.

Don't you think you should have that right, Johnny Fox?

Oh, yes, I do. Oh, most definitely I do.

Can you talk to me a little bit about how life used to be, and how life became, as the years went by?

All right. Before, it was nothing to go into the joint and get buffed up. It was just a playground. That's all it was.

What's "buffed up" mean?

You know, pumping that iron.

Oh.

Just lifting weights, getting big, and getting healthy. You had to follow certain rules and regulations, but you could get high. I could get anything that you could get on the street, and that includes sex from a female. I had money in there, whiskey, dope.

If you first came to Walla Walla and didn't tell me you were scared when you first went in, well, I looked at you and thought, "You're either a damn fool or an idiot."

Why would you be afraid?

Your life. Your life.

Other inmates would take your life. They ran the joint. There wasn't no bullshit. They've ran the joint. You could die in a heartbeat. I seen kids raped right in front of me. The guard was standing right down at the other end. Only the strong survived. You just did what you had to do.

When I first went to Joliet, they gave me a knife. I was 19 years old, didn't have a feather on my face, but I did what I had to do. If I could go back now, I never would have went to the penitentiary.

Well, what do you mean? Who is "they"?

Friends of my uncle. My uncle had just gotten out, and they came by the cell, and they said, "You're his nephew?" And I said, "Yeah." They had heard a couple of guys were going to fool with me.

They said, "Here's a knife."

"Here's a knife. Do what you gotta do, kid." And when that cell opened up, and they ran in there, I did what I had to do.

What happened to you then?

Nothing. They didn't charge you for doing something to another inmate.

Oh.

You were just a number, or a statistic.

So they'd just come haul the body out?

Yeah, you just set him out on the tier. Set him out on the tier, get him away from you, and just give somebody the knife. As long as you ain't got no blood in your cell or on you. They'd put you in the hole under investigation and put you on the shelf for six months, but the paperwork just got lost in the shuffle. And you were just a number. I had to lay on the concrete. They didn't even give you a mattress. They fed you every other day when you were laying on concrete.

Why were you laying on the concrete?

Because it was the hole, and you were in the hole for disciplinary action.

Oh.

It just made you tough. You got one meal.

One meal a day?

Yeah. Yeah. If that's what you want to call it. If that's what you wanted to call it.

You'd get vanilla extract bottle of chicory.

What's chicory?

Chicory was a substitute for coffee.

That's what they gave you in the hole to drink. And you got that with your meal. They'd cut the top off, and they'd make that into a cup to serve you in the hole because it'll slide through the bars, where they don't have to open up the door to feed you.

Oh, I see. Wouldn't you get thirsty?

Well, yeah. You had a toilet. You pushed the button, you hold your finger on the bottom of this little spigot, and that's how you drank it.

Oh, you could drink out of the toilet?

Yeah.

Then every ten days, they took you out for a shower and let you shave. They had a big old wooden door that said, "Silence is Golden."

And that's when they had goons, what they called a goon squad, and that was inmates. They had arms that were 19, 20, 21 inches around in the biceps. And if you were in there and made noise, they'd open up the door, and then inmates would come in and knock the shit out of you. Choke you. Throw a wet towel around your neck and choke you out, and you'd wake up on a strip bed. And that was a wire-framed box spring, or a wire frame that you were tied down to. They'd have you four-pointed, your legs and each one of your arms, and usually they had your head back. Those inmates never went out in the population.

Well, I imagine they did not. They would probably not be too popular in population.

No, they weren't.

Were they like given special privilege for doing this job?

Yeah, they got anything they wanted. Just living up in the hospital, watching TV, and that.

Oh.

Joliet was really strict. You marched everywhere. You had to wear a coat in the summertime. You had to wear a cap. And you stood for shake-downs everywhere you went.

And then all of a sudden, bingo; one day, I was in the hole, and they told me, "Come on out, brother." And usually when they call you out in the hole, they're going to whip your ass. I told them, "I ain't coming out" because I'd been singing, and I told them, "Brother, I ain't coming out." I said, "What do you want me to come out for?" And he said, "Well, you need to shave and shower." And I told him, "Oh, no, I'm not coming out." And he said, "No, come on out. They just passed a new ruling, United States Supreme Court, that we have to give you a shower every day, that we have to feed you three times a day; we're going to give you a mattress with two sheets and a blanket and a pillow. You're actually going to get to exercise and that."

And I thought it was a trick. I told them, "No, I ain't coming out." And they said, "No, come out." I stuck my head out, and I didn't see the goon squad anywhere. I went upstairs, and I took a shower, but I wouldn't wash my face because I thought, "As soon as I get soap on my face, they're going to rush me and start dealing with me," 'cause I was singing. I was singing in the cell.

I was paroled not too long after that. And then when I went to Walla Walla, I could not believe it. When I first went in Walla Walla, I could not believe it.

The first night I was in the receiving unit of Walla Walla, a friend of mine and a guy that I rode the chain with came by, and we'd smoked something like PCP in the receiving unit. And I was looking right at the guard while I was smoking it. And he told me, "Don't worry about him." And I was really uncomfortable. I said, "I can't do this. I can't do this." So I went in and laid down and just slept the rest of the night.

And it was cold. It was in January. It was really cold up at Walla Walla then. They gave us these orange jackets, the bright orange hunting jackets. I walked down by the cellhouse, and when I went in, I looked and seen all these convicts standing around with long hair. It looked just like you'd gone into a regular bar on the street. You know, long hair, greasy clothes, vests, biker patches and all that, bandannas. I just looked, and there was a haze, where you could tell there was just a fire. There had just been a fire in there. You know how the smoke just hangs there?

I took off this jacket, this state property, and they lit it on fire and threw it in the garbage can. And we walked on down to the cell.

Then a bunch of brothers that I know, bikers and Indians--just different convicts--came by.

And I didn't have to wear the state clothes that they gave me. I had a pair of boots on, but they gave me Levis, sweatshirt, flannel shirts, a Levi jacket, and a couple bandannas. I was asked right then if I wanted to prospect for the bike shop. I told them, "I'm too old to prospect."

What does "prospect" mean?

Be taken underneath the wing, and if you're good enough to get into the WSPMA--Washington State Penitentiary Motorcycle Association--then you get a patch. And you get to wear that patch.

Is that like joining a gang?

No, it's a ...

A club?

A club.

I see. A club?

A club, yes.

I understand.

It's an association.

An association?

Just what it says: Motorcycle Association. There's no gang.

It's a club?

They do not allow gangs in prison.

Of course they don't.

No. There's no gangs in prison.

I see. So you were invited to join the association?

Yeah.

But you decided not to join?

Yeah, because I was too old. I made my bones years ago.

Why were they so good to you when you walked in the door there?

Because I knew everybody there.

You knew all these people?

Yeah, I knew them from the street and all that.

Oh, the streets.

Plus, I rode a motorcycle and I sold drugs, weapons. You'd come to my house if you were hurt. If I had to, I could pull it out of you. I'd sew you up, do whatever I had to do if you were in that little ...

Club?

Clique. It was a clique.

I see. I understand.

So that was a lot different than Joliet?

Oh, yeah. Yeah, Joliet was really different. Yeah, I started out right from the diagnostic people going to the hole.

Because you had to make your bones?

Yeah.

And you were just a kid?

Nineteen years old. I had to do what I had to do.

You had to survive.

Yeah.

So they let you out of the hole, and then you were back in general population. And, at that point, had you made your bones? Were you okay then?

No. No, I had to do it three other times after that.

Really?

Yeah, I wasn't going to be no woman, and that was it. After I did what I had to do, people stood back and watched and said, "Yeah, the youngster's got heart." Then I was kind of adopted. There used to be honor among thieves.

There wasn't all the child molesters and that. To be a bank robber, a jewel thief, armed robber, you know, there was honor. There wasn't all this craziness, like there is today. All these sex offenses and that.

What would they do with the sex offenders?

Oh, kill them or turn them into a woman, real quick.

So back in Joliet, if a person were a sex offender, coming to prison, they're either going to be "made into a woman" or be killed?

Yeah. Or you're going to lead a terrible life.

I went to the hole right away at Joliet for what they called reckless eyeballing. I looked at a guard. It was cold. You didn't put your hands in your pocket in Joliet. We were standing outside, and it was cold. God, it was cold. And I stuck my hands in my coat, and this guard came up, and he hit my arm and said, "What are you doing?" I looked at him, and I said, "What?" And he said, "Where's your eyes supposed to be?" You were supposed to keep your eyes right in back of the next person in front of you.

He kept talking to me, and I kept looking at him. I always have kept good eye contact when I talk to people. And he said, "Get your hands out of your pocket." I got my hands out of my pocket, and I kept looking at him. He gave me a ticket for reckless eyeballing. And I went in front of the Captain, old Zeke, and Zeke, he said, "Well, I knew you was cold, and you didn't know no better." "But ...," he said, "reckless eyeballing."

Let's get back to the subject of Walla Walla. Walla Walla was wide open. Wide open.

How could that be?

Because they got some bug up their butt. They were going to try this new thing, where the inmates had a resident council.

Did you ever do hole time there?

At the Walls?

Yes.

Nope. I got one tag, and that was for a cup of coffee. They took 30 days good time. I was working at the metal plant at night, so we ate at 2:30 in the afternoon. And something happened at the metal plant, so they ran us into the dining room, and we ate another meal. I didn't eat, but, I had a cup of coffee. And one of these bulls wrote me up. One of the guards wrote me up for getting a cup of coffee, and I lost 30 days good time.

That was my first tag. Because it was a major tag there. They called it stealing. They said that was stealing.

Oh. How does that affect you mentally, when you know they've taken away 30 days of good time for a cup of coffee? Does that get you down?

Gets you down? Yeah, Jean Marie, what do you think it did to me?

I don't know. What did it do?

I wanted to kill 'em. Thirty days. Thirty days. My first tag. I'd smoked weed in front of them, been in fist fights. I hadn't even gone to the hole. They came in my cell and tried to find knives, couldn't find no knives. I was always one step ahead of them.

And it was a stupid cup of coffee, and it wasn't my fault. I asked the bull. I said, "Man, is it all right if I have a cup of coffee?" He said, "Sure, get a cup of coffee."

Did staff ever abuse inmates?

Oh, quite a few times. Quite a few times. Beat 'em up, reach up and grab you by your hair. Other little bullshit things, like tear your pictures up of your kids or break something in your cell they knew you treasured. Drop your T.V. while they're cell searching, or really trash your cell while they're cell searching, and just make your life miserable. You know, just little petty-assed bullshit. They couldn't do that to people on the streets because nobody would stand for it. But in there, you gotta stand and take it.

Few years later, they told me, "Oh, you got a contractor's license for painting, huh?" I said, "Yeah." They said, "Oh, you're a certified welder also?" I said, "Yeah." They said, "How would you like to go to Monroe?"

One time, after I got to Monroe, I got bad news, and they let me out of that cell. I got out on the yard, and it was pouring down rain. They knew I had to walk; I had to get out of that cell to walk. Because my wife died when I was at Walla Walla, and my kid was really sick after they transferred me to W.S.R. The best thing is just leave me alone, and let me get out and walk. And they did.

There was a time there, where I used to feed them guards. I'd make them sandwiches and that. They'd say, "Stand for a shake-down," and I'd tell them, "I can't. Dirty as a dog." I'd be Saran Wrap from my ankles clean up to my neck, and I might have 25-30 pounds of beef jerky on me. And I'd tell them, "I'm dirty, man. I got beef jerky on me." And they'd say, "Oh, you do?" and I said, "Yeah."

And they'd tell me, "All right." And they'd give me a pass. I'd go to my cell, and they'd come by, and I'd kick them out theirs. One time, I just wrapped it in butcher paper. And the guard said, "What have you got there, Fox?" I said, "A machine gun." I had a leg of lamb. A whole leg of lamb. And he said, "What have you got there?" And I said, "A machine gun." He said, "No, what have you got there?" I said, "A machine gun." He said, "Go on to your cell." And I went on to my cell. And when he came down, there I was cutting it up.

Johnny Fox, what would you do with it?

I'd pass it out to my friends or sell it. For a joint, I'd give them a sandwich. I ran a little--it was...

A little sandwich shop?

Yeah. Success comes to those who hustle wisely. And I was always hustling because I usually drink four fingers of whiskey. And there was guards that would pass it in. Money talks. You can buy anything you want for money.

Why would these officers let you get away with this?

Good old boys. They got paid.

They got paid? Oh, they got paid.

I'd give them cash.

Oh, you'd pay off the officers?

Yeah. I had one; I'm not going to say his name. I was dipping snuff for a lot of years. He'd bring me in a can of Copenhagen laced with blackberry brandy, Black Velvet or Jack Daniels. Every day he'd bring me in a can of Copenhagen.

There'd be certain staff that were bringing in. I'd give them 20 bucks for a fifth. And I sold shots for $10 a shot. They never used to shake down them guards. I had a guard open up my cell. He threw in two ounces of weed, and I thought it was a setup. He said, "Give them to the guy next door." I told him, "Fuck you." And I flushed those two ounces of weed down the toilet. Then he really got upset over that. I told him, "Don't you ever in your lifetime do that again." Because I really wanted to go home.

My wife had died, and then I had a kid I wanted to come home to. I quit doing everything. I just squared up. And I said, "I'm going home, boys. My kid needs me."

Right now they got really good programs at W.S.R. They got excellent programs. Your program, Jean Marie. Guys used to come by, "Man, what the fuck are you doing, laying on a mattress, crying?" I tell them, "I'm in Clarity Training." They tell me, "You're doing what?" I say, "Clarity Training." "Hey, Johnny man, have you took leave of your senses? What, are you flipped out?" But, you know, I would feel better after that.

Until you're ready to work them for yourself, they're all bullshit. You just gotta say, "Hey, this peer pressure ain't where it's at. I want to better myself."

Those programs are what's keeping me out here now.

What do you think about Ken DeCharme?

Ken's all right. He's open-minded. He lets a lot of programs come in that's going to benefit a lot of convicts, a lot of convicts like myself. He lets them volunteers in. Man, volunteers don't come in there packing dope or anything. They come in there and help us. And that's what you need. You need the help from the outside.

Ken's all right. Ken's all right.

Is there anything in closing that you'd like to say?

Just because a guy's committed a felony and convicted of it--you know, give him a chance. Because there is programs in there where, if he really wants to change his life around, he can. And no matter how violent you are, there's programs in there, there's people in there that can help you.

I learned a lot through my programs--that you just gotta open up and let the goodness come out of you. You can't keep it stuffed. And if you do get stepped on, oh well, just pick yourself up by your bootstraps, wipe your nose, and keep on trucking.

That's all the convict wants; just give them half a chance. They want to forget that madness up there. But there's a lot of people that don't want to let them forget about it. Other than that, I don't know. I don't know.

My son was molested when I was home the last time by a friend of mine. I didn't know he was a child molester. I just gotta forgive. Let go and just forgive. I go to the sweat lodge every two weeks, and it does me good. You gotta find something to believe in. You've really got to change your whole life around, and you gotta stand up and take accountability.

Nobody put me in the penitentiary, except Johnny Fox. I put myself in there. I had to make them bones. If I didn't make them bones, I never would have went to the joint. I'd still probably be with my wife and have a whole lot of things, be a whole lot different. That's all I gotta say.

Thanks, Johnny Fox.

Any time.

Section Two

Who Are the People in the System, and How Are They Treated?

Lyle Poolman

I'm speaking with Mr. Lyle Poolman. Mr. Poolman, who you are within the system?
Well, I'm "ex" within the system as of this year, with the Department of Corrections.

In 1985, I applied for the Associate Superintendent of Programs--most commonly called Associate Superintendent of Treatment in most major facilities--at the Washington State Reformatory and was hired. That was with a little bit of surprise to many folk because at that time, I was what was called a correctional unit supervisor, and the next step from a correctional unit supervisor is to that of a correctional program manager. I kind of leapfrogged that position and went straight into a position of an associate superintendent. I also did that without having ever worked in a major institution. So it was a big surprise to a lot a people.

In 1985, I did go to the Reformatory as the Associate Superintendent of Programs/Treatment, which is responsible for all the counseling and treatment programs, volunteer programs, religious programs, reading material programs, clerical--the records office, and supervision of the Washington State Reformatory Farm, the minimum security institution. The cell blocks were under my institution, and supervision of about 125 staff, and six or seven programs.

And then, in 1992, the long-time Associate Superintendent of Custody retired and Ken DuCharme, the Superintendent, asked me to become the Associate Superintendent of Custody. On paper, those are lateral positions, Associate of Treatment and Programs and the Associate of Custody. Although, in all frankness, in most institutions the Associate Superintendent of Custody probably has a lot more say-so in how the institution will run. I supervised several programs but predominantly was responsible for the security of the institution, which included a captain, 8 lieutenants, 26 sergeants, 250 or so uniformed staff, correctional officers, and the security of the institution.

And I was quite actively involved with the remodeling of the prison that was going on. I was the liaison with the institution and architects and engineers and capital programs, and that sort of thing.

In 1993, I applied for the Superintendent's job of the new prison in Spokane, Airway Heights, and believe was down to the final two applicants in that, had anticipated getting that job, and I did not.

Ultimately I applied for, with no anxiety of getting out of corrections but with a need to do something different, the position of Administrator of Juvenile Courts in Skagit County and was selected from 48 applicants for that position and took it in January of 1994.

Mr. Poolman, I'm interested in your insights into the Department of Corrections.

I think one of the things that you find, predominantly in the older, established institutions, and certainly the Reformatory meets that definition, is they get pretty set in their ways, in terms of how they operate.

In terms of personal experience, I kind of walked in there, and there was certainly nothing that you could pin your hat to, but I think there was really a lot of curiosity and skepticism from people.

I think there was, and is, typically in those older institutions, somewhat of a general attitude that custody is the name of the game. That is kind of the attitude, at least in general terms, from a lot of the uniformed staff. If you're not custody, who cares who's there, anyway?

I think those institutions are almost alive, those old ones. They just kind of breathe and operate on their own. And the Reformatory will be coming up on a hundred years here this next decade. You have people that have worked there for decades, and you have people whose fathers worked there.

So it's just kind of a living, moving, evolving thing, in terms of how it does business. I was real fortunate that, when I got there, the Associate Superintendent of Custody and I got along extremely well. I think that was because he immediately saw that I was not some totally innocent, naive guy coming in saying everything is wonderful, and everybody can be cured, and everybody can be treated.

I'd been around for a while and had a real basic understanding of that. My philosophy was/is that you cannot run programs, you cannot provide treatment until you first have security. That's the basis for everything. And nobody wants that more than the inmates in general. They want to feel safe and secure in their institution. Certainly, you could wait the rest of your life for one inmate to come up and tell you that, but, nonetheless, that's what they want. So it's really extremely important that the first thing you do is have a safe, secure institution, and then you are able to run programs that are meaningful.

I also made a point of being really visible in that institution and spent a lot of time in the sergeant's office, and the lieutenant's office, and with the captain, and talking to officers and not divorcing myself from security, which I think frequently happens in other places. I became a member of the team down there, ultimately, as a result of that.

You said that you went through a transition from Programs to Custody. How did that change your outlook on things?

I don't think it changed my attitude very much at all. It changed where my energy and times were spent.

It was real frustrating to me to think after all the years of work I'd done there, that some of those programs would collapse if they weren't nursed and kept running and people prodded. So programs were still important to me.

It was never difficult for me to see the relationship between programs and custody and that custody had to come first. That isn't an issue of importance. It's just an issue of the only way things will work.

One thing you can't do at a big prison is you can't make anything work by yourself. Or you probably can't make anything fail by yourself. You have to have buy-in from people to make anything happen.

The volunteer program was extremely important to me when I was there, from a couple different angles. One is programs are one of the best securities you have. As important as the guy in the gun tower, or at the gate, was having programs. Because people needed to be involved in things--active. (Besides, they might just get lucky and change the way they do business in life and improve themselves.) If they were sitting in a program Tuesday evening for three hours, regardless of whether they got anything out of it or not, they weren't out running the big yard, scamming a game, looking to go over the wall, or do something like that. Kind of the issue that idle hands are the devil's playground. You know?

People need to be occupied. Keep them busy to maintain their sanity, and if we get lucky, maybe it would even change the way they look at the world.

One of the things I probably felt the best about was in taking some chances with programs, not just doing the same standard things, but going out on the edge to some degree with some different types of programs. My thought, "Why not? If they don't work out, then we just throw them out of the institution. But, who knows? So try some different things."

Then, secondly, the amount of energy I put into trying to do training down there. When I was there, we implemented the mandatory training for volunteer sponsors, and we had volunteer nights quarterly.

We were doing literally hundreds of hours a year of training of volunteers and volunteer sponsors to make them more effective in the way they did their business and to make things work more smoothly.

Is that what you attribute to the vast success of the volunteer programs at Washington State Reformatory?

Oh, no. I attribute the vast success of the programs at the Reformatory to the Superintendent wanting those things to happen, to the people that run volunteer programs, wanting to make them happen and working hard, and to the correctional staff for making them work and taking the extra effort to see that they work, and just a multitude of things.

You said, "If the resident got lucky, he might change his view of life."

You've already stated that you think it's a highly effective security measure. Do you think they have any effect on the individual?

My feeling is there's no panacea in any program for people changing their way. The only thing you can really see that dramatically changes criminal behavior is age.

We like to think that education's the answer to everything, and yet I'm not sure that can be substantiated any more than you could because that person was involved in a religious program or a self-help program. The fact of the matter is most of those programs work for some people.

And sometime a guy working in the kitchen that has a solid relationship with the staff cook down there over six months makes a difference in that guy, just a positive role model. And sometimes it's Clarity Training, and sometimes it's Tai Chi, and sometimes it's--who knows what? But some different things work for different people. And some things don't work for anybody at any given time.

But, you know, it's important to have a lot of good programs. It worked for some of the people, some of the time.

We have a real poor concept, in terms of how we judge success and recidivism. Not only in this state but in this country, too. A lot of the time everything comes down to dollars. And just for the sake of dollars, let me present recidivism.

Basically, what recidivism is, if they return to prison, they've failed; if they don't return to prison, they've succeeded. That's a pretty narrow definition, but that's basically what it is. There are some real flaws in that. I mean if we get an inmate out of here, and he's from Vancouver, and he crosses a bridge into Portland and murders 35 people, and gets 35 life sentences or 35 death sentences in Oregon, he is a success statistically in Washington because he never returned to the prison system here.

So some of that's kind of hard to read, what the real numbers are. And I think one of the things that we really neglect to look at is there's some real gray area in there that's important for people to see.

If people get something out a program, get something out of counseling, get something out of themselves when they're in prison, and they go out and they manage to stay out, and hold down a job for 2 years or 3 years or 18 months, earn income, pay taxes, not create any pain to any other people out there, before they once again succumb to weaknesses of the flesh, to peer pressure, to substandard living conditions; they get two years, or two and a half years, or one year, as opposed to walking out the door, and within seven hours, or seven days, be out there doing dope again, supporting it by burglaries, etc., and back in the joint in ninety days or six months. You've gained a year or a year and a half there, and you've gained $40,000 in correctional costs saved because he was out two years rather than six months this time.

And so you've really saved a lot. And even though ultimately he failed, he'd had enough skills to make it a couple years, and the savings to the taxpayers both monetarily and socially is great. But we never measure that. And I don't know how you would measure it. But I think people need to be conscious of that. Yeah, he failed, but it was after two years. And had he not got a certificate in welding, he probably would have been back in 30 days.

So, there's some gray area there to look at.

Mr. Poolman, would you speak to the issue of women and their involvement at Washington State Reformatory? A lot of women come up to Washington State Reformatory.

You're not talking about correctional staff?

No. We will get to correctional staff.

I think one thing that's been long established is that probably the greatest factor in determining success or failure for an inmate being released from an institution is the support system he has in the community or doesn't have in the community.

I think that R.C.W.'s, when they speak to visitation rights, they're saying very explicitly that within the confines of the concrete rectangle up there, it's incumbent upon corrections officials to try to have a life as near normalcy as possible within those confines.

Obviously, a life without--be it a corrections center for women with no males in the institution, or a male institution with no females, is certainly not normalcy.

So we encourage that. There's some real problems that it doesn't take a brain surgeon to figure out that come with that territory.

But it's important that the people maintain their relationship with their wives and their girlfriends while they're in the institution.

It's absolutely necessary that volunteer programs and religious programs and self-help programs include females. It's important that those inmates learn to relate appropriately with female folk working in there.

One of the common denominators (certainly not every inmate in every situation, but by and large) is that they have a low regard for females.

If not in terms of their treatment, then seeing them as just objects. I hope that one of the things that occurs up there is a little more appropriateness in that arena.

Washington State Reformatory has an extended family visit program?

I have kind of mixed emotions about that. Let me address it from a prison manager's perspective first. From that perspective, I have an extremely positive view of it because it's a great management tool. I don't want that to sound wrong.

There is a percentage of inmates that watch their Ps and Qs, program, stay out of trouble, don't do dope, so they can participate in that program. So as a management tool, it's wonderful.

The part of it that is hard to swallow is some of the abuses that come with it. I saw one inmate up there that was married at least three times, perhaps four times, to four different women over a seven-or eight-year period of time. All of whom were women who'd come in as volunteers, people he'd contacted, a friend of a friend's girlfriend that he would marry, have trailer visits with, divorce, take up another relationship, be back out in the trailer again.

I know there were a lot of inmates that aggressively sought out women to marry, just for the opportunity to have a trailer visit. And so you saw some pretty sad situations. You know?

I think of one in particular, a young girl coming up there and starting work as a volunteer. Then she got involved in a relationship with an inmate and was terminated as a volunteer. Now she was coming as a visitor to visit in the visiting room with the inmate.

Then I saw her marry the inmate and then later begin trailer visits with the inmate. Then I watched her go through a full-term pregnancy and have a baby and saw her come up to the prison with a new baby in her arms. By the time I'd left there, she was coming in with a five-or six-year old, school-aged child, visiting and going to trailer visits.

That was a pretty sad commentary. I'm thinking that baby was conceived inside of that prison, spent four nights of his week in the prison, and visits in a trailer in the corner of a prison yard. So there are some things that don't sit right there in terms of the motives that some of the people had.

I suppose some of the motives of the women were abusive also. I don't mean to be throwing a blanket on everyone that's involved in that program. There's many people involved legitimately. There's also people who abuse it.

I supervised the mail room in the prison, and I would see many women who I knew were on public assistance with two or three kids, sending both money and packages, food packages, clothing packages, etc., etc., into their husbands. I didn't know how on their income they could even afford to feed their children, yet they put $100 a month, or whatever, on the books of their husbands so they could buy cigarettes and what have you. There were just some real abuse by some guys towards those women that way.

Can you talk to me a little bit about women employed there?

I'd mentioned earlier, old, established institutions as compared to new institutions. When that change was made in the early '80s to hire female correctional staff, that was way harder at the Reformatory than it was for a brand-new institution. That was pretty easy to pull off.

Much more difficult when you get into the Reformatory or the Penitentiary, where for 60, 80 or 100 years, it's been a totally male domain. People that have been there for years just saying, "What in the hell are you talking about?" You know? "This is a man's job; this is no place for women."

And I think probably still there are a lot of people who believe that. But lots and lots of people now believe that the female correctional officer can do the job and be very professional and adequate at doing it.

I think there's been lots of studies that shows that there's a decreased amount of violence in areas supervised by female correctional officers.

The flip side to that is there are some problems that come along with it. There's personnel issues that I was constantly dealing with, where staff B felt harassed by staff A and wouldn't work with staff C if staff D was there, because of that male-female thing. And then we'd lose staff occasionally, female correctional officers, who became over-familiar and involved with inmates.

Frankly, that wasn't very frequent. But whenever it occurred, you could hear the I-told-you-so's ring for a thousand miles in a thousand directions. So it just fed the fodder. Even though it was frankly pretty infrequent that that occurred, it did occur.

Do you think women do a good job as custody?

It's like saying, "Do you think men do a good job?" I saw some women that did and some women that were horrible.

How could they deal with working on the blocks? They walk on the blocks, where men are ...

Showering? There were a few exceptions, positions, that females did not work, but basically that was the name of the game. This is the job, and this is what it entails.

If you're hired here, here's what you have to do, and that includes working the blocks, and there's going to be some unpleasantries that come with it. You're going to have to walk by and supervise the shower area, and you're going to have to walk by cells, and there will be men in there who will be masturbating, and there will be men in the cells who exhibit themselves to you and then claim they weren't.

That's the price of admission. It comes with the territory, and some women could handle that, and some couldn't.

Just as some men could handle aspects of their job and couldn't handle other aspects of the job. Women officers had all the responsibilities that the men officers did, plus they had the additional agenda of being a female officer in a male institution on top of that. So, not a place for the weak-hearted, I guess.

Is there something that we haven't covered?

Do you want to talk about treatment of inmates?

All right.

The overwhelming majority of the inmates in the institution are just fine to get along with because they come in, and they only want two or three things: they want to be safe, they want to be secure; they want to not be hassled; they want to be left alone; and to be able to find a way to do their time, whether it's two years, or a lifetime.

The fact of the matter is most of the inmates that come in there, who may have been despicable in their behavior on the street, have come into that institution, and, for the most part, are sleeping eight hours a day; they're getting three square meals a day; they're working; they're exercising; they're doing something constructive during the day and hopefully have had their drugs and alcohol taken away from them. With those factors in place, most of them are decent people. They're just fine to get along with.

Unfortunately, back on the street, with drugs and alcohol, no sleep, bad friends, and poverty, it's back to being a real jerk again.

But most of them are just fine in the institution.

"You leave me alone; I'll leave you alone. These are your rules. Make sure I understand them, and I will follow them." There's always that 10% in there that continue to loot, rape and plunder. "Well, I'm not in downtown Seattle or Tacoma; I'm in a prison. But that isn't going to change the way I operate. I'm still going to be a sexual predator or a strong-armer, or a drug dealer." They continue to do their business, as they always have, including a lot of people who really abuse the staff.

I'm not saying all of them. I'm just saying some inmates really abuse staff and can be so good at it that it leaves little recourse for the staff. I experienced that myself. You can just about get enraged because of the abuse you take from John Doe Inmate in there.

One thing I tried to really pound home with staff is that it was rarely, if ever, individually pointed at someone. Inmates need to punish someone, and his anger is coming out at any target.

Probably more than anything, the issue of retaliation against that inmate, which is real easy for any staff to do. I don't think anybody would deny that occasionally there'd be knives found in cells that could really impact an inmate's life and time and that it may have been put there by a staff.

It's not our job to punish people who are in there. The punishment is having their freedom taken away. If we start reacting to inmates as they react to us, then how do you tell us'uns from them'uns? You know?

It seems like you've had a lot of responsibility through the years. It must be a huge amount of stress having so many things going on at the same time. How have you been able to deal with it on a personal level?

I think I've been good at being able to pick up the job at 7:00 in the morning, and, in large part, being able to leave it at the institution when I drive out. Things will be the same tomorrow, whether I fret and stew about it from 6:00 at night till 7:00 the next morning or not.

Things aren't as complicated as they seem. You need to brush out all that peripheral stuff and just see what's there. Do the right thing, and be honest, and be fair with people. Be reasonable, and exhibit some common sense in making decisions, and be direct with people.

Do those five or six type things, and life isn't nearly as complicated as it appears.

I tried to always keep in mind there's just nothing that's ever going to happen to me, or while I'm at that prison, that hasn't happened before and will probably happen again. My only obligation is to work hard, do a good job. When something goes sideways, I try and fix it and make it so it won't happen again. That's all that can be expected of me.

I want to thank you for all you've done at W.S.R.

Oh, you don't need to do that.

I want to. You've left an impact. Thank you.

You're welcome.

The Professor

Is this the microphone?

This is the microphone right here. My name is Jean Marie. I'm at Washington State Reformatory speaking with the Professor.

Why do they call you the Professor?

Well, it goes back to when I first came into the system in 1974. I was a real calculating individual. But, on top of that, I was also real bright. The academic level back then of prisoners was very low, so anybody who had obtained high school graduate status or had actually gone to college was an anomaly within the system. And that's how I kind of got my name. I could figure things out quick, and that sort of thing.

I see. Can you tell me what your association with the Department of Corrections is?

I'm an inmate, and I have been an inmate for almost 21 years this month. I'm a three-time offender, this being my third time. And I've been heavily involved in the system through my criminal activity.

Couple of things ...

Okay.

Number one, you refer to yourself as an inmate.

Yeah.

Why is that?

Well, because convict isn't used any more. I mean, we convicts are dinosaurs. So to try to fit in that--almost chameleon-like--you use terms that everyone's using: inmate or prisoner, as opposed to convict. You're never a resident. And you try to fit in.

Who are you trying to fit in with?

Well, the other Pepsi Lite generation of inmates that are in here and the administration. When you start using terms like convict around them, they get real antsy and shaky, and it takes them back to the old days really quick.

What's the "Pepsi Lite" inmate? What's that mean?

When I first fell, back in 1974, the majority of the crimes were for monetary purposes. They were done because a guy was a dope fiend and needed to get money to satisfy his habit; or he just wanted money to buy things, and he didn't have an inclination to work; or he did work and didn't make that much money.

Nowadays, there's a lot of just senseless crimes. We can call them the Pepsi Lite because they're senseless burglaries. They did a burglary just to burglarize something, and then they'd vandalize somebody's house, or they drive by and shoot someone--drive-by shootings. The sex crimes now are on an explosive rate. And I think that's all just indicative of the whole generation I'm talking about, probably from about the late '70s, beginning of '80, all the way up to present. The whole thought pattern for criminal activity has changed.

Do you have any insight as to why that might be?

Drugs, first of all. The rampant use and society's complacency with the drug usage. That's one thing. Not taking a position on it, either helping people rid themselves of a drug habit or saying no, that we're not going to have drugs. That's probably one of the biggest things.

The other thing is family values have deteriorated. And then the established politicians' knee-jerk reaction laws aren't really there to punish; they're there to appease a voting segment of society.

And so, consequently, we end up with nothing to guide people. People need guidance, and there's not much of that out there.

You said that when a prisoner uses the term "convict," that causes administration to react?

Right.

Can you tell me a little bit more about that?

Well, the '60s-'70s were a time of convict rule, almost. A federal judge passed a ruling that said we should be able to have some self-government. And, consequently, here and at Walla Walla, they started self-government. They said, okay, what we're going to do is we're going to man the perimeter of the prison, and you guys run the inside. Well, that's like turning the nuthouse over to the nuts, okay?

Not that we're not trying to become citizens, but when you've never been a citizen, you need direction on how to get there. If you've never built a boat, you don't just hand somebody a bunch of wood and say, "Here, build a boat." You give them a person that's sailed boats and built boats and that sort of thing, and that gives them direction on how to build one.

Well, consequently, during the '70s, all that was just rampant. I mean we convicts ran the prisons, basically. And so, when you use the term "convict" a lot of the staff--administrative staff that was involved in the '70s--look at that kind of, well, with a leery eye. So if you're trying to get along in the system, if you're trying to move through it comfortably without causing any problems and get the most out of it, you try to become part of it, okay? And to become part of it you have to use the terminology that they use. And the terminology that they use is residents and inmates.

Thank you. I'd like to learn a little bit more about you as an individual. Can you tell me how old you were the first time you ever committed a crime, broke the law?

Seven or eight, easily.

What did you do at the age seven or eight that would break the law?

Probably it was petty theft, as I can think back, or something along the lines of malicious mischief---that sort of thing. One of the first incidence that I can recall, at seven or eight years old, different gentlemen ran trout lines on streams for crawdads and that sort of thing. They used them as bait, and they sold them as bait, and I'd go and let them all go. I just didn't like to see the crawdads in the traps, and so I'd let them go. Well, that was illegal. That was against the law to release somebody's trap. So, consequently, I got busted for that.

You didn't like to see the crawdads --

In traps.

Trapped?

Yeah.

So, as time went by, did you continue to break the law?

Pretty much, in other ways. I became a self-made entrepreneur. I had a paper route. I was about 10 years old, and I had a paper route. After my paper route, I would collect, so I always had a few dollars on me. I would take my money and go to paper machines, use one coin and take out all the papers, and then I'd take all those papers and sell them on a whole different route. So that would increase my profits tremendously.

And did it ever cross your mind, even at this young age, that perhaps you were doing something wrong?

Oh, yeah. I was aware of right and wrong. I just felt that I wouldn't get caught, you know? I was too slick; I was too bright. And I didn't. The consequences aren't something that a criminal thinks about, you know. He doesn't sit down and say, "Okay, I'm going to plan this job and what are the consequences?" That's a falsehood that leads into that knee-jerk policy-making.

Well, at 10 years old, you're probably not quite a criminal yet.

Perhaps.

But you are stealing?

I'm stealing.

And you're not, you're not too concerned with the morality of it though you're aware of that. You're mostly concerned with whether or not you're going to get caught?
Right.
And did you ever get caught?
No.
Okay. So continue on. What was the progression of this?
Mmmm ... minor crimes of that nature, but progressing in dollar value up until I was 15, when I committed my first armed robbery.
And what did you rob?
I robbed--the statute of limitation's well over, so I don't have to worry about that--I robbed a Carnation distributorship. They pick up the money, and they have these big thick wallets for each delivery man. And then they turn them into ... he was an old guy, an accountant, I would presume, bookkeeper of some sort, who counted up all the day's sheets of money, and that sort of thing.
You said that was an armed robbery?
Yeah.
You used a gun?
Yeah, I used a .22, a wired-together .22. I remember it distinctly. Yeah, it was quite something.
Where did you get a gun when you were--what, 15 years old?
Fifteen years old. That gun there was just one of those old--it was a gang-related gun. It had been passed around, and passed around, and I had bought it for a minor amount of money.
So, Professor, approximately how much money was involved with this particular robbery?
About 5600 bucks.
Okay, so you are a 15-year-old child now, and you have 5600 dollars?
Well, I would say I was a 15-year-old young adult, and I had 5600 dollars. I think there's a transition that some people make from being a child to young adulthood that isn't taken into consideration. There's many individuals, young adults, out there nowadays, far more than in my day, I believe, that are acting and doing things that are in the adult vein.
So you believe people of 13, 14 and 15 should be tried as adults?
That's not what I said at all. What I believe is there needs to be serious consideration given to the individual, not just one of these knee-jerk reactions, and let's just lump everybody into this one category. If you're 13 and above, we're going to lock you up as an adult for a violent crime, okay? There's many 13-year-olds that don't understand the full consequences of their actions, and there's some that do.

So you feel that there are some people of this age who should be tried as adults?
That's still a difficult question for me to answer in a yes or a no. I feel that occasionally you will find an individual that is 13 or 14 years old that committed an act that had full understanding of what they were doing. In that case, they may be tried as an adult.
And you feel that you were one of these?
I feel that I was a young adult at 15, yes.
As a 15-year-old young adult, then, what did you do with the money?
Well, one of the first things I did was I bought myself a motor scooter. And then I spoke with my mother about living with my grandparents. And that's what I did. I moved up to be with my grandparents.
With your motor scooter?
With my motor scooter. Great fun.
I see. So did you commit any crimes when you were living with your grandparents?
Continuously.
What kind of crimes were they?
Armed robbery. That's all I've done. I was an armed robber. And so, consequently, that's what I did. The man who taught me how to armed-rob, he was an armed robber.
There was a man who taught you how to armed-rob?
Basically, yeah. He said if you're going to do crime, you might as well do it and get the money, and not just fiddle around and go to prison for no money.
I see. So, he's telling you, if you're going to take a risk anyway ...
Right.
Make the risk worthwhile?
Exactly.
So, you started robbing places or people who had more money?
Right, right. Usually not people. I'm robbing a business, you know, so it's the insurance company. I know now that's distorted thinking. What I tried to do is I tried to rob large grocery stores and that sort of thing. Stay away from anything small or try to get the maximum amount.
Is that a scary thing to do?
Robbery?
Yes.
Yes and no. See, what it is, it's a control thing. There's some place in my life, during that time, I didn't feel I was in control. So with the power of a pistol, a gun, a weapon, I became in control. I became stronger. And, hence, I was able to go in, point a gun at someone, demand the money, take it and extricate myself out of the area.

And in a way it's scary, but I think it falls more in the line with that adrenaline rush. You know, some people take drugs to get high, and some people sky dive or drive cars. I think there's a whole group of criminals that commit crime just for that rush. There's a rush that comes along with it.

So now you're robbing large grocery stores?

Grocery stores, those sort of things, yeah.

Well, what does "those sort of things" mean?

There's a lot of different things that fall under that category. There's large liquor stores; there's jewelry stores, like that.

I don't want you confessing to crimes.

Oh, I wouldn't confess to a crime. Statute of limitations has run out on all of those.

So what are you doing time for now?

Armed robbery, bank robbery and first degree assault.

I see. Can you tell me about that?

In 1988, myself and another individual entered a bank with the object of robbing the business. When we entered the place, there was police inside, and the robbery itself never actually took place because there was a shoot-out there. My partner was shot a couple of times through the heart, and he ran off about 500 meters and collapsed in a driveway and died in the arms of the police officer.

Our whole intent was to rob the place, and when I entered the building, we encountered police officers. Instead of retreating, I chose to continue on with the robbery, and in trying to continue on with the robbery, I was consequently shot numerous times: through the hip, arm, broke my leg, you know, other parts of my body. And finally, after being shot so many times and really incapacitated, I turned and I shot. And then I turned to try to abort the robbery and leave. And my leg was broke and, you know, I was pretty messed up by then. I just got outside the bank and collapsed from loss of blood and that sort of thing.

So were you taken away by the ambulance?

An ambulance came, and they saw I was shot up pretty good, so they began medical treatment on me and put me in the ambulance, and they rushed me to the hospital really quick. I was there for about nine months.

Okay, nine months of treatment ...

Right.

... for the gunshot wounds?

Right.

And when were you incarcerated?

Well, we went to trial. I was still in a wheelchair and still undergoing treatments. But we went to trial, jury trial, where I was subsequently found guilty on the robbery and the assault, and at that time, I was given 212 months and sentenced to prison.

And what prison were you sent to?

Well, as I said, I was still in a wheelchair, so I'm non-ambulatory, and they took me first to Shelton. Everyone goes to Shelton first. That's the receiving unit or diagnostic center, as they say, so I was there in the hospital there at Shelton, and they didn't know exactly what to do with me because my arm was paralyzed, and my leg and hip were pretty badly damaged, and I had to have continuing surgeries. And so, at first they sent me to Washington State Reformatory. I got up here, and they'd just finished some renovations at the hospital and that sort of thing, and I wanted surgeries done so I could get out of the wheelchair, at least attempt to start getting out of the wheelchair. Because of that, they sent me back to Shelton with the objective of sending me to Walla Walla, which they did. I went to Shelton again, and from Shelton I was sent off to Walla Walla.

How were you treated?

At Walla Walla?

At any of these places.

I have to say that at Washington State Reformatory, the hospital treated me really well. At Walla Walla, I was put in isolation, denied phone calls and contact with the attorney, generally abused. And I couldn't get around at all. They'd take the wheelchair, so, consequently, I couldn't go anyplace. I was bedridden.

So I was kept there and then finally they let me into what they call One South, which is a handicap wing. And when I got to One South, I started legal action, and because of the legal action, I was transferred from Walla Walla back to Shelton, where I received the necessary surgeries. I asked them to send me to W.S.R., Washington State Reformatory, which they did. And that's where I've been ever since.

You used the term "generally abused." Could you be more specific? What does that mean?

Well, it would be like I'd ask to use the phone; they'd say no. I wouldn't get any of my mail. When I did get my mail, they would be reading it in front of my cell, or when I'd send mail out, it wouldn't go out; it would be lost.

There's a lieutenant over there that has a real interesting cruel streak to him. He threatened to place me in IMU, and he had tried to get me placed in what they call the third floor, which is the nut wing, because he says there was no reason why I just couldn't get up and start walking even though I had doctor's reports and all these other medical stuff. So he had a psychologist come in who wrote a report in my favor, which made me stay in the hole longer. Basically, I was in the hole there.

And just through time, and the doctor saying that I wasn't going to get any better being locked up in the hole, did I get out to One South.

And how was it for you at Washington State Reformatory?

Well, by now I was walking with the aid of crutches and a cane, and the whole atmosphere is different, you see? There's a lot of old-timers here. They come here as a transition stage. That's what most of us old-timers see Washington State Reformatory as--a transition point so we can get normal. The punitive punishments aren't here. The guards pulling you out and beating you up. That sort of thing.

It's just not as a hostile atmosphere here as other prisons, and so you would come to W.S.R. and kind of be able to start relating. And your skills at getting in contact with people are rebuilt, and there's just a lot of things like that that take place that are nice about W.S.R. You can get in contact with humanity a little bit.

You made references to officers pulling you out of line and beating you up?

Historically at Walla Walla and at Clallam Bay, places of that nature, the officers are very disciplinary and punitive. You're coming out of the kitchen at Walla Walla, and there might be six guards standing in front of the exit door. They'll tell you to step over to the side, and they'll start shaking you down roughly. They may strike you in the testicles with their hand, push your forehead against a brick wall a couple times while they're all laughing. And if you're not just a punk or something, you usually end up going with a couple of them, and they end up dog piling you, beating you up and taking you out to the hole. And then you get infracted. So it's a losing situation for the convict, but the guards get a good kick out of it.

Is that they why they do it, for a kick?

They do it because they're angry and frustrated, I think. One of the things at W.S.R. is that they try to develop a professionalism about their status. And that's instilled into them not only by the sergeants and lieutenants, but by administration too.

Well, at Walla Walla, there's more of the "good old boy" kind of thing going on over there. There's a lot of alcoholism with the guards, a lot of drug abuse with the guards. It's a factual thing. There's guards over there that have committed crimes, and you just don't hear about it in mainstream news. There might be a little blip in a Walla Walla paper.

They're not as professional either there or in Clallam Bay. They're just not as professional. I guess they're trained about the same, but I guess it's the support that they get. It's not an enviable position, being a correctional officer, at any time. It's a job that has to get done, but not many people want to do it. And, consequently, when they start just pulling any John Doe off the streets, a wheat farmer out of the wheat fields over there or an apple picker or something, you don't get a real high quality individual.

And at Walla Walla, there's a lot of nepotism--fathers, sons, nephews, that sort of thing going on. And it's almost like a welfare state, where it leads from one family to another in an unbroken chain as their source of income.

So, Professor, you say that you have been incarcerated now on three separate occasions.

This is my third time.

The first time you were incarcerated what were you charged with?

Armed robbery.

And the second time?

Armed robbery.

And the third time?

Armed robbery.

Actually, the second time was assault. They dropped the robbery.

And how many years did you do on the first one?

Five or six.

Second one?

Five.

And now, you've been in how long on this one?

Over seven.

Would you just generally speak about some of your experiences?

Well, like I say, I first came in in 1974, and we were running about 1,000 to 1,200 people here at Monroe. It was called the Gladiator School. And the reason it was called the Gladiator School is because when you got here, you knew that at some point you were progressing to Walla Walla. This was a training ground to go to Walla Walla.

What took place here at Monroe during those early years was you learned. If you were a property offender, you left as a violent offender. So you learned to be more angry; you learned to be more violent. If you didn't learn that, you'd end up being a punk, a sissy. If you let people run over you, or take your stuff, or your clothes, your watch, or whatever, you ended up being abused. It could be physically abused, sexually abused, and certainly, at the very least, mentally abused. So, consequently, that just led you to become harder and harder.

Nowadays, 20 years later, there's not even a vague resemblance to that.

So, that's what nobody was asking: How did someone come in as one thing and leave as a multiple rapist murderer? These are the kind of questions that need to be asked.

So, this being the Gladiator School, I did a lot of hole time. Not only was I going to the hole, but the whole group I ran with, we all went to the hole. A lot of reasons: fighting with the guards, fighting with other inmates, stabbings, riots, you name it. So it was a very wild period of time.

You mentioned going to the hole. Can you tell me what that was like?

Well, Monroe had several holes. They had an upper max and a lower max, and then they had the hole that was behind the kitchen. And none of them were pleasant. I went to the hole a few times, and I would allow my mouth to get me into trouble. I'd be taken down to the hole for fighting or beating up a guard, and I'd be down there talking stupid and crazy to the other guards, and all of a sudden I'm being handcuffed to the bars and beat up. That took place back then.

Excuse me, Professor, I'd like to interject right now. What do you mean, they'd handcuff you to bars and then beat you up?

Well, your hands would be handcuffed above your head, usually, and then you'd be there naked, handcuffed, and then they would come in and give you rib shots and might kick you in the testicles a few times.

It was done because of the lack of professionalism. They would be pushed to such an extent--the guards were--that they would need to retaliate. So they would take you down there and give you a good old-fashioned ass- whipping.

To the point where you would bleed?

Occasionally. Just depends how stupid you stayed. I mean, if you were like myself that was stuck on stupid, the more they whipped on you, the madder you got. So ....

So they'd continue to hit you for a long time?

Usually they'd get tired before they'd--you know ....

It seems like if someone or several people are striking you like that for an extended period of time, that could cause some kind of internal damage.

I'm sure it could.

Do you feel you were the only person ever treated this way?

Oh, no. No, no, there's plenty of guys that could give you stories about it, both here and at Walla Walla. Actually, I got worse ass-whippings at Walla Walla than I ever did here. Over there, they really work on you. Here, it wasn't so bad. Here, what they'd do is they'd take you down, might give you a good 15-minute butt-whipping, put you into the hole, and you'd be there for a year, okay?

Over at Walla Walla, now, on the other hand, they'll take you down and give you a good hour whipping, take you to the hole, leave you there for a few days, bring you back out, and give you another couple hours whipping.

You speak as if this is not an unusual event?

It's not an unusual event. It doesn't happen at Washington State Reformatory anymore. But it still happens at Clallam Bay, Walla Walla.

So for a man to be put into isolation, taken out and beaten, put back into isolation, taken out, beaten, and this goes on for an extended period of time--how would that affect that person?

Well, what you really need to ask is: What happens when they say, "Okay, your release date is here; we're letting you go" and they parole you from the hole? Now, you've been whipped on now for five or six months, a year, and your release date comes up, and they let you go. They do that all the time at Walla Walla. They don't do that here at Monroe anymore, but they do it all the time there.

It's like Walla Walla's never changed. They've locked it down more; there's no self-government there. There's no self-government here, but at least we have a rapport with administration, staff and guards. There's none of that at Clallam Bay, Walla Walla. I'm not saying it's easier time. I'm away from my family and friends. It's difficult time here at Monroe.

But what happens at Walla Walla is they make you hate there. When you leave Walla Walla, you hate. You need to punish somebody, see? They owe you now. So somebody has to pay, and that's what nobody's saying. What's up with that? When you leave Monroe, you're looking to go and become a citizen back into the community. You're looking to move on, you're looking to get with your family, your friends, and just--ah, I'm done.

You come out of the hole, and you've been whipped on for so long, and they use a dog chain over there. They put that around your neck. They put you in IMU and give you a finger wave, a digital probe every time, and laugh and video it, and it's a good old boy time. They hose you down. They'll bring a fire hose in and hose you down just because you knocked your tray off of the wall and called them a bunch of son-of-a-bitches.

There might be some rhyme to the madness, to have to subdue somebody for something, you know, if the guy's all the way off the deep end or something. But to do some of the things that take place within this prison system and then to release a man after doing that to him into the public is so out of line that the people that are doing it need to be punished. It's not happening, and it isn't going to happen. Because the public thinks all their needs are being addressed.

The public is angry, and they're frustrated, and they're tired. They're angry because their money is going down the tube, okay? They're putting their tax dollars out; they're not seeing nothing. They call up the Department of Corrections and say, show me something that's getting corrected. The system is really counterproductive to correct anything.

The next thing is they're looking around, and they're saying, "Hey, what's up with this? I can't even send my kid to school anymore without guns and everything going around." The issues aren't being addressed. And they're tired. They're tired of the same old rhetoric that comes out of the politician's mouth--Democrats, Republicans, doesn't matter who it is. That same stuff is coming out.

And that's what's going on. They're not angry with the convicts themselves. If they thought the convict could get some help and get out, be right, and be a citizen, that would be fine.

Now what they want to do is they want to hang signs around your neck; they want to publish bulletins on you, etc., etc., etc. The public is saying, "We're willing to give up our civil rights, our rights under the constitution, to punish people more." What are they talking about here? They shouldn't have to give up anything to get these things right. The politicians continue that rhetoric that doesn't mean anything but only inflames. They don't understand that.

This is the most punitive time since they used to hang pickpockets in this country. We're locking up more people in this country now than any time before, and violent crime's down. These are statistics that can be easily looked up. Violent crime's down. Crimes that are up are sex offenses and property crimes. Drug crimes are up 250 percent. They're bringing people in here for possession of crack, one chunk of crack that they were trying to sell to make money so they could go buy some more because they were so strung out.

Nobody's addressing it. It's punitive. See, the politicians have used scare-monger, terrorist tactics, and they've scared the public into thinking that they're addressing these issues. They're not, you know. They're throwing good tax dollars after bad.

When you get somebody into the system who can actually do something, like Chase Riveland, Tom Rolfs, Ken DuCharme, they're hindered by people that start throwing out all kinds of half truths and deceptions.

So, that's what's happening with prisons. What it's about is the treatment issues aren't being addressed; the professionalism isn't across the line; and there's no rhyme nor reason to what they're allowing.

This is a serious issue. Crime and prisons is a serious issue, and if people don't quit with this rhetoric about we have a war on crime going, it's going to be just like the war on drugs. It's been a failure. They've put billions of dollars in it; it didn't work. We have more people being strung out. Heroin's the new number one designer drug out there now. Yippie-yi-yo. They're just going to have a bunch of cowboy youngsters out there with more pistols and everything else because the issues aren't being addressed.

Well, it sounds like to me, Professor, that you've been through a lot.

A lot.

You described yourself earlier as a criminal?

Right.

Do you feel you are still a criminal?

Oh, no.

What brought you to the point of being something different than a criminal?

Well, I think that beginning experience was being shot, laying in the hospital recuperating. My interactions with a lot of individuals through the hospital system.

There was a young man that I met in Shelton who had been diagnosed with full-blown AIDS, and we used to have long talks, and he was always very sad. He knew he didn't have the time to make it up to his mom and dad. And one of the things he always said, and he was pretty wise for such a young man, "It's never too late to make the right choices." And that was a real eye-opener.

Then coming to Monroe. They have a lot of self-help programs. I got involved in them. A lot of programs that gave me tools to start asking myself those real tough questions, like, "Who am I?"

In reality, what I was is a thief, a liar, a cheat--that sort of thing. So to get to that point was a huge step.

And then a next step was to ask that next series of questions, such as, "What do I want to be?" I wanted to be a husband; I want to be a member of my community and not be remembered for my criminal past, but for what I can actually give to my community in a positive way. I wanted to be a caregiver in some way, a therapist or a caregiver. I wanted to be a part of the citizenship of this state and not just a drain or a criminal.

Which led to a third question: How do I get there, how to bring me back into being a human being, to a point where I can be a citizen, where I can become a part of my community? All that was offered here at Monroe. You know, it's not offered anyplace else. It's offered here at Monroe, though.

Then I had the chance to say now I've asked all these questions. I've taken these programs. Now I either got to start walking that talk, or I gotta be a liar, cheat or thief. I got to be that manipulator, that deceptor. I chose to walk that talk, as difficult as it may be, and it's not like I've walked it perfectly for the last five or six years, by far. But I've walked it a lot better than I walked it in the 14 years prior.

We can't continue thinking of criminals as disposable human beings. We can't disenfranchise this whole segment of society.

I just read in the paper the other day that the people outside prison were called "citizens," but the people inside prison were called "criminals." Well, that's right; we are criminals; we've committed a crime. But, you know, that's separating us, see? The Blacks have to live over here; the Whites have to live over here. This part of the bus for you; this part of the bus for us. You can only drink out of this water fountain; you can't have these kind of jobs. The majority of people in prison are poor, under-educated, and they're becoming more and more disenfranchised from society.

I'm becoming back in tune with society. I have a different group of friends; I've reestablished a lot of family contacts. I've gotten married, which is a huge turnaround. And there's just things like that that are taking place that are incremental and are just as dramatic as the traumatic things that happened in my life. I don't want to be the "Professor," you know? I just want to be the Citizen. I want to be known as the "Citizen," you see? Not the "Professor." I don't want to be the slick guy anymore.

Marty

Marty, what is your current position with the Department of Corrections?
Actually, I'm no longer with the Department of Corrections. I work with children as a residential counselor.
And so you used to work for the Department of Corrections?
Right. I did.
And what was your position with the Department of Corrections?
I was a correctional officer.
And where was that?
At Walla Walla.
Why are you no longer a correctional officer?
Because I fell in love and married an inmate.
Could you tell me what that meant to you in your life?
You don't always pick the person to fall in love with. Love picks you a lot of times. And it meant that I lost a lot of friends; I lost a lot of my family. I was isolated and pushed totally away and treated like I was scum of the earth because I fell in love with someone.
I've interviewed quite a few people, and some of them did time at Walla Walla. Can you tell me what the conditions are like in Walla Walla?
They don't really care about the inmates. They don't care if they're rehabilitated. One story that comes to mind was of a young man, a big, black young man, probably 19, 18. He gave me a kite one day, and the kite is the form that they have to fill out in order to see someone, and you have to read it and sign it. I couldn't understand what he wanted, so I went to him and asked him who he wanted this kite to go to and what he wanted it to say. I had taken him away from everyone so no one would know what I was saying to him, and I finally asked him if he could read. He got very upset. And I said, "This stays between us. Tell me." He told me he hadn't got past the first

grade. That's why he had to go to stealing because he couldn't fill out applications. I went to his counselor, told her that he could not read or write, and she told me, "So?" She was too busy. She did not have time to be bothered with him.

How long were you a correctional officer there?

Over six years.

Six years. How would you say the general treatment of the inmate is?

They really don't care. They run them through like cattle. If they're sick, oh well. I've seen kids have pneumonia, and they wouldn't call a doctor. They just had the nurse come out, and she says, "Oh, yeah. You can hear him breathing." Yes, you could hear him clear down at the end of the tier, breathing. And they didn't seem to really care.

I sat and held a man dying in my arms. They didn't want to send him to the hospital, and they couldn't get a doctor to come and look at him. When they did get him to the hospital the next morning, he died 45 minutes later. He was full of cancer. He had no--no pain killer. He died in pain. No one deserves that type of death. No one.

Why wouldn't they get him to a doctor?

Because it's too expensive for the doctors to come in at night, and they didn't want to be bothered, so doctors wouldn't come in.

How did you meet the man that you're currently married to?

I met him in the unit that I work in. He was there.

How did you get involved with an inmate? It's--it would seem to be a difficult thing for a correctional officer to become that romantically involved. Or is it?

When you work side by side with them, you have to oversee everything they do. You're with them every day.

When I realized that I was in love with him, I quit. I got out of there so it wouldn't hurt him or anybody else.

And after being a correctional officer for so many years, and then being involved with an inmate, did you feel like you were retaliated against, or did any problems occur in your life because of that?

Oh, yes. Obscene phone calls, nasty letters.

Who would make an obscene phone call to you?

Well, they never could find out. They were made from telephone booths and other places.

And who do you think were making them?

Um--

You don't have to give me a name.

I would say fellow correctional officers because of the context of what they said.

I see. And was anything ever done in retaliation against your husband?
He was thrown in the hole, and they shipped him out immediately.
Where was he shipped to?
Washington State Reformatory.
I see. And was he treated fairly at W.S.R.?
Yes. He's been treated very nice here.
What are some of the things that you would just like the public to know?
They keep saying that they want to rehabilitate these people. How can you rehabilitate someone that you treat like a dog, or like an animal? Like the boy that couldn't read. They had programs there at Walla Walla that could have taught him to read, but his counselor was too busy to see that he got into that program.
Isn't that what they're paying them for to make sure that these kids, or these people, get into programs that they need to be into? The public is yelling that these people should be into school so many hours a day or working so many hours a day. How can we get them in school or working if their counselors are not doing their job?
In the six years that you were at Walla Walla, did you ever witness an inmate being abused in any way?
Yes. If an officer decided they didn't like the inmate, or the inmate had done something to irritate them, he would spread it to all the other officers, and they would watch him. I mean, this man could not do anything that everybody wasn't onto him about. They would literally almost shove him into doing something.
And, in fact, I have left roll call with them, and they would say as we walked out, "Well, who are we going to harass today to get thrown in the hole?"
You mean a group of officers would say that?
Mm-hmm. I've actually heard officers brag about how they took a man down and rubbed his face across the concrete or the asphalt when they were taking him down. Even though they have to have a video camera, they thought it was real funny. And they had a video camera there, and they acted like the inmate was moving his head when actually the officer was moving the inmate's head.
Was it difficult for you to be a correctional officer?
Yes. I was told more than once that I was too kind-hearted. You weren't allowed to call an inmate Mr. Jones or Mr. Smith. You were supposed to call them "inmate." I was called in on more than one occasion because I called them Mr. Jones or Mr. Smith.
I see. Now, one of the things you said to me is that you wanted to use another name because you were afraid of retaliation on your family?
Right.
Can you speak to me a little bit about that fear? What do you think might happen,

or what did happen?
Letters, things in your cars, dirty Kotex, used Kotex, harassment on the phone--the same thing.
What do you mean by those things? I don't understand. Has this historically happened?
Yes.
Can you tell me a little bit about somebody else's experience that you know of?
A package in the mail to a daughter or a son. The child opens it; it's a dirty Kotex, a used Kotex. Cards opened, "Your mother is a rat, your mother is a bitch"; or other things.
I see. It sounds like correctional officers are a tight-knit group?
Yes.
And if you go against that group at all, then you're ostracized?
Right.
Do you find that they are ever a forgiving group?
No.
Never?
Never.
And once you've made a mistake in their eyes, that's it, you're out?
That's right.
And they can make life very difficult for you?
Very, very difficult. People that have been your friends for years see you on the street, and walk clear across the street.
Has that happened to you?
Yes.
Tell me about that.
Walking down the street, I saw a person that had been my friend for 15 years. The person crossed over, wouldn't look at me or have anything to do with me.
A child was killed, of another friend. I called to find out how they were doing and was told, "We don't want you around. You can't call here. We don't care about you." Even though you still care about those people, because they've been in your life for 15 or 20 years, you're told you're nothing anymore.
Your children are not allowed to go to school. If they make friends with an inmate child, they have to break off that friendship. That child is not allowed to be your child's friend because his father is in the penitentiary. So, you're teaching this child is ostracized and for no reason except he has a father that made a mistake.
Sounds very sad.
And your child loses a friend.

Yes. Both of the children, it sounds like--

Have lost.

Right. So did you relocate out of that community?

Yes.

And how is it going for you now?

Really good.

Do you visit your husband here at Monroe?

Mm-hmm.

And were people at this prison aware of what had happened before?

A lot of them, yes.

And yet they still treated you okay here?

You get one or two that will give you a hard time. Every time you go through, you have to be patted down just because they're standing too close to the metal detector. If they stand too close, it will make the metal detector go off. Or if they move their foot toward the metal detector, it will go off. There are little tricks to make it go off. And there has been people that have done that. Very few over here.

You're talking about officers?

Right.

I see. Well, I'm glad things are better for you.

Me, too.

How much more time does your husband have?

Thirty-six more months.

So it's getting close?

Getting close.

Well, I really appreciate your willingness to share this with me. I can see it was very difficult for you. You were tearing up a lot.

Still hurts.

Yes, I can see that it does. In conclusion, is there anything that you'd like to say?

You talk about reforming these people. How can you reform somebody unless you treat them like you want to be treated? If you treat them like they're scum, they're going to be scum.

And what about you, as the wife? What about treatment for you?

At least treat me like I'm a human being. That's all I ask.

Detective Gebo

I'm speaking with Detective Gebo. Do you want an alias, Detective?
No, I'm comfortable with my own name.
All right. And are you aware that this conversation interview is being tape-recorded?
Yes.
And are you further aware that the contents of this interview will be used in a book, and the book is going to be read by the public?
Yes.
And that's all right with you?
I expect it will be.
If you'd like to see a transcript of this before I publish it, I'd be glad to do that for you.
That would probably be a good idea.
Okay. That would be fine.
I'm here to learn about what it is that you do. You're a detective?
Yes.
With the Seattle Police Department?
That's right.
And what does a detective with the Seattle Police Department do?
Detectives, whether it be with this department or almost any other large municipal police department, are divided up by prime specialty, type of crime. Some people are property crime investigators, like burglary, auto theft, that sort of thing. Others are person-oriented type investigators--robbery, sex crimes which we now call special assault. I'm in the homicide unit. We investigate homicides, serious assaults, kidnapping--those sorts of crimes.

A homicide detective generally (and there are a number of them in this police department) responds originally to the scene of a suspicious death, or a murder, or a serious assault; conducts a scene investigation, which may be so simple as to take a few photographs and some measurements, or as complex as at an arson fire, where there is a huge scene, with heavy equipment, and basically an excavation type of thing. The same thing as the Green River investigation. Some of those were more archaeological than investigatory because the body is in a decomposed state in an outdoor scene, where you actually have to find all the pieces rather than a whole body laying out on the pavement or something.

But, back to the original response, we do that. From that point, it's our individual responsibility to determine what happened, coordinate with the medical examiner's office, and others to determine the cause of death. At times, we are the individual that notifies the family of the death of their family member; also we interview witnesses that were at the scene and of course, apprehend and interview the offender. At that point, then, we coordinate with the prosecutor's office to charge the individual.

And then that part of it moves into a trial phase, or actually a trial preparation phase, where you are recreating what took place for the purposes of trial presentation in front of the jury or a judge, using the assistance of a prosecutor. They would like to flip those roles around and say they're doing the preparation, and you're the assistant, but, in most cases, it's quite the opposite. We are the provider of most of the information, most of the court exhibits, most of the analysis of the evidence, and then testifying in court.

Let's say a call comes in, and there's been a homicide. A dead body is found. How would it be determined who would go to that call?

In this police department, we have quite a large number of investigators. Generally speaking, the homicide investigators are divided up into two-person teams that are supervised by a sergeant. There's a list that is typed up that has the teams listed in order.

The next-up team on the list is summoned to the scene. The first response is usually always with the uniformed people and supervisors that would make a determination if it's something that we should go to or not.

I see.

There are deaths that occur, serious injuries that occur every day in the city that don't require our response. The original responders can take care of it. The medical examiner's staff can take care of unattended death situations, where there is no thought that there was foul play. Those things happen all the time.

So it's a rotating basis?

Right. No real control over whether you're going to get the fire at the warehouse or one transient-type person killing another in the alley downtown.

There are times when there may be a number of calls in a fairly short period of time--

three, four, five murders in a week. There are other times when weeks may go by with no calls, which doesn't happen often, but it does happen. We seem to average around 60 to 70 murders a year.

Your jurisdiction is the city of Seattle?

Just the city limits. There are federal buildings in the city limits, and they have their own security force. However, by agreement, if a murder occurred in the federal building, or a federal courthouse, or places like that, we have an agreement with the federal government that we will do the primary investigation.

So now let's say you're on the scene. How would you know how to proceed?

Well, I don't know that anybody knows instinctively. There's a lot of seasoning, experience that goes into becoming a homicide detective. Generally speaking, all of the investigators that work there, and all the supervisors that work here, have a long history of experience going back to the very beginning of their police career: training, special training, experience built on top of experience. Eventually, it's a voluntary assignment. People that are here because they asked to be here and want to be here. It's a very specialized assignment.

You have to put a bid in for it?

Yes. And the folks that come here generally stay for a long period of time. It's not a rotational basis or anything. I've been here 14 years, and I'm not a senior man. There are people that have been here a lot longer than I. So it's a very specialized type of work. The people that are there have gained a lot of experience elsewhere before they ever came here. Then once they're here, there's specialized training that they're sent to, and over a period of time, they gain more, and more, and more experience and skill.

The state of the art, of course, is changing in just the simplest of things, like cameras, for example. Over the period of time I've been here, we've changed cameras several times because they've gotten better. So that's part of it. Things like measuring tapes, of course, they're pretty easy to use. But we use computer-based diagramming that was never available before for outdoor scenes or very complex scenes.

You said that most people here have a specialty?

Well, I guess some of us have specialties. Not everybody does. In the mid-'80s, I got some specialized training, and I do a specialized analysis of cases all throughout the Northwest. I look at a set of circumstances, do an analysis, develop an offender profile, develop interview strategies for a known offender, and develop investigative techniques for the investigating agency. That is what I do in addition to--to regular investigative work.

You realize that the Chief of Police recommended you to me?

Mm-hmm.

That's a real nice compliment to you, I think. Out of the entire police department, he selected you. I'm wondering if you have any idea why?
There are only about 30 or so others like me in the world that do the same type of thing.
What is it that you do? If only 30 people in the world are doing this, you're very specialized.
That's true. I am.
Is it so specialized, you can't even tell me what it is?
There have been some dramatizations of what I do, books that were written about people that do exactly what I do. Look at a set of circumstances, develop an offender profile from behavior that you see at the crime scene, step into the shoes of the offender, and develop a picture of what took place between the victim and the offender.
I assume you're the only one in this area who does it?
Right.
Have you been successful?
Yes.
How long have you been doing this particular thing?
1986 is when I got this specialized training.
And how did you happen to do that?
The FBI had established at Quanico, Virginia, an investigative group that they call the Behavioral Science Unit, which is the group that was doing this for the FBI and the group that was doing this for the world. They had a federal grant to branch out and bring in police investigators from the United States, and then it branched out to the free world. You went to Quanico and lived and worked there for a year. Sort of a master-apprentice type of relationship with the people in the Behavioral Science Unit. Then when you were done, they sent you back out to your region to sort of be a disciple.
Something I'm picking up from you is you're fascinated by it.
Oh, yeah, it's a great experience.
I'm interested in learning about the criminal mind, and obviously you're a specialist.
In the area of violent criminals, the folks that I have most to do with, they didn't, one day, just wake up and stretch their arms and say, "Well, I think I'll go out and kill somebody today" or "I'll go out and commit a rape today," or, "For lack of anything better to do, I'll go assault somebody with a gun." It's not a spontaneous thought process unless they're psychotic, and their mind just snapped one day, and they're no longer in control of what they're doing. Even that is a developmental process.
There are little marks along the path of somebody who is losing their mental stability,

little flags would be raised saying, "Oh, oh. This person's having some trouble." And as they go down the slope toward really losing the whole thing, people who could have seen it, or should have seen it, later on can report to the psychiatrist or the psychologist and say, "Oh, yeah. We saw that happen."

The same thing is with a criminal. It is a long, developmental process that takes place. Probably begins at a very young age, where you have a breakdown of that individual. Things like the family and society are built into this whole process, where you end up with somebody who has no morals, has no conscience, has no concern for their fellow human being, is very compulsive, and finds joy in pain and suffering--not in their own, but in others.

It isn't exactly the same. I'm using terms that are recognizable by other people. We know what joy is. We know what comfort and support is. It's the same idea. You have to look at the way some of these folks conduct their lives. They are putting as much energy, as much of their life, into committing violent crimes against other people as you and I do in the pursuit of happiness.

Because, in some way, it is bringing them happiness?

If you looked at the way that they're living their life, you would never say, "Hey, that person has achieved happiness." Because they're not. They're not insane; they know what they're doing is wrong; they know that they're hurting people. But it's almost like it's a drive.

Would you classify that as addictive? Are they addicted to this kind of behavior?

They're almost compelled to do it. Power becomes their addiction.

Power?

The power over another person, the ability to control, to determine who lives, who dies, the possession of another human being. And that can be something real simple, where you actually are taking the person from A to B or forcing the person to do what you want them to do. But, in some cases, they've got a prearranged and prepared place to go.

Why?

Because they want to, and they can.

Because that feeds their need for ... ?

For power.

Control?

For control, that they don't have anywhere else. Certainly, if you go back in their early development, they had a lot of choices to make, and they could have done other things. But at this point in their life, this is it. It's the most important thing.

You said that this could start at a very early age? Childhood, maybe?

The start of it is, sure.

And what would the start be? You're talking about the criminal mind? This is "criminal" behavior?

Yes.

What would start a little child on the path of criminal behavior?

A little child starts a fire outside the home, playing with matches. But this young person is doing this on purpose to get attention, or because they are fascinated with the fire, and it draws a lot of attention.

That then develops. The next step is the attention is no longer just Mom and Dad come rushing outside; now the fire department's come. All those big trucks, and all the sirens, and all of the people. You do that several times, and now you have no other real power anywhere else in your life, but, you can do this. And look what you can do. You can mobilize millions of dollars worth of equipment, hundreds of people; you can destroy buildings just by lighting a fire. Then that supersedes everything else. You know that it's wrong; you know that people are endangered. You may even know that you've killed people. But you still will continue to do it.

Some of the things that you said would characterize the "criminal mind" would be lack of morals, lack of a conscience, lack of concern for other people, compulsive behavior, and taking joy in the pain or suffering of other people?

And all of this is compelled. They feel a sense of compulsion to do this, to achieve a sense of power or control over something or someone. You said one example of this might be they might actually take physical possession of another human being, take this person to a place. So once they have the control over them, what are they going to do with this person?

In some cases, it's the torture and sexual abuse. In other cases, they think that, given enough time, you will become attracted to them and will live together happily ever after. They think, "I will just hold you prisoner until that day occurs. If it doesn't occur, and you die during the course of all this, that's the way it goes."

And then they'll go get somebody else, maybe?

Probably. But, fortunately, there's not a lot of those of guys running around.

There aren't?

No, and that's good.

There are a lot of people who are developing violent criminal behavior that eventually do offend. It's sort of like a cup. Every human psyche, if you were to typify it as a cup, will hold so much liquid, and you pour some in to seek satisfaction. And, in most cases, you get to the level where you're satisfied, and you don't pour any more in there. But if you continue to pour in and pour in, eventually, it's going to flow over the side.

In the area of a sexual offender, let's say. He begins at a very young age as a window peeper, and then maybe he will graduate from that to make a covert entrance into the house when it's empty. But he's been peeking in the window, and he knows who lives there, and maybe he'll go play with the underwear or do something else that he's thought an awful lot about. And maybe that will be all he'll ever do. He will find some sense of satisfaction in doing that and will never do anything more.

But others continue to develop. Then the next step would be to go in the home when the person is there. And then the next step is maybe even to touch the person when they're in the home, when they're asleep in bed. You might not even realize that this person was in the room with you. And then eventually maybe act out, attack the person in the home.

That takes time to develop. They don't just one day say, "I think I'll go break into that house where that woman is." That doesn't usually happen. It takes time.

And that's a problem. You were asking about development. It's a problem in our society. We see this behavior in young people at a very young age, and yet we do nothing about it. We've almost given up on the fact that young men are window peepers. That's potentially a dangerous thing to do. But we don't do anything about those people when we identify them.

We can't ignore them, because I know that when we end up with a serial rapist who has committed hundreds and hundreds of sexual assaults, 100% of the time that young man was a window peeper. That doesn't mean that every window peeper becomes a rapist. But every rapist was a window peeper.

We need to address that. There's a lot of problems in the world today. Every day in the paper you see we have a lot of problems. But violent crime is a problem that needs to be addressed. It's not so much that you just keep throwing money at it and hire more policemen because we don't do anything but react. We're not proactive at all. The police department, investigators like me, we don't do anything to stop people from offending.

We've got to find some way to cut off these careers of violence that begin at a very young age and are easily identified.

There are lots of people that have that long list of criminal behavior traits I gave to you who are pillars of the community. Successful people in business, or sports, who have the very same list. And we look upon them as being wonderful people because they do have that drive, they do have that obsession, with success. They have the ability to step on other people to get to the top. But we look upon them as being successful. That is a problem. That's something that we've got to address.

Why should we pay attention to these people's psychological profiles?

What you need, and what you have to accept, is the fact that once certain people have offended, and re-offended, and committed certain types of crime, they are just about not salvageable.

You're talking about certain types of offenses?

The vast majority of murders are a one-time event, a personal thing. This anger, or whatever it might be, has been developing for a long time. Eventually it boils over and erupts with someone ending up dead on the floor, and the killer is standing there with tears streaming down, calling the police. It would probably never happen again in their life.

That's not the same type of individual that would kidnap you, take you to someplace that they had already prepared, keep you there, torture you, find some sense of satisfaction in the tears streaming down and your cries of pain, and torment your family with telephone calls. That's not the same kind of person. That kind of person, once we identify them, probably doesn't need to walk among us again. And whether we lock them up or whether we do away with them really doesn't matter, but they have gone so far outside the bounds that we probably don't want them around ever again. That's why we need to pay attention to what they're doing.

However, I think that some of the societal reaction to violence is based on media hype because it may not be as bad as people would like to think.

You made the point there really aren't a whole lot of these people.

Correct. The problem with these people is that they gain attention, and others, who are sort of inadequate, then look upon that behavior as something that they can admire and engage in it themselves.

I don't know how school-age kids ever got the idea that it was cool to carry guns to school because we certainly didn't do that when I was in school. I don't know how that began. But somebody thought it was neat. Once it started, we didn't have a very quick reaction to people doing that, and now we have shootings in the schools. Well, that's unacceptable.

You talked about the person who takes possession of another human being, and their hope is that if they hold possession of that human being long enough, that other person will love them. If a person were kidnapped, would it be a clever ploy on the victim's part to pretend to care about that person?

How can I accurately advise somebody when I don't know what the guy's doing? And you wouldn't either when you first confront him.

You don't know whether he has been interrupted just rifling the glove box of your car or whether he has just killed somebody down the street. You may have a real good idea in your mind about what you're going to do, and, in fact, you're doing something that he thinks is neat.

Some rapists, for example, want you to show fear. And if you don't, they'll inflict more harm until you do. If you had decided that you were going to be strong and not show any fear, you're going to get hurt a lot more than if you had been compliant.

Now, the other is true, too. That there are some who, were you to be compliant, don't want that. They want you to be excited and upset, and they will interact with you until you do.

So it's real hard to say, "Do this each time and it will work" because you don't know. You don't know if the guy that is stealing your car with you in it is most interested in your stereo or most interested in you.

There are those who would advocate, "Fight to the death. Don't give up no matter what." There are folks from both genders who are very practiced in hand-to-hand combat and are willing to fight to the death. But if you're not, you're going to lose. The best option is never to get yourself in a position where you can get cornered. Be aware of your surroundings and park your car in safe places, and if you have the feeling of being followed, or being cornered, or being trailed, go to a place where there's other people; go to a well-lighted place where this attack or kidnapping can't take place. Lock your car; lock your door and windows at home. Don't leave your windows ajar at home. Time and time again, the cases that we've seen, where assaults or murders happened in the home, the offender gained entry through an unlocked door or an open window.

We have the ability to harden the target so that the vast majority of the offenders will not choose you. They might choose somebody else, but they might not be able to get to you.

Do you feel like citizens should carry a weapon?

I don't. I'm frightened of weapons. I think the proliferation of them in our society is part of the problem. We've made it attractive to people. It's just reverting back to the fictional Wild West days that everybody carries a gun, and if somebody wrongs you, you pull your gun out, and you straighten it out.

I saw a sign the other day that said, "A well-armed society is a polite society." I would take it that you do not agree with that?

Polite to the point where, in cases we investigate every year, assaults and murders started with somebody cutting somebody off in traffic. Somebody died over that? Because somebody had a weapon, or they both had weapons, and because somebody's turn signal didn't go on, or because they got too close to the other person's fender--then let's both pull out our guns and shoot at each other?

How does your work affect you personally? Does studying the *criminal* mind affect *your* mind? Does working with this sort of abhorrent behavior constantly affect your personal life?

Oh, I'm sure it does. If you were to ask my friends and those close to me over the years, I'm sure it's had an effect. Whether it's been something that has destroyed me,

I don't think so.
Recently, I was at a small community where a man was breaking into a funeral home to have sex with the dead bodies. A type of behavior that is very, very bizarre and very rare. In fact, it's so rare that in the '70s, the criminal code in the State of Washington was revised, and the state legislature left necrophilia out of the criminal code. It's back in the criminal code now because of this one man's behavior.
That department didn't know even how to address that kind of thing. On the one hand, they know something about what a burglar is, but what do you do with somebody that's willing to do this?
My assessment of him was very on target, and it was helpful to them. They did apprehend the man. My advice to them about how to interview him, and that sort of thing, was very helpful to them. It resolved their problem.
So I guess there is a burden to that.
On the other hand, there is also a feeling of satisfaction that I am able to help and nobody else can.
Is there anything else that you'd like to say?
My career has been a long one, but it's not over. I hope that what I do will continue. I plan to do the same thing for a number of years longer. But I wonder how I can share my knowledge and my experience with others and carry this on even after I'm gone? That's sort of what we're up to now.

James

I am conducting an interview at Washington State Reformatory with James. Hello, James.

Hello. How are you?

I'm fine. Thank you. Are you aware that you're being recorded?

Yes, I am.

How long have you been incarcerated?

About nine years.

How old are you now?

About 29.

So you came in when you were 20 years old.

Twenty-one.

And what were you convicted of?

First degree murder.

Can you tell me something about that?

It was an alleged murder-for-hire.

Tell me what you were alleged to have done.

I was alleged to have taken another man's wife's life for an insurance policy.

So you were accused of doing a contract killing?

Yes, that's correct.

And how much were you supposedly paid for this?

About $10,000.

$10,000.

Yes.

I'm going to ask you to talk to me about this story and how it supposedly happened. This is all alleged, and you were accused of it?

Right.

You were also convicted of it?

Right.

Would you talk to me about what happened?

Well, allegedly, I used to run with a pretty rough group of people. I got away from the criminal element for three or four years, and then they came and contacted me. I was working at the time, living with my girlfriend and my two kids. They offered me the proposition of making the $10,000. It was something that I had thought about for a while, and being how money is usually pretty short, I decided to get involved. It was for $10,000. I never received anything but a 35-year prison sentence.

My partner, he's been out. And the driver of the car, he did six years. He's out, back on the street with his family. The man that allegedly hired him is doing life without possibility of parole.

There are a couple of things I don't understand. First of all, you said you were running with a "criminal element"?

Right.

What does that mean?

Well, it just means people that are, you know, robbing, stealing, and hurting people. Stuff like that.

You're not talking about organized crime?

Somewhat of an element of that, yeah.

You said you never received anything?

Never received a penny.

Why not?

Well, it was kind of like I was the cannon fodder. They got it done for their reasons, and I was never paid anything, absolutely nothing.

So what were their reasons? Why did they want this woman dead?

It was, allegedly, a divorce and she was going to take him for everything that he had, and he didn't like that. They come up with this story, just to get rid of her. So that's when it ultimately happened.

Did they turn you in? How did you get arrested?

My partner was arrested. He pled guilty to first degree manslaughter in exchange for his testimony against me.

How was this woman killed?

She was shot.

She was shot?

Yes.

You said you were living with your children at the time?

Yes. With my girlfriend and my two sons.

Have you ever been married?

No, I haven't.

Okay, but you had two children with a girlfriend?

Right.

You know, it's hard for me to understand this. And I think that for anybody who's going to read this, it's going to be difficult for them to comprehend a mind set that could do this. Could you maybe explain a little bit about what could take somebody to this place, how somebody could make a decision to do this? I mean, you're living with a woman you love, I take it?

Right.

Two children. And somebody approaches you and wants you to kill a woman. And, allegedly, you decide to do that. Can you talk about that mind set a little bit?

Yeah, it's really something that I've thought about over the years. The way I dealt with it, I just dealt with it as a--as a--as a business proposition. It was the money. It wasn't her as an individual because she was innocent and didn't deserve what happened to her. It was the whole issue of the money; that was the issue for me. Nothing else other than that.

When you talk about it as a business issue, it sounds like that old cliche' from a movie, where you're separating "business" from "personal."

Exactly.

Exactly?

Exactly.

This is business. This isn't personal?

Right.

So even if you take a life, it's not personal?

Right.

Do you still have that mind set?

No, I don't. Since I've been incarcerated, I've changed a lot. I've grown up a lot; my ways of thinking have changed. If I had to do it all over again, I wouldn't do it.

I'd like to think I'm a better person. I think that this time I'm doing here in prison has turned my life around, and made me think about things before I do them, before I act.

Have you been at Washington State Reformatory all nine years?

Yes, I have.

What happened to the woman that you were living with and the two children?

Once I went to jail, we separated, and she went to live with her mom. Took my two sons, and I've seen her one time. She came up to visit, and I hear from her occasionally through letters and pictures of the boys. And that's about it.

Have you ever seen your children?

Yes, my son was three years old when I was arrested. I never did get to see my youngest son. I haven't seen him, except for pictures.

Do you think about that?

Yeah, I think about that a lot. I could have took a lot of different routes in life and been more productive for her and the kids and been a responsible individual. But being young, and wild, and crazy, you don't think about them things at the time. It's something that I've had to deal with over the years.

Prior to this alleged crime, had you ever been convicted of anything else?

I did some jail time for two burglaries, back when I was a juvenile. That was the extent of my criminal record.

Why were you running with this crowd?

Because it was exciting. There's nothing like the adrenaline rush of excitement. There's nothing that can replace that. No drug, or anything, that can replace that. And, you know, wanting to fit in.

You wanted to belong to a group? Belong to a family?

Yeah. Yeah, and to be accepted. Because I come from a dysfunctional family. Family life wasn't all that great. Lived with various, different families and stuff, growing up. My dad was an alcoholic. My mom was a great lady, but it just wasn't the ideal family life.

What was your life like as a child?

Well, we never really had a lot of anything. My dad was pretty much a selfish individual. He was a drinker, a cowboy, a drifter. And my mom was pretty much the stable one. There wasn't a lot of love and affection coming from my dad's side.

Was he ever abusive to you? Did he hurt you?

Not visibly, no. No, he never beat any of us kids or anything like that. Sometimes he'd be verbally abusive and not really caring about anybody but himself.

Did you have brothers and sisters?

Yeah, four sisters and one half-brother.

Four sisters? You say your mother was a really fine lady. Are you still in touch with your mother?

My mom passed away while I was here at the Reformatory. I'd had one trailer visit with her and my brother about 30 days prior to her passing away.

What did she die of?

I think it was a heart attack. That's what I understand.

And how did that affect you?

Up to that point in my life, it was one of the hardest things I've ever had to deal with, losing my mom, because we were--we were really close. I don't know. I don't know how I deal with that. I just kind of just shut it off and not think a lot about it. That's how I deal with things sometimes.

Did you attend the funeral?

Yes, I did. Yes.

How do they do that?

They shackle you, your hands to your waist then they put Hinkle shackles on you; then they transport you to the ... to the funeral home. They unshackle your legs so you can walk, leave your hands shackled. You attend the service, and they transport you back here afterwards.

Are you allowed to go to the grave site?

No, you're not, no. You have a choice, either the chapel or the--or the--the way I understand it, either the chapel or the grave sight. And I chose the chapel.

I see. Oh, dear. It's rough.

I kind of disassociate myself from a lot of things, and I just don't think about them. That's how I deal with things. It's not as bad as it used to be. I'm a little more in touch with my feelings nowadays than I was years ago.

Talk to me about being disassociated from your feelings.

Disassociated with my feelings? Well, I had a psych evaluation one time, and the report said that I really had no use for people around me. I'm in touch with reality; I know the difference between right and wrong, but I don't have use for a lot of people. I don't associate with a lot of people. That's the way I've always been, and you know, I'm better than I used to be. Talk a little more and stuff like that.

Is that a lonely way to live? Do you feel lonely?

No. I don't think so, no.

Do you feel anything?

No.

Do you wish you could?

Yeah, sometimes. Sometimes. I just always found it easier not to have to deal with things. I just shut them off and don't even think about them and go on from there.

How long have you done that?

Probably through all my childhood and probably up to a few years ago. I try to deal with stuff differently nowadays and try to think things through.

Do you think this is a protective mechanism that you learned as a child, to protect yourself from being hurt?

It's very possible. I've heard it termed that way before. Kind of a wall that I put up. I don't let anybody around me or next to me, so I don't have to worry about being hurt, or anything like that. You can always count on yourself. You don't need to count on anybody else.

What number are you in the sequence of children?
The first one from my mom and dad. My mom had a son prior to their marriage, and my dad has three or four other sons from a previous marriage.
But you were a first-born child of this marriage?
Right. Right.
And then after came four sisters?
Four sisters.
How did you get along with, or feel about, your sisters?
We used to argue, and fight, and everything else. You know, as I've grown up, I've grown to love my sisters more and appreciate them more. I guess we just got along average, like any brother and sister.
Are you in touch with them now?
Yeah, I talk to them on the phone. They don't come and see me or anything like that because they really don't agree with why I'm locked up, and they kind of have a problem with that I'm a dangerous individual.
Are you?
I can be, yeah.
But in your daily life you seem to be pretty easygoing?
Yeah, pretty easygoing.
Are you stimulated into anger easily?
Not really. I mean, it takes a lot to push me to the point to where I'll react violently. But when I get to that point, it's no turning back, and whatever happens, happens.
Has that ever happened to you while you've been incarcerated?
No, it hasn't.
So, you're speaking from experience prior to nine years ago?
Right.
It sounds like you've kept yourself pretty well under control for the last nine years?
I guess so. It's just part of growing up and maturing.
So you came to Washington State Reformatory when you were 21 years old?
Twenty-one, yes.
Washington State Reformatory is an adult institution, and 21 is pretty young. How was it for you?
It was a different experience. I'd never been to prison before. My first trip through, and my last trip through. I guess it really didn't bother me. The time that I was locked up for 30 days bothered me a lot more than being locked up for this amount of time here. When I was younger. Why, I don't know, but it does.
Tell me about your life here. What's a typical day?
Typical day for me is I wake up at 6:30; then I go down to breakfast. I work in the

print shop until 4:00 in the afternoon. I come back from there; I eat dinner; I weight lift four or five times a week. Usually, the rest of my time is spent in the cell, watching TV or reading books, until here recently. I met a gal, and I've been visiting a lot. That takes up my evenings now.

Tell me about this woman that you met. How did you meet her?

I met her through a friend of mine in here. One of his girlfriend's girlfriends. We wrote for a while and talked for a while and seemed to hit it off real good. So I lucked out.

How do you feel about her?

She's a very special lady, and I love her a lot. She has two kids. The kids and I interact great. We get along great. We're hoping to be married here, so I'm really looking forward to that and excited about it. It's nice to have a female interaction instead of just hanging out with the fellows all day. It's nice to have conversation.

So you're thinking about getting married?

Yes. I've never been married before, so it's kind of a new area for me. I'm kind of nervous about that, which is natural, I guess. But I'm really excited about it.

Here at Washington State Reformatory, you're allowed to have extended family visits. Is that correct?

That's correct, yes.

Can you talk to me a little about what that is?

Basically, you submit the paperwork. If you're married, or your mom or dad, or sisters, or stepsisters visit, you are allowed to go out in the trailers that are here at the Reformatory for 46 hours every 50 to 90 days. It's pretty much like a home setting. They bring food in, and you can cook and everything like that. I've only been to one, with my mom and my brother, so that's about all I really know about it.

Do you have a personal opinion about them? Do you think they're a good idea?

I think they're a great idea. People think a little more before they're willing to give up their trailers or jeopardize anything like that. Losing their trailers makes people think.

You mean before they might get into trouble, get into a fight--

Right.

--or break a rule because they're thinking they don't want to miss their visits?

Exactly. Right.

How would you describe yourself?

I'd describe myself as pretty easygoing. I'm about 210 pounds.

Pretty muscular. You work out, you said, three or four times a week?

Yes.

When you lift weights, are you doing it for your health, for strength, because you're bored? Why are you doing it?

I do it as a tension release, and I enjoy it a lot. I enjoy spending the time in there lifting the iron, and it makes me feel better. That's pretty much how you work out your frustrations in here. That's how I do it, anyway.

So they have a pretty well-equipped gymnasium here for you guys?

Yes, they do.

Who paid for all of that?

It comes out of the Inmate Welfare Fund.

You pay for it yourself?

Yes. The inmates all contribute a certain amount to anything that we purchase in here, as far as recreational equipment and things of that sort.

There would be those that would say you're given too much in here.

I can see where people out there would say, "They've committed a crime. They need to go to prison and be punished. They need to do hard time." And I'm sure if they had their way, we wouldn't have as much as we have in here. But you gotta have that, you know, for people on an individual basis to try to change. I mean, you just can't lock a person up and forget about them and give them nothing and expect them to go back out into society and be productive. It doesn't work. A lot of the recreational stuff we have in here keeps people in line. It gives them something to do.

You were given 35 years? Did I hear that right?

That's right, yes.

And you've done nine. Now that means you have quite a few more to do?

Yeah, couple more.

Couple more?

I'm almost on the downhill.

That's still a long time, James.

Yes. I'll have been incarcerated longer than I was on the streets. You know, by the time I get back out, I'll be 44 years old, almost 45.

It sounds like you think about that?

It's one of them things I don't spend a lot of time thinking about. I just take it day by day. I know when my release date is; I work on it that way.

You're contemplating getting married. So that means that the woman you're marrying is going to spend a lot of years with you while you're incarcerated?

Yes.

Have you thought about that?

I've thought quite a bit about that. I mean, is it fair to ask somebody to live this kind of life? Trying to hold a relationship together and being locked up has got to be one of the hardest things in the world to do. You can't contribute a whole lot, as far as financially. If they have problems, you can't be there for them all the time.

It's something I have a hard time with. I really don't enjoy that part of it, as far as not being able to be there, to be financially supportive for things that they may need.
And you'd like that? You'd like to be able to help financially?
Yes, I would, yeah.
Do you work here?
Yes. We used to have a little more money than we have now. There was a bill passed, which has taken a lot of money away from the working inmates' work, that used to support their families. That's put additional hardship on them. That's something everybody here that works in the industries deals with now.
So it makes it difficult to contribute very much to your family on the outside?
Yes, it does.
How do your families on the outside survive? What do they do? What does your fiancee do?
She works. She works.
It sounds like you have feelings about it?
Yeah, I do.
It might be, after a period of time, not being able to support your family in the way that you want to, not being able to be there when you want to be there would wear on a relationship?
Without a doubt. It's easy to say, "Well, I'm going to be there for you forever through this, through good times and the bad times." That's easier said than done.
But when we get right down to reality, your family out there doesn't have you there. If they want to see you, they gotta come up here. And that's always one of the tough parts about it.
Marriage is a risk. Do you think so?
Yeah. I've known people in here that's gotten married, had one trailer, and that was the end of it, never to see their wife again. And I've known people that's been married for quite a few years.
I find your insights into yourself, about your feelings, interesting. On one hand, you say that you're able to block them a lot, that, in fact, you have no feelings at all sometimes?
Sometimes.
And, on the other hand, you're very sensitive in some areas, particularly about the marriage that's coming up. And also, James, I know that you have a very dear friend in here, another person who's incarcerated.
Right.
Could you talk to me a little bit about that?
I've known him going on four years. He's just one of them people that you meet in

here that you just naturally get along with and have some things in common. And, over the years, we spent a lot of time talking and becoming really close.

You're like brothers?

In a sense, yes. I'd describe him as somebody that I can always count on and depend to be there if I got a problem or need somebody to talk to. And, you know, vice versa. If he gets into trouble, or whatever. You know? I mean I'd always be there for him and do whatever I could to help him out.

Friends.

Friends. It's pretty rare that you find that in a prison setting because pretty much people are users, using the word "brother" and "friend" real freely, with no foundation to it. I don't use the word "friend" loosely. There's not a whole lot of people I like in here.

You'd already said that you don't have a lot of use for other people.

Right. Right.

But you do care about this individual?

Right.

And you do care about this woman that you're going to marry?

Right.

And you care about her children?

Yes, I do. Yes.

James, is there something that you'd like to say?

Sometimes people get into situations in life where they wish they could turn back the clock and do things different. The prisons are full of them. On the other hand, there are people in here which I firmly believe should always be in here and should never get out. But I believe an individual deserves a second chance if he's willing to work on changing.

And not everybody locked up is a bad guy, you know? Sometimes they just got into situations that they wish they hadn't and ended up in prison for one reason or another. And you should know the whole story before you pass judgment on anybody.

Section Three

How Do People in the System Think?
Why Do They Make the Decisions They Do?

Albert D. Rosellini

I'm in Governor Albert D. Rosellini's office. Hello, Governor Rosellini.
Hello.
My name is Jean Marie Christenson, and I'm going to be interviewing you today, and I'm going to be taping that interview.
That's fine. Be happy to cooperate.
During my campaign, I had a photographer go to the different institutions--juvenile facilities; penitentiaries; of course, the Reformatory; and the retarded children schools, and film the conditions that were existing at that time.
And then, later, after I was elected and made the improvements, we took a dish of films of the improved conditions, which we showed when I was up for reelection. I think I still have those films someplace if that would be of any help to you.
Oh, that would be wonderful.
I'm sure I have the original ones. I don't know if I have them or not, but I'll be happy to look and see.
That would be wonderful.
I'm wondering if you would speak for a few moments about yourself. You're an interesting person.
Thank you.
I'm just going to turn it over to you.
Okay. Well, I was born and raised in Tacoma and learned to speak Italian before I spoke English because my parents couldn't speak English.
My parents were peasants that had come over from Italy and couldn't speak English, had very little education. In Italy in those days, I guess, and when they first came over, they only had first or second grade. I went to St. Leo's grade school there; that was a Catholic school. Then I went to the public schools.
We moved to Seattle for a few years, then went back to Tacoma. I finished high

school, Stadium High School in Tacoma, and then went one year to the University of Puget Sound. Then I wanted to go to law school, but they didn't have a law school there, so I started going to the University of Washington Law School. And a couple years later, my folks moved to Seattle, and we've been here ever since that time.

I married, got married to a young lady from Seattle--young at that time, of course. We have five children, fifteen grandchildren, and three great-grandchildren now, so we'll have a big Christmas.

A big Christmas.

The last thing I ever thought of, when I was at the University of Washington, was that I'd ever get into politics. If anybody had told me in my last quarter of law school that I would ever run for political office, I would have told them they were plumb crazy. Yet, within a year that I was out, I was running for the state senate.

What took you to that point? Did someone encourage you?

Yes, these were depression days, and there wasn't too much activity, and I was struggling by, trying to make a living as a lawyer. I was lucky if I took in a hundred dollars a month.

And, in any event, I decided that I'd run. Principal reason was I had a little cubbyhole in an office in the Northern Life Tower. One of the principals in that law office was a member of the legislature, and so he kind of encouraged me. So I looked at the legislative districts and picked the district that I thought I'd have a fair chance.

I ran in 1934. That was in the state senate against the incumbent senator at that time, the late Tiger Jim Murphy, who was also the Democratic King County Chairman. And through sheer hard work, I came within 80 votes of beating him but didn't. I lost out. But the following day, after the primaries, I got a letter from a fellow named Magnuson, who was running on that same ticket as a Democrat--for the prosecuting attorney of King County. And he was impressed by the run I'd made and mentioned that if he were elected, he'd be happy to have me come in with him by helping in the finals. I said, "Well, I don't think I want to come in as a deputy prosecutor, but at the same time, I'll help you, as a good Democrat."

So I went to work and helped him. And then, after he was elected in November, I decided that I did want the job. So I went in with Magnuson in January of 1935 as a deputy prosecuting attorney. We took an office over that had been in the hands of the Republican Party for 32 years, and, one by one, we kind of cleared them out and appointed some of our people.

But I stayed there and then four years later, while I was still in the prosecutor's office, I ran again for the state senate, and that's when I was elected. And stayed in the prosecutor's office another two or three years and then had my own law practice here in Seattle with a fellow who later became prosecuting attorney himself and later a

Superior Court judge. He's retired now.

And I stayed in the senate. Two years later, I was elected majority floor leader and remained as majority/minority leader for the 18 years that I stayed in the senate.

Then I was elected governor and stayed there eight years.

You know, I just can't help but notice the roses on your tie.

Oh--

And the roses in your lapel. I've heard stories about people wearing roses to support you. Where did that come from?

Well, I'll tell you where it came from. I hadn't thought of it, but when I was running for governor, at one of the campaign meetings, one of the ladies got up and said, "Well, is the name Rose-illini or Ross-ellini?"

At that time, the name that was well known throughout the world, actually, was the name Roberto Ross-elini, who happened to be a big movie producer down in Hollywood and who had just married Ingrid Bergman. And his name was Rosselini, with two S's and one L.

So I told this lady it didn't make any difference what I was called, as long as they could remember the name. But it was R-o-s-e-l-l-i-n-i, Rosellini, not Rosselini. And she went home and came up with the idea of making these little red roses by hand. And it became the symbol of the campaign, so that we had slogans, "Roses for Rosellini," and that became the symbol of the administration, too, of course.

And after I was in office a year or two, the American Rose Society even came out with a Governor Rosellini rose bush that is still being produced.

It's a beautiful red rose, and we have some--actually a lot of them in our home.

At that time, when they first came out with it, there were public plantings of it all over the country, back at the White House and different places, and actually down in Olympia on the grounds there.

That's wonderful.

Governor, I'm here today to talk to you about the correctional system in this state. You certainly have an incredible history of leadership in the State of Washington. I'm looking at a book called *The Guide of Papers of the Governors of Washington.* The list of reforms during the time you were in office is incredible. You just did so many things.

And certainly one of the things that just seems to be throughout the entire paper is your concern for people in difficult circumstances.

Maybe you could talk a little bit about the correctional system as you recall it and some of the things that you did personally while you were in office with the correctional system.

Well, amongst other things, when I was in the State Senate, I took on the study of institutions themselves.

I had had some experience both as a criminal deputy prosecuting attorney, involving a lot of criminals that were sent to prison, and as a defense attorney--but my real interest came in 1945, when a young boy who was 16 years old was killed in the King County Jail, a place where, under the law, he had no business being. They were supposed to put him in a juvenile detention home. And he was killed by one of the other inmates. That naturally sparked a big inquiry.

I was majority leader of the state senate, so I immediately introduced a resolution in conjunction with Judge William Long, who happened to the juvenile court judge here, who had been talking to me about doing something. I sponsored a resolution asking for a creation of a committee to study juvenile conditions around the state.

We passed the resolution, and then I had the presiding officer appoint me as the chairman of that committee. So for two years, myself and the other members of the committee, we did a very comprehensive study of all of the juvenile facilities in the state. We visited most of them around the state. And in order to be sure that we did a professional job and knew what we were doing, we retained the services of the National Association of Crime and Delinquency. And they sent out a young man to work with us, with our committee, to guide us on the studies that we were making, sort of as our executive secretary.

We came up with several ideas at the end of the two-year period; we recommended several things. The Youth Protection Act, for one thing, called for the youth being separated in separate facilities, and other things relating to youth care and treatment. When we were studying the youth facilities, we also studied the schools for the retarded, and I was able to see the deplorable conditions in the schools that we had there and the fact that there weren't enough.

And when we started the institution study, we studied both the penal institutions, the mental hospitals, and girls' and boys' schools. Over a period of two years, we studied them all. The prisons were dungeon cells, where conditions were as bad as any place in the deep South--improper care and no treatment. No work programs or anything of that nature.

And, of course, mental hospitals again were--well, they were so bad they had lost all their accreditation from the American Psychiatric Association and from the American Hospital Association. They were considered amongst the worst in the country.

Those are the things that led me to believe that something needed to be done. And the administration at that time just wouldn't do anything about it. We made our report; we recommended certain things, but no follow-up. Nobody wanted to spend any money. They didn't have a voice speaking for them, nobody in the governor's office. So, that's probably why--well, that is why, when I ran for governor in '56, I had that as one of the major issues. We certainly were going to clean up and upgrade the institutions that were so bad.

That's when we took these films during the campaign. To show conditions, to show the people what the conditions were like, so they would get to visualize these, and I promised people that if I was elected, I'd do something about it.

I have a couple of questions in that regard.

Sure.

You mentioned that a 16-year-old had been killed in an adult facility. And today it seems like more and more minors are being tried as adults. Do you have a comment on that or a feeling about that?

I don't think there's anything wrong in trying them as adults, depending on if it's that serious a crime. And if they're tried as an adult, and they're convicted, they could go to an adult prison under the law. If they commit those type of crimes, I don't see anything wrong with it.

In those days, the law provided that anybody under the age of 18 should not be incarcerated in the King County Jail, and that's where this young fellow had been killed. Judge Long, who was the juvenile court judge here, had a campaign to have something done about the conditions, both at the juvenile facility and the way they were handled at that time. And he had talked to me even before this thing happened and probably influenced me into being concerned about this area.

You said that you were a prosecuting attorney of King County?

The deputy prosecuting attorney, yes.

You made a name for yourself by handling some of the most difficult cases, both in the Superior Court and the state supreme court, and you won all but two jury trials in the six-year service. That's a pretty outstanding record.

Well, I don't mind saying it myself. In those days, I was a pretty good lawyer.

So as an assistant prosecutor, and then later to become senator and then governor?

Right.

Did your view of things change as those roles changed for you?

Not particularly. I always was a strong believer in punishment, including, of course, capital punishment. But I don't think I ever could accept the need for the way prisoners were handled. Give them something to do, rather than just sitting around in cells doing nothing. And we did push for that a lot when I was governor and set up all types of work programs for them. But, aside from that, I always felt that punishment should be severe.

And when you say "punishment," you mean length of time that they would be incarcerated?

Length of time, primarily, yes.

I've talked with inmates. They say that you were a fair governor. So you must be able to hold a strong balance between being strict and also fair.

Well, I guess I always had a lot of compassion for people, you know? And certainly a lot of compassion for the unfortunate ones. Whether they're homeless or whether they've committed a crime and tried to balance it properly.

It's hard to do sometimes.

Very difficult.

As governor, you're the top law enforcement individual in the state. And that's why I have always been a strong believer in capital punishment. I've always felt that it is a deterrent, in my judgment.

I've been on all sides of that question. I've defended people; I've prosecuted them; I've argued it in the state senate; and I had the ultimate decision of whether people should hang or not.

Did you ever have to make that decision?

Oh, yeah. A lot of times. When I say many times--in the eight years, at least eight or ten times.

How did that feel to you, to make that kind of life and death decision?

Well, it's the toughest decision, of course, anybody has to make. You know?

Yes.

Until the two hangings last year, nobody had been executed in the state since the last one I executed in June 1963.

That's because of several reasons. Dan Evans, who followed me, didn't believe in capital punishment. And there was some litigation in the United States Supreme Court that--well, there was some question whether they could go ahead with it or not. But finally it was decided that the states could execute people any way they wanted to. Probably the worst one that I had to decide was the one in '63, a young fellow--27, 28 years old. He had a series of crimes, but in the last one, he killed some cab driver, stabbed and robbed him at the airport. And, you know, you can believe in capital punishment, but at the same time, you know that you're the last one that has the decision. And then you have all the societies that are against capital punishment.

So we went all through that. Whenever they had an execution, I'd always stay in my office. The warden didn't believe in capital punishment, but he followed orders. And the pattern was always the same. He'd call about 11:30 to say everything's fine. And he called again about five to 12:00, and I said, "Fine, go right ahead." And, you know, you watch that clock, and you know that somebody's going to die unless you say the word. And at five after 12:00, he'd call me and say, "Governor, everything went on time."

It's a tough decision, you know? I mean--you rationalize: the jury decided, the judge

decided, and you don't have the right. But, at the same time, you know, you're the only one that can save that life.
So it's a tough, tough decision.
Did you ever stop an execution?
No.
No?
Not that late. I stopped several that I commuted before that, but not at the last minute.
There was never any instance where there was any reason to stop it.
I've always felt that the governor, while technically has a right to stop it, doesn't have the right to do so, or shouldn't have the right to do so, unless there's something--mistaken identity or some real issue--that they hadn't come up with before.
And, like I say, I've been on all sides of this question. It's been kind of interesting. Capital punishment in this state had been repealed once back before my time. The legislature repealed it, and then back in the '20s sometime, somebody got killed on the capital steps while the legislature was in session. So they immediately reinstated it.
You know, listening to you, it hits home to me, the pressures that must exist with the job of being governor?
Yes.
It must be incredibly stressful at times. Can you talk just a little bit about how it feels to be in that powerful of a position?
Well, there are so many decisions you have to make. You know? Some of them--the worst one, like I say, is this question of execution. But we've had others. We had one related again to prisons. We had one young fellow who had been convicted down in Georgia someplace and had escaped and was up here; and the governor down there asked to have him extradited and brought back down there for the punishment. It was a tough decision. This kid had straightened out and was working on a farm over there in eastern Washington. Anyway, I refused to extradite. I figured, "Well, he had been rehabilitated." It wasn't a murder charge, but it was a pretty serious charge down there. But he had straightened out, and it was 10 or 15 years later.
But there were other decisions, of course. Even little decisions on how much money you're going to allow schools, or prisons, or social welfare--those things. It's a tough decision. You know, the best political job in this country is United States senator because you're one out of a hundred people that make that decision.
And you're in there for six years; you're far away from home. But here, as Harry Truman used to say, "The buck stops here." Any executive position, that is, mayor, county executive, governor, you're the one that makes the final decision. That's why people in executive offices don't last as long as United States senators and

congressmen, and people like that, because they don't make the decision. They're just one vote out of hundred in the Senate and almost five hundred in the House.

It's a tough job, but I was definitely happy with what I was doing. I had a big law practice and was doing fine long before I decided to run for governor. My folks, they've been real proud.

Yes, I'm sure they have.

When I first started running, some my best friends said, "With your name and your religion, you'll never make it in this state." There was a lot of prejudice against Catholics.

Catholics?

Especially Italian Catholics.

Even when I was up for reelection in 1960, we couldn't carry the state for Kennedy because of religion, you know. But when I broke that barrier of religion and nationality, the folks were really proud.

You know the best things I did for institutions was to find the right individual to help me run it. I always said, even before I was governor, the key to any good administration is finding the right type of people to run the right department.

Took me nine months, when I became governor, to find the right head of that Department of Institutions. But I found, I think, the best in the country when I got Dr. Garrett Hines. I brought him out here. I didn't know him; he didn't know me. But--well, as a matter of fact, this same organization that I worked with--National Probation and Parole Association--I called their director back in New York. I asked him if he had a young man, and he said, "Well, there's one fellow in Michigan that would do a great job for you. He's a little older, but he's up to a challenge." So I called Governor Williams, who was governor of Michigan and a friend of mine and asked about this fellow. He says, "Well, he's great," he says. "I wouldn't want you to steal him from us, but.... Anyway, I got him out here. And working together, he did a great job for us. You know, took some money--a lot of money--to upgrade these institutions. But we not only upgraded all the prisons and juvenile facilities but also the mental hospitals. As I indicated before, they had lost all their accreditation. And we got them all fully accredited before I left office. And that, like I say, took a lot of money. But more important, or just as important, were the programs, too.

But Hines was just tops.

Do you mean programs inside institutions?

Oh, yes, uh-huh. Programs inside institutions--different types of programs that would give them something to do in prison, like I say--instead of idleness, which is one of the greatest problems. Keep them busy.

Do you feel like there should be psychological programs in prisons? Should we try

at all to help these people, or is it just a matter of incarcerating them?

Oh, I think there should be programs: psychological, work programs and different types of programs. I think there was way too much idleness; that's what causes a lot of the problems, riots and things like that, that have occurred in the institutions. Of course, one of the big mistakes, I think, that was made was grouping everything together under this monstrous Department of Social and Health Services. That's the worst mistake that's been made in this state, as far as state government is concerned. In my lifetime, anyway. The idea was that it would be more efficient and more economical. It's proven to be less efficient, completely inefficient. And as far as institutions themselves are concerned--all types of institutions, you see--there's always a real push for the tax dollar. The biggest lobby, of course, is schools, and rightfully so. They deserve every funding that they get but don't get enough. The next one are the social welfare people, general welfare, and other things. And then the ones that we call the voiceless ones are the institutional people. Nobody really looks after them. And what I'm getting to is the fact that if you don't have a strong voice, probably in the governor's office or somebody near the top, they're left out in the cold when it comes to shelling out the tax dollar, you know? That's one reason I think this Department of Social and Health Services isn't much of a service to these people because they are just a small part of the department, and nobody really speaking for them. Nobody close to the governor is speaking for them. There is the overall secretary of the whole department, but they've got so many things to look after, the institutions have gone downhill a lot.

How would you set it up?

Well, I'd dismantle the Department of Social and Health Services, number one, and get rid of that and have the separate departments. Not exactly like they were worked before, but at least having somebody that's directly responsible to the governor in charge of the major departments. You can group the institutions all together in one group, and the adult correction and juvenile correction all in one group. Definitely, I think they should have that and have it directly responsible straight to the governor.

So at least they'd have a voice.

They'd have a voice, a voice for the voiceless ones.

You always fought for women's rights. Would you speak a little bit about that, and your philosophy on that?

My philosophy on that is women should have a strong voice in the home and government affairs, as well. I felt that women had a place in my employment circle.

Was that was unusual for that period of time?

Yes, it was.

How do you feel about this last election?

Well, I was surprised, like most people, that it would be that much turnover. I think it just indicates the dissatisfaction of the people. I'm a strong Democrat, but I think that it's healthy that it happened--a change. I'm not too concerned about it. I think it'll change again.

It's reminiscent for me of the 46th election, when Harry Truman was President. He came by. As a matter of fact, that's a picture of where I met him on my wall.

That's a wonderful picture.

He was campaigning on the train in '48. Nobody gave him a chance. Dewey, they thought, was a cinch. But he was campaigning, and I was in the state senate, and I wanted to meet him, so I drove over to Ephrata. Got up there and went through the line and got a picture. I went through the line twice. He looked at me and said, "Weren't you here a little while ago?" I said, "Just wanted to make sure."

We got to be good friends later.

He campaigned hard and campaigned against the do-nothing 80th Congress and came through in good shape.

I'm a good Democrat, but some of my best friends are Republicans.

Good and bad on both sides.

I would be interested in what you've been doing since you left public office. Can you talk a little bit about that?

Oh, sure. Well, I have an office in Seattle, and I have an office in Bellevue. I do primarily consulting work, rather than routine law work. I didn't get back to that because--well, several reasons. One, I had appointed one-third of the judges at all levels when I got out of the governor's office, so I thought it might be a little embarrassing to them and to me, too, if I went in and pled a case before them.

But then I got into a little more lucrative work. Been working for some national companies, primarily in Washington, D.C., handling some of the letters that they have back there. No lobbying, as such, but working with some of the officials back there for some of the matters that they wanted done. And I've done a lot of that back there and some here in the state of Washington--consulting work.

In my Bellevue office, I'm associated with a company--not as an investor but as a consultant--that is a building an industrial park in China.

This is more than an experiment. It's something that they're doing. They've already got the lease from the Chinese government. Longest lease the Chinese government has ever given anybody. They're going to build an industrial park over there to manufacture goods for the world market with Chinese employees. It's located in Tiensin, which is the third largest city in China, near the port of Tiensin, which is the third largest port and the closest port to this area. So it should mean a lot for the state of Washington, too.

In addition to that, I'm also on the Board of Directors of the Washington Convention and Trade Center, helping to run that. I'm on the Advisory Committee for the King County Dome. And I have been, for years, chairman of the state of Washington for the United States Olympic Committee. And that keeps me busy too.

These are all non-paying jobs, of course, you know.

Then I've done a lot of real estate work and have managed my own properties. I've got quite a few pieces of property that I manage and buy and sell real estate as my own personal business.

But I enjoy all of it. It's a lot of fun.

It sounds like you have remained incredibly busy.

It occurs to me that when a person goes into politics, you really open yourself up to highs and lows. I mean, some days you can be real popular, and then some days, you're not popular.

That's for sure.

And some elections you win, and some elections you don't win. How does that feel? How do you deal with that, that roller coaster?

Well, that's true. You said the right thing. You're up one day; you're down the next day. And, you know, there's a lot of glory and pride and happiness in winning, and a lot of sadness in losing. I've lost and I've won both. But, you know, you've got to accept the philosophy that you win some, you lose some. That's true of life in anything you do, all things the same way.

When I lost the governor's office, naturally I felt bad about it. I was trying for a third term, which had never, at that time, been accomplished. People said, "Well, why should Rosellini have a third term? Not even the president can have a third term." The prohibition against the president running three times had just been enacted at that time.

Anyway, I felt lost. For the first two or three months, I felt lost. But within two or three months, I got so busy on other activities here and in Washington, D.C., I didn't want to take another job. Lyndon Johnson offered me several good top positions, but I didn't want to live in Washington, D.C., because I'd been home in the Puget Sound area all of my life, and I wouldn't give it up for anything in the world.

But it's a hazardous profession, politics. And you can't win them all.

Was it ever frightening for you? Did you ever fear for your life?

No, I never was. We had several threats when I was governor. I remember once the sheriff of Pierce County called. Somebody had called his office--they were on their way down to kill the governor.

He was a friend of mine. He rushed down himself to protect me. But I never traveled with a bodyguard or anything.

Since the Kennedy assassination, which happened when I was in office, the State Patrol just insisted that I have some guards around the mansion. Before that, we never even had guards around there, and then, you know, it gets pretty dark driving up there. And I had a driver, State Patrol driver. But after that, they always had security people--one or two, at least--around. But prior to that, I had no security whatsoever.

Well, I just want to thank you so very much for allowing me to come here and talk with you today.

I appreciated your coming down. I've enjoyed talking with you.

And thank you from everyone in this state, for everything that you did for us.

You know, we didn't do everything right, but we had--and I say this in modesty--we had a good administration. Good, practical people. It took me a while to appoint some of them, but I always got the best I could. The men and women we had there were the best cabinet this state's ever had. Now that's saying a lot.

Yes, it is.

I wouldn't take that back for anybody. We had a good team, and we worked closely together. And we built a lot of bridges.

You had a huge highway program.

You go across my bridge, don't you?

I've been across your bridge many times, Governor.

Well, you know, the funny thing, I wasn't even on the highway committee in the senate. But there were so many things I felt needed to be done. I think I advocated about ten different bridges in my inaugural address. And we built every one of them, including I-90. We started that one--cut the ribbon and they just finished it. Anyway, it's been a lot of fun.

I appreciate your generosity in giving me this time.

If you find something missing, call me up.

Thomas

All right. I'm here today at Washington State Reformatory in the visiting room, and I am speaking with Thomas. Thomas, what is your association with the Department of Corrections?
Right now I am an inmate in the Washington State Reformatory, and I've been under that status for almost 30 years.
Thirty years. How old are you now?
Fifty.
So you came into the system when you were 20 years old?
Yes, I did.
And what did you originally come in for?
First degree murder.
Have done all of your time on that same beef?
I have three counts of first degree murder running consecutively. And right now, I'm on my second of the three counts.
So once you were 20 years old, you became incarcerated, and you never left the institution from then on?
No, I haven't been out since.
Wow.
Yeah, I know. Long time.
Yeah, it's a long time. Where have you done most of your time?
Well, I can break it down into three units. I did roughly three years in a county jail. I did my next ten years at Walla Walla, and then I've been here at Washington State Reformatory for almost 17 years.
Did you plead guilty to your ...
No, I did not plead guilty.
Can you tell me what you were accused of doing?

I was accused of robbing service stations and killing the attendants.

More than one service station?

Yes. There were three separate service stations.

And killing attendants in all three of them?

Yes.

Were you in a gang at the time, or were you by yourself?

No, there was another gentleman involved also.

Three years in county jail. Isn't that unusual?

Not for that time period, prior to about 1968.

Once you were convicted of a crime in King County, you remained in the county jail while your state appeals were in process. And shortly after that, because of the rash of escapes from the county jail, they started sending people to another institution to be held because they just figured it was not a good risk to have people there for that long a period of time. Sometimes people may have been there for two, three, four, five years, depending on how long their state appeals took.

Thomas, when you say that people spent that length of time in county jail, it kind of surprises me. I've visited county jail, and that is a very difficult place to be. Can you comment on what it's like to spend that length of time in a place like that?

About the only comment I can give is staying in the county jail for any period of time longer than necessary is torture because at county jails they have no facilities for you to do anything except sit around. There are no recreational facilities; their health care is bad; everything is just terrible. There have often been men who have begged to be sent to another institution, or to any institution, because the conditions had to be better.

It's probably one of the most depressing places that a person can spend their time because you're not actually serving time; you're just being housed. You can't do anything; you can't accomplish anything. About the best thing I can say is it is hell and it's overcrowded.

Is it dangerous?

Yes, it is dangerous because the people in there, they are mad, they're frustrated, whether they've gone to court or not, because of the way they're being treated. And quite often, there's a lot of physical abuse there prisoner to prisoner. Sometimes the jail officials tend to abuse the men there because they don't like working under those conditions any more than the men like being held under those conditions. And it's just a very frustrating place. Because again it's almost as if you're a nonexistent person. You're an animal herded into a cage until they decide what they're going to do with you.

You say that there's two kinds of abuse there? There's prisoners abusing other

prisoners?
Right.
And then there's officers abusing prisoners?
Yes, and the officers abusing prisoners is not always a physical abuse. Sometimes it's a mental abuse, where a man needs to make a phone call, and the officers kind of look and say, "Well, so what? I'll let you do it when I get a chance to." Or the officers don't like the idea that they, more or less, have to wait on the inmates because the inmates can't go do things for themselves. So you run through that. If you have a visitor, sometimes the officers may be a little slow in getting your visitors in to see you or any number of things. It doesn't necessarily touch you physically, but it gets to you emotionally, and sometimes that's even more detrimental to a person than the physical attacks.
So it's the mind games that the officers play on the men, taking their frustrations out on the men. They never stop to think that we don't want to be there even more than they don't want to be there.
And what about the abuse you're talking about from prisoner to prisoner? What's that?
A lot of that is because when you go into county jail, you instantly have nothing. If you're fortunate enough to have family or financial support, then you can possibly buy cigarettes. Well, you can't smoke in the county jails now, so that's left out. Some men, from being in there for such a long period of time, they don't have any way of getting any money. So when an inmate comes in that has something, he's generally victimized.
I may come in, and there's someone sleeping in an area that I would prefer to sleep in instead of sleeping on the floor, so I may go over and force that person to give up that area they're sleeping in. Just basically putting a minnow into a tankful of sharks.
It's a place where you have no way of venting frustrations except on one another, whereas if you were at another institution, you could possibly have these frustrations build up, but you could go out to the yard, and you can run some of the frustration off. Or you can go walk, or you could go over to the gym and play basketball or handball or lift weights to get some of that negative energy out. In a county jail, you have no way of doing this, so it comes out against someone else.
That was quite a few years ago. Has it changed?
It has changed as far as the length of time a person stays in the county jail. But, if anything, it has gotten even worse. When I was in the county jail, the tanks, as they called them, held a maximum of 40 men. And once you reached that 40, no one else was put in there.
Now you may have the units in the county jail that's supposed to have a maximum of

40 people in it, but they may have 60 to 80 people in there, with people sleeping on mattresses on the floor. So it's even worse. Every time you take a deep breath, you're bumping into someone, which increases the tension, which increases the potential for violence.

So over the years, maybe physical structure has been improved, but the conditions have gotten even worse.

After you spent your three years in the county jail, where did you go then?

I went to Walla Walla, and I was on death row there because I was still under a sentence of execution.

I know nothing about that.

Death row is kind of hard to describe, even though I did seven years there, because you're in an area where you spend 23 hours a day in your cell. You're let out, depending on the weather, for one hour a day. During that one hour a day, you have to shower, get your exercise, and do anything else that is done outside your cell. Then you are back into your cell.

It's really depressing. When I first got there, there were only about three people in the area. That eventually reached to about 16. All these people sitting there under a sentence of death. It's really strange because we all know why we're there, but we all try to pretend as though we're not where we are.

And it's really sad because you're treated by some of the officers as if you're dead already. You'd ask an officer for something, and he kind of looked at you and would say, "Well, I don't see why we should waste any good money on you because you're going to be dead in a little while." You get little comments like that. You tell an officer you need something, and they say, "Well, so what?" And you've just asked for something like, "Hey, I need some toilet paper." "So what?" And so, you have to go without toilet paper until another officer comes along or you have an opportunity to leave your cell to go get it.

I would not say that it was as torturous as the county jail, but it's another type of torture because everybody treats you as if you have a contagious disease. They don't want to be around you. They don't want to talk to you, almost as if your death sentence is going to rub off on them.

While we're talking to one another down there, we all knew that we're under a sentence of death, but we never talked about it. We always talked about the way things used to be, what we would like to see, what's going to happen in the next two, three, four years, as far as our lives are concerned, just overlooking the possibility that we could have been executed. We didn't even want to think about it or accept the fact that it was going to happen.

While I was there, I had two dates. The first one, I got a stay of execution about a week prior to the date. The second one, I got down to 23 hours.

When you say "dates?"

That was the date you'd be executed.

I see.

When I got to the second date and got within 23 hours--although I had in my mind, "They're not going to execute me; I'm not going to let it happen," the thought kind of came, "Hey, these people are really going to do this."

And the whole area down there took on--you know, they didn't want to be happy. They didn't want to laugh and joke, but we didn't want to be sad and depressed either. So you're kind of caught in that middle ground. They were feeling sorry for me, but they were more feeling sorry for themselves, like, "The next time, it may be me." And it's kind of hard to talk in those situations. The whole area just takes on a real gray feeling. When the stays finally came through, it was almost as if a party took place down there. People could talk again. They could laugh and joke, and it made life a lot better.

And I did not realize, when it was happening to me, the effect that it had on the other men until there was a gentleman down there who had a date. And I realized how I felt at that time, which gave me an indication of how they felt. What can you say to the person? How do you treat the person? Do you treat them as if you've been going through this for the past 20 years, and nothing's going to happen? But you can't do that because, you know, this person may not exist, may not be alive 24 hours from now. So do you treat them any differently? You don't want to, but you do. Do you try to treat them as if nothing's happening? You want to, but you can't. So it kind of puts you in a very weird state.

I guess the only thing I can say about death row that would mean anything is that it is probably the most depressing place in the world because you're all in there for one reason, and you don't even want to think about it or talk about it. You try to pretend as though it doesn't exist.

The conditions that you're describing on death row sound a lot like solitary confinement.

It basically is because you're segregated from the rest of the institution. You don't even see the other men in the prison unless for some reason you have to go to the doctor. Two or three officers will come get you. You're strip-searched on the way out. You put on a pair of special coveralls, and then you're escorted from the area where death row is to the hospital. At that time, you walk through the population of the prison. This is the way it was then. When people would see you, and although they didn't know who you were, they knew where you were coming from, and people would wave and say "hello," you know, try to convey, "Hey, we know you're alive." And it was kind of interesting because you were seeing people that you don't know, and you're really happy to see them because for maybe two, three months, maybe a year or two, you just saw a maximum of 16 people, not including your correctional officers.

So it was almost like taking a vacation to be sick, to go to the hospital. Then you come back, and you're in the dungeon again.

Could you describe that cell?

I can describe it. The cell was about six feet by nine feet. It had a metal slab attached to the wall for a bed. You had a mattress, two sheets, pillowcase, and two blankets. You had your universal appliance in the corner, which was a sink that had a toilet attached to it. Right above the sink, there was a stainless steel piece of metal attached to the wall that you used for a mirror and about a 12" by 6" shelf above that. That was your whole cell.

Were you allowed to write letters, read books, or ...

We could write letters, and we could receive letters although everything that left the institution and came in was censored. If you said anything that the people decided was inappropriate, or if the people corresponding with you did the same, it would be blacked out. Although it may not be anything as far as we were concerned, if they found it offensive--sometimes you wouldn't even know about it. They'd read your letter and say, "Well, we can't let this go out," and the letter disappeared. But we were allowed to communicate with people through the mail.

Visiting was something of a joke because if someone cared enough about us to come visit us, they had to write the institution, get permission to come up and visit. They write to the institution and say, "We'd like to come up and visit him on a Saturday afternoon." The officials in the institution had to give an okay for that visit to take place for an hour, maybe two hours, depending on the availability of officers. Because, again, I'd have to have three escorting officers, and once I got to the area where I was going to visit, one had to stay in there with me during the entire time of that visit. So it was kind of difficult although in all visiting situations there are officers present. What made it even more difficult is if two inmates off of death row had people request to visit on the same day, the administration decided which one of them would go to visit. And it made it kind of difficult because of all the screening and procedures that people had to go through to come visit.

If you had a mom or someone you wanted to visit you every Saturday, could she set that up?

She would have to write a letter each time she wanted to come up to visit, and the institution wanted at least two weeks notice. So if she wanted to come up every Saturday, she'd have to start writing letters two or three months ahead of time to request it. And normally the institution would not have allowed that because of the manpower required for a man on death row to visit.

So in a typical year, how many visitors would you say you had?

During the time I was on death row I had four visitors.

In the entire time?

The entire time.

So we're talking seven years--

Mm-hmm.

--you had four visitors?

That's right.

It doesn't sound like you'd see the sunshine a lot. What I'm thinking is such little time being exposed to light has got to work on your body and your mind, of course. But just physically, it would seem like you'd become weak. Does that happen?

It does happen because, again, you're in that cramped space in the cell, and there's not really much you can do as far as exercising or walking or anything. So you spent the majority of your time either sitting on the edge or the bed or laying down.

When you go out to the yard to exercise, there was some times when you might play basketball as a group or something; in about two or three minutes everybody was gasping for breath because you did not have the energy or any lung capacity because again, you spent most of your time not moving. It was not a very healthy place.

After I'd gotten off death row and some people from the outside had gone in, one of the people said, "When I went down on death row, I could smell death." Although no one had been executed, no one had a date for execution, just the place itself, he said, reeked of death. He said he didn't even want to stay down there, even though he had agreed to go down and asked to go down and see the men. It wasn't that the men smelled bad or the place was unsanitary; it's just that, I guess, death has a particular smell, and he said, "Here's all these men waiting to die." And, technically, they may have already been dead because they can't do anything to maintain their health, or whatever.

I appreciate this is probably very difficult for you to talk about.

It is in a way, but it's something that is a part of my life. It's something that I had to learn to deal with.

Would you describe prison food?

How do you describe prison food? On the whole, prison food is destroyed through the preparation of the food. We get mashed potatoes where the peel is still on the potatoes, there's lumps in it; the potatoes are only half boiled or cooked before they mash them. You get beans on the line. Sometimes when you pick it up, it runs off the spoon because it's syrup instead of beans. Other times, you think you're chewing on pebbles.

You just have no idea what the food's going to taste like or how it's going to be prepared when you get it. There's no consistency. If it was consistently bad in one category, you could adjust to it. But it's bad in a different category every time you get it, so it's almost like, "Oh, boy. Why don't they just take me out and shoot me? Don't force me to eat that food anymore." It gets that bad sometimes.

You were not executed. However, you've now been given life without chance of parole?

No, I was given three life sentences running consecutively.

How many years does that add up to be?

If I did the minimum on each one, it would be 40 years. I know that somewhere out there in the future, there's a date that I'm supposed to walk out of prison, but I don't know when it is because the people that are going to make that decision haven't decided when they're going to see me to make the decision. It's a terrible position to be in.

Does that weigh on you? Does it wear on your nerves?

It does. It doesn't bother me as much because of me being in prison. It bothers me because of the effect that it's having on the people outside that love me and care for me; right now their lives are on hold because I'm in prison, and I don't have a clue as to when I'm going to be getting out. And it makes me feel bad because as long as the relationships exist, I feel as if I'm saying, "Okay, you don't have a life because I don't have one."

And there's sometimes when I stop and think that it would probably be better for all people involved, whether it's true or not, if I said, "Hey, why don't you just go live your life, and if I'm a part of it, just let it be a part that you pass through every once in a while." Because it makes me feel bad, realizing that they're being denied a lot of things because I'm in here. And they care about me.

And I think that aspect of it bothers me more than the fact that I have to be in here.

Let's talk a little bit about Walla Walla. You got off death row?

It was like going from total isolation to an insane asylum. I did the time when they were experimenting with prisoner self-government. There were men sitting around the institution drinking pruno, or whatever. There was people over in other corners, smoking or shooting up, whatever they wanted to do. The officers basically felt they had no control.

It was really uncomfortable. There was no rule; there was no order; you didn't know what was expected of you, what you could, and couldn't do. And it was just really strange.

As we all know, over time, things have changed and have gone from that extreme to the opposite extreme, where right now we can almost do nothing.

What a huge environmental shock for you.
Yeah, it was. It was almost like putting a starving man in the middle of a room with a banquet table and saying, "Help yourself." And you stand there, and you die of starvation because you don't know which way to go first. I think I was in the population for three days before I went and enrolled in school. And shortly after, that I got involved in the Lifers' Club there and the Black Prisoners Caucus. And from that point on, out of my 24-hour day, I'd been busy doing something 23 hours of that day.

It was almost as if I'd been given a life that possibly should have been taken. Now I had to do something with that life, and I couldn't see myself just sitting around, not using that time to either benefit me or someone else.

You used some words, and I'd like to ask if you could define them for me because I'm not familiar with them.

I can try.

Okay. One was "pruno." What's pruno?

Okay, pruno is the terminology that we use in prison for homemade alcohol. In the institutions in this state, we call it pruno. In some other institutions, they may call it "Raisin Jack." And the reason it was called pruno in this state is because they'd get prunes, they would get some yeast, and they would allow it to rot or ferment, and then they would squeeze it off, and you'd have an alcoholic beverage. So they call it pruno, but it can be made out of almost anything.

You said people were "shooting up." What is "shooting up"?

"Shooting up" is the terminology that you use in the drug culture, which means that you're using intravenous drugs. So they were sitting around with their hypodermics and whatever they were using at the time. It could have been mescaline; it could have been heroin; it could have been cocaine. Whatever drug was available at that time, they were injecting it intravenously.

You said that the officers would do absolutely nothing about any of this?

They were almost powerless at that particular time because self-government was a new concept. If someone got put in the hole, they'd say, "Oh, just put them in the drunk tank, and let them out tomorrow."

So the officers were at a point like, "Why do anything because it's just not going to make any difference? If they're not causing any trouble, leave them alone."

So this self-governing thing you're talking about? This is quite literally that the residents made their own rules?

To some extent, yes. Within the rules that the institution had to have, like, "No, you don't climb over the wall. No, you don't go home at night." But within the institution rules, what we did inside the institution, we basically made those decisions ourselves.

And although the program was a dismal failure, if it had been implemented ideally, it's something that could have been really successful.

You take men in any prison system who, from the day the prison was designed up until that day, have been controlled. Then you say, "Okay, from this point on, you're going to govern yourselves." You'd just go crazy because the institutions had no guidelines on how to implement self-government.

If it had been set up to say, "Okay, we're going to establish a form of self-government, but it's going to be done within certain parameters." If you're dying of thirst, you don't go up and give a man a large glass of water and say, "Drink it". You give it to him in small sips, so the body gets adjusted to it. And if self-government had been administered in small dosages, it probably would have been very successful.

So after ten years at Walla Walla, you were then shipped to Washington State Reformatory?

Right.

Why?

The Director of the Department of Adult Corrections felt that here at Monroe, and at other institutions, there was no control, there was no leadership, and he wanted to send some people to these institutions that could possibly add a little maturity, a little leadership. And I was one of the people that was earmarked to come here.

Well, I didn't want to come here because this place was known then as a Gladiator School. There was a bunch of youngsters here that were wild; they were crazy. Every other week, there was a stabbing, a fight. The institution spent more time on lockdown than it did off of lockdown, and I just figured, "Hey, there's nothing I can do here." I didn't have a choice because I'm in the Department of Corrections. I can be transferred anywhere they want to send me, at any time.

I feel with the help of some of the other men that were transferred from Walla Walla at that time, we were able to add a little maturity, a little stability, and leadership into the population, and it reduced a lot of the violence and tension in this institution.

So things have changed?

Yes. The inmates grew up, and they were no longer acting like teenagers.

The administration and staff has changed. We have a superintendent by the name of Ken DuCharme now, who will listen to our problems, our concerns, although he may be powerless to do anything about it. At least we know that he will listen whereas in the past they'd say, "Well, hey, I don't want to hear about it. It's your problem. Deal with it." Well, if you have the feeling that no one cares, then you really don't care.

Also, educating the men in the institution probably helped more than anything else. And it took a little time, but most of the people right now realize that by acting like a fool, you're going to lose more than you gain. And the men in prison, they have seen what it is to lose, and lose.

Is there anything that you would like the public to know?

Oftentimes we're viewed as what we are. We're the problem children of society. We have been unable, or unwilling, to follow the rules and do things in a proper manner. And society's way of dealing with us is to lock us up off in a corner of the world and to forget about us.

If you have children, and that child does something wrong, you're supposed to punish the child and instruct them. After that child has been punished, it's welcomed back into the family with open arms, and you still love and care for that child.

Although I am not your child, I am society's child. Therefore, being punished doesn't bother me that much. Being instructed on what I've done wrong, and ways to correct it, doesn't bother me because obviously I needed it.

What bothers me is that we are never really forgiven. We're never really accepted back into the family. We're never really given that love that we once had because we did something wrong. Would they do that to their biological children? Most people would say, "No, I wouldn't." Then why do you do it to society's children?

Harley

... okay, what's planned now here?

I'm going to ask you a couple of questions. This is the microphone.

Harley, I appreciate you coming up here and talking with me. What is your association with Washington State Reformatory and the Department of Corrections?

I'm doing life, which is 35 years. When I started, I had--let me see. Okay, well, I'm here for first degree murder and delivery of controlled substance. I got ten years on the delivery and 20 years on the murder, which gives me 15 years 2 months to do--13.4 for the murder and 3-year minimum on the drug beef. They saw me again in '89; I picked up 14 months. And then in '91, they saw me on the murder beef and give me 15 more years on that. So it raised my murder beef to 35 years, instead of 20. So now I'm doing 24 years, 2 months.

I did most all my time at Walla Walla. I did nine years, two months inside the Walls. I did eight years out at the building, shy of a day or two. Then I was transferred to Monroe, and I'm here now.

How many years total have you done already?

Nineteen years.

Nineteen years you've already done, and you've done the majority of those at Walla Walla?

Yeah.

Can you tell us a little bit about Walla Walla?

Okay. When I first got to Walla Walla, it was 1976, summer of '76. And when I first got there, I'd never been in any juvenile systems. As a matter of fact, I never was ever locked up before this beef.

I came to prison when I was 25 years old. When I got there, they just dropped you off the chain and let you go. You just got dropped off the chain in the back of the walls in the industrial area, and they walked you to the wing, and then you was just cut loose and sent to a cell. It reminded me a lot of what I assumed would be doing time like on a ship. And there was a lot of freedom. They had resident councils at that time. The institution was wide open.

And when I first got there, I looked around: they had like a people's park, a big yard; they had a water tower. Blood Alley was still in operation. It closed that summer.

My first night I went out up against the walls, and I can remember leaning up against the walls and looking around and going, "Oh, my God. What did I get myself into?" I had about 15 years to do. My cellies, they checked me out. I left the cell at chow time, and by the time I came back in my cell, they said it was all right for me to stay. They had checked me out and seen what I was there for and everything, and said, "Well, you're all right." So--and that was the first day.

Okay. Now I have a couple of questions about what you've said so far. You said it was like a ship, and so I'm wondering if you can tell me how it was like a ship? You said it was wide open. What do you mean by wide open? And you said Blood Alley still existed. Can you tell me what Blood Alley is?

The housing was--when you went by, there was plants and little activities in little pockets. Otherwise each cell kind of was its own--kind of like a little house. They wasn't bare cells. There was curtains; there was rugs; there was--there was little niceties in the cells and stuff. It just seemed like there was a lot of activity going on. I never was on a ship. For some reason, it just reminded me what it would probably be like on a ship, in them little old cubbyholes. And that was my first impression for ever being in a prison.

As far as wide open, what I mean by wide open is in comparison to the way the systems are run now. They had resident councils, which worked with administration. They didn't care what you did inside the walls as long as you never hurt no officers. You could do whatever you wanted to do. Nowadays, it's a whole different thing. It's more restricted. Your movements are more restricted. Your recreation is more restricted. And that's what I mean by wide open.

And Blood Alley? Blood Alley was on the way to the movie house, on the opposite side, between the old recreation and the hospital. There was a lane, a sidewalk that you walk down, and you could go into the movie house. It was called Blood Alley because there were so many stabbings there.

When you say you could do anything inside of the walls .... Can you tell me a little more about what "anything" is?

Let me go like this. Let's say anything you was man enough to do, anything somebody else had, anything that you could get your hands on, anything you could get to your cell was yours. You had free movement in the joint. You had like hourly gates. Matter of fact, I'm not even sure if you had gates at that time. I don't even think they brought hourly gates in until '79 riot. But before then, you just put out your sign, and they'd let you out, and you'd just go out in the breezeway, or run here, or run there, or go jump some rope, go to the gym, go hang out with the fellas, go do whatever you wanted to do. Just anything to entertain yourself.

Including conducting business?

Including conducting business. Now you never had TV's when I first got there. You only had radios. They got TV's in Walla Walla in 1977. Matter of fact, right after the first of the year, around January or February, because I got one of the first color TV's that came in. But TV's got there in '77.

And you think that made a big difference?

Well, it was a more of a controlled situation. They wanted TV's. That's why they'll never get rid of TV's in these institutions, because TV is a quick communication for them to us. They're never going to get rid of TV's. They can say that they don't want you to have TV's, but the administration wants you to have TV's. On a lockdown, all you gotta do gotta do is turn on the TV, and they can communicate with you. They've got their own station. It's the best babysitter that you can have. They'll never get rid of that, no matter how big a public outcry there is.

Back then, the clubs ran the institutions, ran what was going on inside the walls. And it was kind of a little society of itself. Nowadays, they disbanded the clubs, and they got these things that they call clubs, but they're administratively controlled. And if they're administratively controlled, they're not really a club; they're an organization. In order to have a club, you have to have some guidelines to be in it. Not just anybody can be in it. Organizations they have nowadays, anybody can be in them.

Back then, not just anybody could be in it. They'd check to see what sort of individual, what your beef was, before they'd even allow you in it. They wanted people who they considered to be solid.

What does "solid" mean?

Well, "solid" was someone who wasn't a rat, someone who didn't tell, someone that would stand up for himself. You know, somebody who could be trusted.

Okay. Do you consider yourself a convict?

Yeah. There's not many around no more.

There's a whole bunch of people consider themselves convicts because the guidelines to being a convict has been changed over the 19 years I've been in.

So a lot of people call themselves convicts now, and I don't believe they are.

Would you tell me what the guidelines to be a convict used to be?

It was a man who would do his own time. You'd stand up against the institution; you stayed out of another man's business; you never talked to "the man" without at least somebody there. You stood by your brothers, whether they was right or wrong, and afterwards you'd deal with them if they were wrong. But you stood by them. You got an ethic. Like right now, it doesn't matter what you've done; you can still hang out with the fellas. Back then, it did make a difference what you were here for. Because if you were here for certain crimes, like say, you was a rapo or a child molester, there's already a flaw in your character. You couldn't run with the fellas because they know if times really got hard, they couldn't count on you because there's already a flaw in your character. And no matter what they say, there's a flaw in that character.

And it'll come out when times get hard. Certain things just weren't acceptable.

You said you're doing time for murder?

Right.

I'm not sure if this is appropriate or not. If it's not, stop me. Can you tell me--

Here's what my beef was. Mine's a drug murder. I got involved in some drugs. I was selling drugs, and then there was a little group of us running around, about four or five of us running around, selling drugs and getting involved in merchandise, and a few other things. And then what winds up happening is one of the guys wound up working on both sides of the fence. He wound up working for the police. He wasn't a kid. We never fooled with kids. He was the same age I was, my equal, my peer. He was an adult. He was 23 at the time. I was the same. One of his friends saw him talking with the cops, and he was working on the other side of the fence. So me and three other guys, we killed him.

It was an execution?

Well, yeah--you're not getting what happened. The man was telling. He knew if he got caught telling, he executed himself.

I see. He broke the code.

Well, that's it. See?

I figured if I had been telling, they could kill me. I wouldn't have held it against them. That's the way I feel. I wouldn't hold it against them if they had killed me. Don't get me wrong. I'm not trying to justify it. I'm just saying that's just like convicts. They've got certain standards that you don't do. I'm here for it. I've already done the time for it. I've already done 19 years. I've done the time. So when you're asking me that, it's just hard to come out and say, "Yeah, we decided we were going to kill this guy." A guy don't really like to say that because you feel like they're going to hold it over you, and over you, and over you, and bring it back up.

This is something that I've thought about for years. The police knew, and they considered us dangerous. And he was a drug user, and they knew he wasn't a trained officer. What about their responsibility? They put him into a situation where, if he had got caught--

And he did.

And he did--that he would get killed. And they knew it. And he was not trained to do that. What about their responsibility? They used somebody that was addicted to drugs. They helped supply him with drugs and wouldn't bust him. Where's their responsibility?

Why aren't any of them doing any time? Because they used him, and when he was killed, they were just as responsible. Because they could have saved his life. They were using him and keeping him on the streets and just giving him some money for drugs. They moved him around us, and they used him as a rat, and they were letting him work both sides of the fence. And he got busted.

They didn't keep him covered, and he got killed. They justify their reasons. There's truth in what I'm saying.

Were you in a gang at the time?

No! Man, I've worked all my life. I've worked since I was 13. I had a pretty good job at the time. I owned a home. This is all legal. Everything I had done up to about a four-month period before this murder happened was all legal. I went through a divorce, and I decided I wanted to build some houses, and I couldn't borrow no money from a bank, or nothing like that. This is true, bizarre as it sounds. I got into the drug activity. And, pretty soon, I saw there was some money to be made, so I took the money that I had saved, about $12,000, and I put it into drugs. And I started working with it and selling drugs, and I was involved with drugs. I was thinking, well, I'll make a little money here and maybe go back to building some houses. And that was the whole thing. It just catches up with you. It just kept going, and I took it serious. Since I hadn't been involved in anything all my life--my family owned restaurants--I actually believed it was a business. I took it serious. People don't really understand; to the vast majority of these people involved in drugs, it's a game. They're just out there having fun. They're not really serious; they're not trying to hurt nobody or nothing.

The vast majority of people are just shooting drugs and partying, and they borrow over here, and they don't pay it. And then if somebody comes along, they avoid. It's just a big game. But every now and then, they do business with somebody who's serious about what they're doing. I didn't know it was a game. These people are doing this just for fun. They're playing with danger.

Look at it like this. Wonder if there's ten guys lined up on the wall. There's one guy sitting in front of them, and one guy comes by and slaps this guy in the head. He don't do nothing. So the second guy sees that, he comes by and slaps him in the head. He don't do nothing. And right on down the line. All of the sudden, the tenth guy slaps him in the head, so he turns around, and he stabs him in the neck, kills him. And they go, "Man, what an animal." Well, no. Matter of fact, he didn't even want to kill that tenth guy. They just kept working on him, and working on him, and working on him. But they called him an animal. Pretty soon a man says he's had enough, and he deals with it.

Most people who are killed, they're not even the cause or the reason. They're the end result of what has taken place over time. You understand that? I know you understand that. You've worked with people before.

So then you went to prison?

I went to prison.

Can you tell me about clubs?

Yeah.

Is that just a nice name for gangs?

It can be. It depends on how you take them on. Some people want to call them gangs. Some people want to call them clubs. You can call them organizations, or whatever. To me, a club has a group of people with one program in mind. An association don't have anything in mind. It's just a gathering of people.

And what would be a gang?

Probably just a pack of hooligans, running loose. Let's say just a bunch of guys with no purpose at all. They're just hanging out, trying to get in trouble. That would be a gang.

In this convict code you were talking about earlier, does it include killing somebody for no reason at all?

No. There's certain groups, in order to be in them, they call it "making your bones." Like, you take the Indians. In order to be in an Indian club, all you gotta do is be an Indian. If you got a good Indian club, they'll weed out all the weak little punks out. It's the same way with the Chicano club. When I first got to the Walls, it was the Chicano club. Chicano club was pretty strong. They didn't let the old roodypoots, and the rapos, and the rats hang out there unless they was just using them.

Roodypoots?

Yeah, you know, goofball, or--whatever.

When I went there, any group of 11 people that were violent enough could run that joint.

Really?

Yeah, it only took about 11 people. Eleven people who were hard could pretty much call the shots. Of course, administration could throw them into the hole. But back then, they didn't. They just left you alone.

And, to me, it was better than what it is now. When I came in the system, it was violent. If you was a convict, you could do good time. And if you wasn't, if you was a rat, or a rapo, or a creep, you did hard time.

What they've done now is they've turned these places into bird sanctuaries. It used to be if you'd deal with one of them people, they'd look the other way.

A bird what?

A bird sanctuary, you know.

What's that mean?

A reserve. You know what a bird sanctuary is, don't you? It's a place where birds can go and be safe.

So you're talking about people who have sexual beefs, or something like that, can be

safe?

What you hear the public saying is send them to prison where somebody will do 'em. Well, whether they think so or not, these lifers, they're not completely stupid. What they're doing now is if you deal with one, they're glad you dealt with them, but they still give you time. It used to be they didn't do that. So what people have said is, "Hey, we're not going to take care of your problem. If you ain't willing to take care of it, we ain't." People wasn't against taking care of these people and dealing with them because that's what society wanted. But they're not going to do it if you're going to sit here and give them 20 years.

So you--let me see if I've got this right. You feel like it used to be better because ...?

People didn't want to come to prison because there was violence in prison.

The thing is when you turn these places into bird sanctuaries, they've made it safe for them.

Like I was telling you the other day, here's what society has told people who do crime over a long time: "It's all right to molest our children and rape our women. But, whatever you do, don't take our money." That is the whole philosophy of this system. Society out there is scared if you take their money. And they don't care what you do to anybody else. Here's what society's got to ask: Who do you want to come back to the streets? Do you want a man who robbed? He was trying to get some money because he had no trades; he had no way of making no money, and he figured he was down on his luck. So he went out to do a robbery, and during this robbery, he killed someone. That's a horrible beef. Now you got someone that comes along who's totally out of control mentally. He likes to rape little boys or little girls. Now the man who went in and did the robbery may get life, or maybe the death sentence. Now the guy that just rapes little boys, let's say he does ten years. Who do you want to move in next door to you ten years later? I'd rather have the man that was interested in money living next door to me than the man that was interested in my children or my wife.

They've had programs for rapos; they've had programs for drug offenders; they've had programs for damn near any mental problem that you have. But they've never had a program for anybody that just does crime for money. If you find a man that's doing something for money, if you teach him a trade and a way to make a good living out there, you have a better chance of having a higher success rate with that man than you do with someone who is mentally ill and will be all his life.

Do you feel like you'll ever commit crime again?

Let me put it like this: I won't. It's just like if people ask, "Will you ever commit a murder?" I think I'm less likely than most people to commit a murder because I know the penalties that you have to pay. Most people don't know the penalties. I would actually think about it and avoid it and stay out of situations.

Well, Harley, I think a lot of people would say to you that most people wouldn't commit a crime.

You say most people wouldn't do a crime? Well, once something happens to them, they want revenge. See, they're thinking with a criminal attitude. People want revenge. Matter of fact, society wants revenge. All they can think about is locking up and throwing away the key. So when you say people wouldn't commit a violent act, they can't wait to.

People seem to be acting extremely violent out there to me. They're more violent out there than they are in here right now. There's more violence on the streets than there is these prisons. It's safer in here.

You had made a comment to me on another occasion about gangs coming out of the prisons?

Yeah.

Can you talk to me a little bit about how that worked?

Okay. Here's my understanding of how it worked. I know a little bit more about white groups, being white myself.

But my understanding, especially of the Crips and Bloods, is they originated up out of them California joints. A lot of them originated under them Reagan years when it was "lock 'em up, build more prisons." And what they did is they just kept putting people in prison. So they come up out of them ghettos and stuff. They do hard time in California; they're locked down all the time. So if you just happen to be in the wrong area at the wrong time, you'd get killed. You didn't have to do nothing. It was racial wars all the time.

You're talking about inside the prisons?

Inside the prisons, It was an extremely violent situation because it's locked down all the time, and people have pent-up emotions, and you feel like you don't have nothing to lose. So what happened was people become real cliquish, brotherhoods form, and binds form that are extremely strong. So them gangs built up there, your Black Guerrillas, your Black Brotherhoods, your Aryan Nations, your Angels, your motorcycle groups, your Chicano clubs, and four or five factions of them, and whatever. But what I'm saying is they formed real strong cliques because of the violence. So they became violent.

Well, they also come out with real negative attitudes because you have to walk a fine line when you're in that violent atmosphere. In order to run with the people that are that violent, they gotta feel they can trust you under all circumstances.

And that's where they start becoming more like convicts. You mentally get caught up in it. You don't even realize what you've become. And so they no longer liked society, and they left them prisons, went out on the streets, and got a bunch of kids to run their errands for them. They're the ones that started them small little gangs down there, them Crips and Bloods. You see what I mean? They didn't care what they did with them kids.

That's where it all came out of. That's why you'll see them; they're wearing them buttoned-up shirts, and they're wearing them penitentiary shoes. They've styled them different now, but all that stuff came up out of them prisons. They wanted to dress and act like convicts. And it's extremely violent. You don't want people on the streets acting like convicts.

Convicts got codes that they live by. In order to be a convict, you can't be disrespectful. You expect people to be courteous. You don't disrespect nobody else, and you don't want no one to disrespect you. Suppose you're standing around, and somebody just thinks, "I'll just cut in front of you or kick your dog out there on the streets." That's disrespectful. He ain't over there kicking your dog, and you ain't got no business kicking his. So he shoots you, see?

People out on the streets, they do that all the time. How many times in a grocery store have you ever had someone cut in front of you, or pushed their thing in front of you, or pull their car in front of you? Well, nowadays they're shooting you. People are acting like they're in prison. They're acting like they're in prison out there.

You should teach respect on the streets. Nobody out there is teaching them kids any manners.

I seen an old man in here, and he couldn't read no English. So he came up to one of my brothers, and he said, "Hey, would you read this for me?" So, no shame in his game, you know? And it said he was a child molester. It said, "We know that you have committed between two and three hundred of these." The paper was from the parole board. "We know you have committed somewhere between two and three hundred molestations of children, but we're going to let you go anyway."

Why?

The only thing that told me is they don't care if you rape your children or rape your women. These are not high priorities. The dollar bill is high priority in America. It always has been. The system works on that. The old convicts used to say, "Hey, next time I rob some guy, I'm screwing him. I'll do less time."

So do I think that the system's fair? I think that's who you want out next door. I think society is getting exactly what they deserve. I think they want people to come out and screw their kids. I think that's what people really want.

I was involved in an illegal activity. No excuse for none of it. But it sure isn't the same as going out and doing that to a child. I'm not the same caliber person, and to judge me as worse is insane. It's insane.

Do you think that sexually molesting a child, or rape, should be capital punishment?

I figure it like this: you let the parents do what they want.

I think if a man is found guilty of something like that, the child's closest relative should be given a choice.

If you got capital punishment for somebody that went in and did a robbery and murdered a teller, and you had someone that went out and raped a child, which one should you get rid of? I think you should get rid of the child molester.

See, you got choices to make. There's hard choices to make, and you better decide what you want.

Is there anything that we haven't covered that you would like to talk about?

Politicians have been getting elected for the past 12 to 15 years on making more and more prisons and putting more people in prison. The people in control know that in order to house masses of people with any form of control, you have to make them into small campuses. You have to make them like this, or you can't house masses of people. You'll have no control.

So they've made them like this. They've made them more like a campus style. They know it's a dead-end street because by making them campus style, it makes them a revolving door.

And that's what's happened, see? Now they're going more towards the direction of we still want to house all these people, only now, we want to take everything away from them. The people that are really running these institutions know, man, you can't do that. We can't control 5,000 people and treat them like animals, put them in the hole, take everything away, and treat them like animals because they'll go out of control. They'll be too violent. They'll burn these places down. They'll be like New Mexico. You know what happened down in New Mexico, don't you?

I had some friends that were down there, and they said they wound up getting into where the PC's were at and they got in there with knives and blades, and they cracked the cell. Three or four of them would go into where the PC's were at and started killing them. And the guys next door, they'd be going, "Don't worry, we'll be over there next." So then they'd get these guys, and they'd be stabbing and cutting. Can you imagine being in a cell, and the guy next door to you is being killed, and you know that as soon as they're done killing him, they're going to crack your door? They said it was mass hysteria. They said blood was everywhere. Now I wasn't there. But I was told exactly how it was. And they butchered them boys.

There was masses of people in that joint down there, and they was treating them boys bad. It'll be just some little incident. It'll be some little incident like used to happen at the Walls, and then all of a sudden, they'll go off.

Matter of fact, in '80-'81--when I got to Walla Walla--I had a friend that worked up at the hospital. There was 267 mentally ill in the hospital at the time. They'd let 200 of these go to pill line. When you got a guy that goes out wacko, when he ain't getting his meds, for about two or three weeks, he's all right. And then, pretty soon, he forgets to go to pill line. So he starts bumping off walls. Next thing, you got all these guys running insane.

You see?

And so it was crazy.

What about the mentally disturbed person that you just described? What would happen to that person?

Hey, I've seen cops bragging about some guy out in isolation was taking his shit and making candy bars out of it, hardening it, and then eating it. And they'd be laughing about it. Well, that man don't even know what his name is. He shouldn't be in prison. Come on, he shouldn't be in prison. He don't even know who he is, much less what he did.

If you're going to make these places, why don't you make some housing for the mentally ill? Why don't you make some housing for the sexual offenders? Why don't you make some housing for the drug offenders? And why don't you make housing for the murderers? And let's see who has the least recidivism. And let's see who has the joint that's actually most together and the officers like working in there.

Officer Arthur

Officer Arthur, what is your association with the prison system in this state?
I'm a Department of Corrections correctional officer at the Washington State Reformatory.

I have very little insight into how it would be to be a correctional officer. Would you talk to me for a few minutes about how that is and what your job entails?
As I always tell the residents, I'm here to serve and protect. Officers work in many different capacities in the institution. For instance, in Block 3, the residents are locked in their cells 23 hours of a 24-hour day. They're allowed one hour a day to get some exercise in what they call the Block 3 yard, which is an isolated area outdoors that only ten or less of those people can be at one time. They are also allowed a ten-minute shower, and other than that, they are locked in their cells the rest of the day.

We have to let them out to use the telephones or push the phone in front of their cells. There's what they call a book box that has magazines and reading material, and that's pushed from cell to cell, at the request of the inmate.

And then, meals--they send a food cart down, and we pass food out to them.

I see. This Block 3, an isolation unit. Who would go to Block 3?
They've got three categories of people that may end up in Block 3. They've got their in-transit people that are there at W.S.R. for a short time, maybe a court hearing in Snohomish County, and they're a Walla Walla inmate. So they will put them in that unit as an in-transit status.

The other people that might be there would be investigation. If there's some allegations of some sort that the administration or the intelligence department feels they need to investigate further, they may isolate those inmates from the rest of the population while this investigation is going on.

And the third category would be the people that have out in population somehow acquired a major infraction of some sort and are serving basically some isolation time for that infraction.

I see. You said that they are separated 23 of the 24 hours a day?

They're locked in their cell 23 out of the 24-hour day. They have an hour for yard, and included in that, a ten-minute shower. So other than that, they stay in there, in their cell, and they read and write letters, and that kind of thing, but they're not allowed out of their cell.

I see. How long would this go on typically? If someone did something wrong, let's say, and they need to be reprimanded for that, how long would they stay there?

Kind of depends on the type of infraction, on the seriousness of the infraction. I've had people down there as long as eight months that I know of. And then I've had people down just for a day. It's really hard to say. It's just a whole bunch of things that the administration or the intelligence people decide on how long these people are going to stay. I guess an average stay down there might be five days.

And is it effective; is it a good idea?

You know, there's one more category, and I need to explain this category, too, before I answer that question.

The other category is what they call protective custody, or PC. If an inmate feels like his life may be threatened from other residents, or the administration feels that his life may be in danger, then they will put him in isolation. He's still allowed his one hour in the yard, he's still allowed in the shower, but he has to do those things alone. The rest of the population in Block 3, ten at a time, for example, can go out and have some exercise in the yard. If you're under protective custody status, then you have to do that alone. You're escorted by at least one officer. Now the answer to your question is, as to the effectiveness of it, it's a joke. It's an absolute joke, with the exception of the protective custody part of it. I feel there's a real need for that because we certainly don't want anyone to get hurt up there. And there are a lot of strange people in the prison system as residents. That part of it is probably important. The rest of it's nothing but a joke.

Could you elaborate on the term "joke"? What do you mean by that?

Probably 60 or 70% of the residents that come into Block 3 will tell you that it's wonderful. They get fed in their cells; they're not required to do anything; their life just gets put in hold, and they can sleep and rest, smoke, and have a real relaxed, really mini-vacation. And that's the way they view it, not so much the way I view it. Now don't get me wrong. That type of confinement gets real old real fast because everybody likes their freedom. But, like I said, probably the average stay might be five days down there. Five days is wonderful for those guys, especially if they're working hard and spending a lot of time at whatever they're doing inside the walls of the institution. They, just like anyone else, get tired and run down, and it's a nice little break. They get to catch up on their sleep, and their reading, and their letter writing. And, really, some of them really think it's a great deal.

You don't have a sense that holding a man in isolation for an extended period of time affects him psychologically?

Well, I think an extended period of time will. Everything is just so regimented for those inmates that are in there. So I'm sure that part of it has a psychological effect, as well as every aspect of what we have them do, or allow them to do.

But it's my opinion that a short stay--five, six days, ten days--they're just catching up on their sleep, and taking a little rest, and recharging their batteries.

And a lot of it is under investigation type of circumstances, where many times they'll know that they're a part of this investigation, and they know that they are. Well, first of all, they know that because they're told that when they're hauled down into Block 3. But if they get wind of this investigation going on, and they know in their own mind they're a part of it, they expect to come down there. So they'll come down with their cigarettes, unopened pack of cigarettes, because we can't allow opened pack of cigarettes. We do allow unopened packs. So we'll see them hauled down there from, let's say their work place, and they may have five or six packs of unopened cigarettes in their pocket. And you can't tell me that all of those people up there are walking around with five or six packs of cigarettes. They're preparing for their little vacation. It's not like a Hollywood prison system. They're waited on hand and foot, and the medical people come down three and sometimes four times a day, and walk through and take care of all of their medical needs. The phones are pushed up toward the front of their cell; they're on wheels. Their food is handed to them through the food tray in their cells, and the book box, and they smoke, and read, and sleep. And it seems to be like they're having a great time.

If you're holding a person because you're running an investigation, I don't suppose it's a punitive purpose at any rate?

No. As I said when this started, I don't think that the whole system in Block 3 is effective.

How could it be more effective? Should it be eliminated completely?

Well, I don't know that it can be eliminated because there has to be that control. And basically the isolation part of it is the punishment. It's not like they come down there, and we punish them by giving them less food, or those kinds of things. It's strictly the isolation part of it. I think that some sort of a system may be necessary. I don't agree with the fact that they should be able to smoke down there. I think that's a real biggie. I'm a smoker myself. If I were to go down there, it might be kind of nice to catch up on my sleep, and read, and smoke. However, if I was to go down there and not allowed to smoke, as a smoker, right there would be a reason for me not to want to go down there.

They can smoke right in the isolation unit?

Right in their cells. It's not like they're getting any punishment or something. Even if the system is set up on a punitive reason to be down there, it's just a rest. It's not like they're worried about it or it's a big deal.

Do you feel that this kind of environment causes resentment from the officers? I can almost feel a tone of resentment in your voice. It's like they've got it better than you do in some way?

You know there's a few issues that I really resent. But probably only a few. Some of those resentments are, for example, the medical. The medical that they receive, I don't get myself. I feel that the medical system is all wrong. If the residents have a particular concern, let's say a backache or something like that, and they don't feel they're getting the proper care from the physicians and nursing staff that are up there, they can request to go on the outside and get what they feel is more professional health care. And this is all free. It's all paid for by myself, and yourself, the taxpayers. An example of that is we may have ten or fifteen medical trips a day that leave that institution with a two-officer escort to go downtown Seattle to the best doctors money can buy for a back x-ray. I can't get that kind of medical care, so I do resent that.

I do feel, unlike the majority of officers up there, the payback for their crime is being there. The punishment doesn't start after they walk in those walls. There are a lot of officers, sergeants, and lieutenants that feel every dealing that they have with any of those individuals requires some kind of a punishment. I don't feel that's correct. I think the punishment is the fact that they're separated from their families and their loved ones and that they're separated from society, and they're not free to do what they want to do--the fact that we've removed their freedom.

You said that a number of officers believe that any interaction that they have with a resident has to include some type of punishment. Can you be more specific? What does that mean? What kind of punishment could they inflict on a resident?

There are two types of infractions or wrongdoing, the minors and the majors.

The majors we're not given a choice on. If we come across a major infraction, then we have to act on that major infraction with paperwork, follow-up, and maybe escort to Block 3. Those types of things.

A minor infraction, like during a routine scanner patdown you might find that a resident has another resident's Walkman. That's a minor thing. It's not a major infraction. At that point, as an officer, we have alternatives as to what we can do. We can give what is called an on-site adjustment, which is a "look, man, you know you're not supposed to have this. Whose number is this?" And if it's Johnny's, then "you give it back to Johnny, and don't do this no more." And that takes care of that, and then he goes on with this business.

However, if the officer chooses to write a written infraction on a minor infraction, then the resident has to go to a hearing, a little kangaroo court type thing. And if he's found guilty, which he always is, he may have to give up phone privileges for a week, or do some extra duty, or those type of things.

What started this whole conversation was the fact that the majority of those Officers would write those infractions rather than give the on-site adjustment, where I have found the on-site adjustment is far more effective. Number one, it doesn't create any more friction than necessary between the officer and the resident. It doesn't create any more friction than necessary between the resident and the institution as a whole. It's one of the things that I work hard to do, to keep that friction level to a real minimum. I can't image what it would be like to be locked up 24 hours a day for years and years, or even a year, or even a month, or even a week. But I really can't imagine what it would be like to be in that situation and be nickel-dimed harassed to death.

Do you carry weapons?

No, an ink pen.

You carry an ink pen?

An ink pen.

Are officers in the towers armed?

Not all the towers are armed, but there are, I believe, six towers that are armed.

Are you ever afraid?

You know that's an interesting question. Prior to coming to work for the Department of Corrections, I had imagined what inside those walls may be like, and it was strictly a Hollywood idea of what prison is all about. When I first started there, I don't know that I was afraid. But I was put into the blocks on one side, and there were 160 residents and two officers. All 160 of those cells, at one time or another, are open. There may be a few minutes lag between the tiers being opened. But basically there's a potential of 160 residents and two officers.

And as I looked around, I thought, "What in the hell am I doing here?" One of the oldtime inmates, who had been there for years and would be there forever, came up to me and said, "You know, it's really good that we like you because if we didn't, each one of us could take a little tiny bite out of you, and you'd be gone." And I thought about that--160 bites out of my body, I would be gone.

What happens is, at least in my particular case, being in that situation, day after day after day, you tend to relax to a very dangerous point. You always have to remember there are many very dangerous people up there. There are many that are not also. But there are many that are very dangerous and very unpredictable. And if you're not always sure of who's behind you, you potentially could be in some danger.

You get to a point where you're pretty much relaxed with the area that you're working in. And you have to give yourself a reality check ten times a day. Or you just go on about your business and don't even realize who's there, who's behind you, what they're doing. And that can get real dangerous. I wish I were more scared. I wish there were some fear there. I don't have that fear anymore, and that's when you get into a dangerous situation because you're not paying attention.

Do you ever have an occasion to become friends with a resident?

Define friends.

Well, you interact with them. You like them. You have personal feelings for them.

Yeah, I have certain residents in there, very few, but certainly there are residents in there that I guess you would consider friends. Three or four.

As part of your job description, you have to be willing to shoot these people, if that's required? Is that true?

That's true.

Could you do that?

I don't know. I sat down the other day with my significant other and said, "You know, how would you like to find yourself in that position?" I'm not sure what I would do. Knowing that I would have to do something, but also knowing maybe your definition of a friend is down there. And what kind of shit the administration and the Department of Corrections and society would put me through for pulling that trigger. I don't know what I would do.

What kind of potential is there for riots?

I don't know. I guess in my mind again I've got that Hollywood idea of what a riot may be. I don't spend a lot of time thinking about it, but the reason is because I don't think it would be that big of a deal.

There is officer training, isn't there?

Oh, you bet. We're highly skilled, trained officers.

Could you describe the training aspect?

They have some in-house training in their own little training center. I spent probably two weeks in the training center outside the institution, going over policies and procedures, and what to expect when we got in there, and those kinds of things.

When that two weeks was up, they sent us to the academy for a month. And that went through everything from defense tactics to cell searches, communication skills, transportation concerns, procedures, and all of those kinds of things.

When I look back on the academy--especially the communication, the one-on-one, inmate-to-staff, or officer type things--it was very well done. And I did learn a lot. The rest of it was a lot of law, which I doubt that you'll ever use in an officer's capacity.

Did they teach you what to do in case you were ever attacked?

Yeah, hair holds and those kinds of things. But, I mean, let's face it, unless you're built like a phone booth with a head on it, you don't stand a chance. If he's attacked, he's just attacked. You're at the mercy of your attacker. You might get a lucky punch in, but you've got an ink pen to write this individual up because that would be a major infraction, and that's basically all you've got.

Many times you've got communication equipment, such as the portable radios and regular telephones. But in many, many situations, you have none of those things, so it's just you and him.

Can you talk to me about the Reformatory just generally?

Basically, they've got a lot of individuals that are not capable of being there in the job capacity that they're in.

Are you talking about administration, or are you talking about other officers?

I'm talking about both. On an everyday level, I deal with other officers, sergeants, lieutenants, captains, those kinds of things. And there are many of those people that are just a waste of payroll. Occasionally, I'll deal with administrative people, but I have a pretty good insight on administrative, too. There are a lot of people that are, in my opinion, doing nothing and getting paid for it in the supervisor category.

Did I hear you correctly? You feel there are people in administration who are not doing their job?

That's correct.

Who are not capable of doing their job?

Well, they're not doing their job because they're not capable of doing their job. However, there are some that are very capable of doing their job but are still not doing their job.

Why?

Probably they feel that it's a state job. It's so big that it takes an act of Congress to get someone terminated up there. And they've done it for years and years and gotten away with it. And no one's ever challenged them. And they're good old buddies with the person that got them in in the first place.

It doesn't seem to be "what you know"; it's "who you know" to get promoted in there, especially if you're in the administration.

In terms of your colleagues, you felt that some of them were not worth their pay. Can you describe for me what you mean by that, why you feel that way?

I guess I could just give you some examples. Let's use what's called an R & M, which is an officer strictly used for response and movement. That's what R & M stands for. If I bid for that job and got it, I would go in every morning and get a radio and a set of handcuffs and some utility keys, and I would pretty much wait for directions on what to do. The shift sergeant may call me on the radio and have me do an elevator escort for a wheelchair resident, those types of things.

And you might have five of those people on a shift. And to try and get one of them to do something, like an elevator escort ... I mean, this resident may sit down there in the rain on his wheelchair for ten minutes, waiting for one these five guys to show up, put him on the elevator, and take him up to the third floor.

Or 1:00 in the afternoon--you get off at 2:00--they do what they call dump trailers. Basically, the officers have to go out to the extended family visit area, and there may be two residents that need to come back to the regular population of the institution and their families go home. Probably takes 20 minutes to do that; to walk out there and strip-search this inmate, go through his inventory, make sure his family gets outside the wall, walk him back up to his cell, and go on about your business.

With five guys, and they know it has to be done before they leave, they will hide from that, and hide from that, and hide from that until it's to a point where, had they done it at 1:00, when they were supposed to, they could go home at 2:00, like they're supposed to. But because they hid for an hour, now they've got to go out and do it when they should be going home. It's an everyday problem.

So they're rush, rush, rush, and it's a fight every day to find somebody to go out there and do it.

It's like, "Who can do the least?" It's like they all line up in the morning and look at each other and say, "I'm going to do less than you do." It's like, "Who can get the job that requires the least amount of effort to carry it out?"

What about corrupt officers?

There are none.

Thinking about prison, it's difficult for me to imagine myself being incarcerated. What amazes me is how fast, and how well, the majority of these people adapt. It's like this is the greatest thing that's ever happened to them.

Travon

I am at Washington State Reformatory speaking with Travon. Travon, what is your association with the Department of Corrections?
I'm a inmate, convict, just doing time.
What are you doing time for?
Aggravated first degree murder.
That's the first time I've heard that phrase. Can you tell me what aggravated first degree murder is?
The prosecutor says that, I guess, you're supposed to think it out and then commit it. Plan it.
I see. And how old were you when you were accused of committing this crime?
Thirteen.
You were tried as an adult?
I was tried as an adult when I was 14.
Why were you tried as an adult?
I really don't know. I mean, I really don't know. I can't say. I mean, they just did. I was tried, and that's the only thing I can say about it. I really don't know. They had their meeting, I mean, not their meeting but they had their--how can I put it? They thought it was best. I don't know why, though.
How old are you now?
Twenty-one.
If it would be all right with you, I'd like to go back into your childhood a little bit because you were tried when you were 14 years old, right?
Right.
Tell me a little bit about your life.
I just had a, a regular--I mean this is my first offense. I'd never been in trouble before. I never had no criminal history or criminal record. I was just a regular kid,

playing football, basketball, going to school. Had a big family, pretty good family. Nothing unusual, nothing hurtful, nothing like that, just a regular kid getting into something he didn't know about and getting hooked.

Were you involved in a gang?

No, not at that time. Like I said, just a kid going to school, playing football, basketball, and the regular things, finding his first love, and all that. And then, I got hooked. So, when the gangs started coming up here, I was already in the Juvenile.

Did you get involved with a gang when you were in juvenile detention?

All the people that's close to me, that are around my age--my cousin, my brother, and all that--are involved in a gang, so it naturally led me into being in a gang.

They are involved in gangs?

Yeah. So I just naturally just followed their lead.

I want to watch my words. I don't want you to have any problem with this. So if I say it incorrectly, please correct me, or don't answer the question.

But you're not involved with a gang? You're just a usual kid, playing basketball, falling in love with gals?

Right.

And then you're arrested for a very serious crime. That's sort of a paradox. I don't understand it.

I guess it goes with who you associate yourself with. If you got one person who is really innocent to all crime in the world, and then you got somebody else who has somewhat of a dark side, and he know what's going on, and then you get this innocent kid, and you take him across that line to the dark side, and things just get caught up, and you just get hooked. I mean, that's the way I see it. I mean--and I just got caught up, I guess, and got hooked.

So you were convicted of this crime?

Right. Once I was convicted, I stayed about two weeks in the juvenile system waiting for a transfer somewhere. And when they first came and got me, they took me to Shelton. They put me in a IMU, which I didn't want to be in; but they put me in IMU because they didn't know what to do with me because I was so young, and they were worried about me.

So then they sent me to SOC, Special Offenders Center, because of my age, and them guys planned on keeping me there until I was 21. But I had got in a fight there, and so them guys sent me to Monroe. And I been here and to Walla Walla.

The first time they sent you to Monroe, how long were you here?

About three weeks, and then I got in another fight, and the guys sent me back to IMU for disciplinary behavior. I spent about 90 days in IMU there; then I came back, and I was here for about two or three years, something like that.

It sounds like all these fights that you had to get into, it sounds like it might have been pretty rough for you when you first came in.
Not really, no. Not really. It was, but it wasn't. That's really how it was, but it wasn't. How can I put it? It wasn't rough for me, but it was rough for me. It wasn't, but it was. That's really the only way I can explain it right.
Okay. What were the fights about?
It really wasn't no big fights. It was about my young age, and I think the system was protecting theirselves rather than anything else. Because I was so young, and if something really would have happened to me, I think it would have been an outcry from my mom and my family. So I don't think it was my behavior. I think it was just them guys was protecting their butts when it came to me. That's all it was.
I see. Can you tell me what IMU is like?
It's pretty messed up. You spend 23 hours a day in a cell. You get one shower for ten minutes; you get one hour outside to walk around the yard, to use a phone. I got books.
You were very young to spend time in IMU.
Right.
How did that affect you?
It really didn't affect me. I don't feel no effects. I don't feel no effects. As far as disciplinary stuff, it didn't do anything to me. It didn't affect me at all--to me, at least.
Was it frightening to you?
No, not really. No, I think I can adjust to any environment. When I went into juvenile my first time, I adjusted to that perfectly. You know what I'm saying? And then, when I got up here, I adjusted to the adult system. When I went to the hole, I adjusted to it. I just adjusted to it 'cause I couldn't do anything about it, so I just adjusted with it. I wouldn't let it affect me too much, you know what I'm saying?
You just surrendered to your environment?
Right.
Has the Reformatory changed since you first came here?
Probably a little rougher then, but I think I liked that a lot better because it's real petty now. I mean, it's just real, real petty.
What do you mean by "petty"?
The officers are just petty. Them guys just do petty things.
What was Walla Walla like?
It really messed me up, I think. I really didn't like it there. Them guys have so much control over there that you can get booked for anything. I mean, for somebody saying something against you, you'll get booked, even if it's not true. I didn't like it at all.
You'd get in trouble for little tiny things, or nothing at all sometimes?

Right. Right. Nothing at all sometimes. Over there, I been in IMU twice, I think. Them guys said that me and my friend and two other dudes that we don't even mess around with was trying to unite all the gangs and get them to turn on the white police and the white inmates. They didn't have no evidence; it was just hearsay. But I did several months for that. Several months IMU for that, with no evidence. Them guys just said they had a confidential informant, so I did seven, eight months for that one. The last time I went to IMU was for a fight them guys said I had got into. Another confidential informant said me and him wasn't fighting. Said that he slipped and fell. I spent 11 months in IMU for that.

Eleven months?

Yeah, 11 months IMU. I mean this is for all hearsay evidence. The dude who they said I hit, he even said that I didn't do anything to him. I spent 11 months in IMU for that.

Okay. When you say "IMU," do you really mean IMU, or do you just mean segregation?

No, I mean "Intensive Management Unit."

Why did they send you to IMU and not just send you to segregation?

I really don't know. Them guys wanted me to do a program in there because of my behavior.

Did that create bitterness inside of you? Don't you get angry about that?

Yeah, but I'm so used to doing their little programs up there. It's like it really doesn't affect me anymore. I don't feel anything these people do to me anymore; it can't affect me. Them guys done took everything from me. The little things they can do can't affect me. What they give me is nice, but if they took it away, it really wouldn't matter because I'm still doing time all-in-all. If it's out in population, if it's in the hole; all-in-all, I'm doing time.

How much time are you doing?

Life without.

What does that mean?

I don't got a parole date; I don't got a release date. I just don't got no date at all.

I want to talk for a moment about your physical appearance, if I could. You have a little tattoo of a tear by your eye. Can you tell me about that?

The teardrop, it mean every day I'm in here, I'm crying. I haven't experienced a lot because my childhood was took'n away from me. The things I could do on the outs, I can't do them.

I ain't experienced a lot because I was booked when I was 13. So it's like I cry every day, and this just--I may not cry physically or nothing like that, but it's a symbolic statement just saying, you know, I'm feeling pain every day.

So inside, you are crying every day?

Every day. Every day. Every day I wake up, every day I go to sleep. It's pain. And that's it.

Because you're incarcerated?

Because I'm incarcerated, because them guys took my childhood away. I ain't never been to no prom. I ain't never drove a car. I ain't never did a lot of things. There's just so much I haven't experienced, and when I see it on TV, it just brings pain back. I ain't been with my family in a long time. It brings back pain. I don't know half of my cousins 'cause I been in here. It's just so much pain.

There are people out there right now who would say that someone who would take another person's life has forfeited theirs. How would you comment on that?

It's hard to explain. My crime partner was 15 at the time. I can understand if we were a little bit older. I understand we did wrong. I understand we need to be punished. But you know what I'm saying? To take a 15 or 13-year-old's life, the rest of their life away? We need to be punished. We should be punished, but I don't think the time them guys gave us should have been the punishment. I mean, life without, to somebody who's 13 or 15, you didn't even give us a chance to try to come up out of it, or to be new people, or whatever. I mean, you didn't even give us a chance. You just took it all away from us. So that's the only way I think I can explain it.

Your associate was given life without also?

Right.

Do you ever see him? Are you doing time at the same institution?

No, he's at another institution at this time.

You appear to me to be a pretty independent and self-sufficient young man. Do you think that you always have been that way, or is that something that you've grown to be through the time that you've been incarcerated?

I'm not as independent as I want to be. I want to be real independent. A lot of dudes done help me grow up faster, and I thank them guys. A couple brothers out there really helped me grow up, common sense-wise. I think they helped me grow up a lot faster than I would have anywhere else. And I thank them. That's probably it, I think.

You're African-American.

Right.

In your experience inside the institution, do you feel like that comes into play at all?

It's really going to come into play now that the gangs are started.

The color of a person's skin might come into more play now that the gangs are starting up? Do you see that gangs are more prevalent today than they have been in the past?

Um--

Are you talking about gangs on the streets, or are you talking gangs on the inside?
I'm talking about as far as gangs on the streets coming in and them guys just being here; people thinking that every young black has to be in a gang, you know? Some guys just stereotyping every young black, that they all had to be in a gang.
Whether they are or not?
Yeah, whether they are or not. If you're old or young, you all had to be in a gang. You can't do this, you can't do that because you've got to be in a gang. If you go--if you just put up your hand as a peace sign, you gotta be in a gang. Just because you're black, you gotta be in a gang.
Is there anything you'd like to say?
I mean there's really nothing I could say. I mean, it seems like the community out there are so blind to what's going to happen. Them guys close their eyes to all the truths and then open them to untruths.

But I think them guys just need to wake up, and to smell the coffee because what them guys do us, they going to do you the same. I think that's it.

Section Four

What About God?

Tom Rolfs

I'm with Mr. Tom Rolfs. Mr. Rolfs, would you like to tell me a little bit about yourself? I understand that you've come quite a ways through the system.

Yes, I started in corrections straight out of school at the Corrections Center in Shelton in 1965 and have just a little over a month shy of 29 years of service.

I started as a counselor in the system at Shelton and promoted up to associate superintendent, and then I came into the headquarters office here for a year in charge of a special program development and sighting for new correctional facilities.

And then I went from here to Spokane and spent a year opening Pine Lodge Correctional Center as the Superintendent there. And then came back to headquarters for two years as director of correctional industries. And then I went to Monroe, where I was Superintendent, opening the new Special Offenders Center, and was there for about three years, and then went next door to Twin Rivers Correction Center to be the opening Superintendent of that facility for about three years. And then moved to the Assistant Director position that had a number of institutions, including the facilities at Monroe. And then I've been here as Director since.

It was my opportunity, unlike most superintendents, to be the first superintendent of three different institutions.

It's not unusual in this day and age, when you're opening new facilities frequently, to maybe get an opportunity to be the first superintendent at one facility, but three was a little unique. For somebody who typically has been involved in administration of correctional facilities, it was a little unusual for me to take a time-out period and be in charge of correctional industries. You tend to be either one or the other, but not both, and so that was kind of a unique experience.

Obviously, I've moved around the system a lot. It's not uncommon for people, at least in Washington, to potentially do all of their career in one facility, and I've worked in four different ones, in the headquarters office two or three different times, so I've had a large variety of experiences.

Why is that? Did that just happen that way, or were you being groomed for this position?

If I was, it wasn't something I was aware of. I remember years ago, a fellow who had essentially this position. He had taken a personnel action on another employee, one that a lot of people thought very highly of, and a lot of people admired this employee's long-term status in his position. The Director said to me that he had one year's experience 20 times over and has been in the job 20 years. And that was a clue to me, if you wanted to really make some contribution, you probably could do so better in the long term if you moved around a little bit, got better experiences, and basically became a little bit more knowledgeable about the whole system, instead of focused on a very small piece of it.

There are prices to be paid for moving around a lot, but I think I'm a better person in the long term for having done so, being exposed to not only a variety of positions, and places, and people--the most important of all, a lot of different people.

And that's not to denigrate those folks who choose to stay in one place for a long period of time. Not all of them become stale and narrowly focused. A good many of them I've known have done extremely well where they've been, very reliable, developed good programs, been as much a service to the public as I, or anybody else, hope to be; so I don't make any judgments about people who choose to stay in their same place. It just wasn't right for me.

Maybe you can talk to me a little bit about the D.O.C. in general? How do you see the future of the D.O.C. in five, ten, twenty years?

Well, how I see it, and how I'd like to see it, are probably a couple of different perspectives.

How I see it is as a continued growth experience, as we have seen for the past several years. When I started almost 29 years ago, there were--not counting a couple of small camps--there were three institutions. Today we have 14 institutions in the state, counting our camps, and a fifteenth one on the drawing board of nearly 2,000 beds. In nearly 30 years, we've had phenomenal growth, and the population projects, assuming that there are no other statutory changes in the law, are for continued sustained growth. And as we have always seen, nearly every year there seems to be some further statutory attention paid to dealing with crime and offenders, and each action tends to increase the numbers of people going to prison and the lengths of time that they stay there.

And so I have no reason to believe that that phenomena won't continue, and so we'll get even greater growth over time, beyond what we're getting now.

But you said that isn't necessarily what you would like to see?

No, I wouldn't. You know, every one of us wears different hats, and if I put on my taxpayer hat, I just think there has to be other answers to dealing with crime, and dealing with people who are troubled or troublesome, other than simply locking them up for long periods of time.

I guess I'm not very optimistic about things being the way I'd like them to be, i.e., more problem-solving in the community, with greater sentencing alternatives to prison and fewer people going to prison.

Could you speak a little bit to that, the alternatives to the sentencing?

Well, I suppose there are any number of creative or innovative ways that people can or have used. Normally, when people think of alternatives to sentencing, certainly to prison, they think of shorter stays in a confinement setting, such as a county jail, rather than long-term stays in a prison setting. They think of--oh, community custody status, where they are supervised in the community by community custody officers or community correctional officers, where there is some organized reporting process, depending on the nature of the offender. They may have a very narrow circle of movement, freedom to move, may be involved with electronic monitoring, which we have seen come about in recent years. Mandatory involvement in certain kinds of treatment programs, whether it be substance abuse, chemical dependency, anger management, a host of programs that come into the confinement settings, or treatment settings, or that people go to in the community. Other potential programs are not unlike some of the programs you'll find in Eastern countries, where an offender is assigned to the neighborhood, and the people who live in his or her neighborhood have some obligation to work with him, monitor him, be responsible for him, whether it's the immediate family or often the expanded family, or the whole neighborhood. Unfortunately, we tend to be a rather independent culture, and we're oriented to, "I'll take care of me, and you take care of you." And I'm not sure that it would be all that easy to get people to think in terms of, "This is my community, and everybody that's in it is my responsibility." But I think that does have some promise, and I think that's something that could be adopted as part of sentencing alternative.

With your position as a director, what kind of influence do you have on these kind of decisions? Can you implement these things?

Well, some of them may be dependent on change in the law. Others may be dependent on the almighty dollar and the availability of resources it can buy.

The courts ultimately make the sentencing decisions about offenders, so about the most a person in my position could do to influence that is to do it in the halls of the legislature during legislative session time, in terms of trying to influence the lawmakers about statutes. That's not in the sense of being a lobbyist, but in the sense of being responsive to their interest, and inquiries, and proposals that may come from them or from constituencies that they serve. That's probably the most effective way.

The other way in which I can potentially be effective is with the people who are employees of the Department of Corrections, many of which may be subordinate to me, others who may be peers, or in other divisions, as the case may be, in terms of trying to influence and encourage people to become involved in their own communities beyond the time they put in an institution.

There's nothing that says people that work in corrections as a livelihood can't volunteer, too. They can volunteer in the community, in activities that respond to the needs of people in their community, particularly kids--whether it's coaching a little league team, or working with United Way, or working in a church that is responsive to needs. I would, and do, encourage them in that fashion.

The other way is to be responsible to the interests of interest groups in the community, with a Rotary group or businessmen, helping them understand what corrections in particular is all about and what the effects of crime are in terms of people going to prison. Going to a PTA meeting, or Victims of Crime meeting, and helping people have a broader understanding of what our corrections system is all about and what we see in their lives that have made a difference, either in terms of causing them to get into trouble or causing them to take a new path. And give a broader understanding how people become troubled and troublesome.

It's better if people will begin to take a handle on their own problem and begin to solve it, instead of depending on, or relying on, tax resources and somebody else to solve it.

I have an article written by Chase Riveland.

Yes.

In this article, he calls the "Three-Strikes-You're-Out" policy "drive-by legislation," and challenges either the State of Washington or Washington, D.C., to stand up for some pragmatic leadership. I was wondering, do you agree with this article? Is this your philosophy also?

Absolutely. Chase is courageous in that article because he's a courageous man all the way. He's a very dedicated, caring, bright leader in corrections, not only in this state, but nationally. But he's not saying or mouthing perspectives that are out of sync with most, if not all, professional people in our field. The difference is that--at least for some--is that he's saying it, and they're only thinking it.

I understand you've got a population problem right now? You've got an overload of inmates and nowhere to put them?

While we are above our rated capacity, it is not overwhelming at this point, remembering again what I said earlier--that when statutory changes are made that add bodies for longer periods of time, then you're back to the drawing board. As an example, the new Youth Violence Bill that passed in the legislature this session will add bodies to the adult corrections. We don't know how many at this point, but there will be some 16-17-year-old offenders, who typically would have gone to juvenile in the past, who now will go to adult corrections. And that adds to our population.

There were some law changes made with respect to penalties for people that are involved in firearms that will add bodies to our institutions that wouldn't have been there before. A couple, three years ago stiffer penalties were imposed for burglary, for drug offenses, and for sex offenders that have added bodies to our facilities.

And every time a decision modifies a statute, or adds a statute, that sends more people to prison for longer periods of time, or both; then we feel the sting of that in terms of where are we going to put them, and what are we going to do for them, and with them? We've got enough beds coming on line to effectively meet the demands that are being put on us now. That offers no assurance in terms of what may be the case next year, or the year after, or the year after.

In the health care area, I've heard feedback from citizens and D.O.C. staff about how much is spent on health care for inmates, when they themselves often can't afford this kind of health care. Can you comment on that?

I can comment to this extent. I appreciate and understand the perspective. I think the sad part about it is not so much what we provide to the inmates but what we do not afford or provide to employees or people on the street. And, that notwithstanding, we do spend an awful lot on health care for inmates, and we're working hard right now to try to address that more squarely than we have in the past. One of the key issues to getting a handle on health care costs is having a comprehensive, adequate data bank on health services that you provide and the conditions under which you provide them. We're also looking at some response to health care delivery that we're not able to provide ourselves. Making sure that we're billed for the right things, and we're not overbilled, or we're not inappropriately or incorrectly billed. And that's not making any judgment about the people that do the billing in the community. When you're dealing with high technical comprehensive health care cost delivery, it's easy to make mistakes; and we're not going to be doing anything that any large deliverer of health care services doesn't already do. But once everything is in place, to provide the best quality health care cost containment, we are still going to be spending lots of money on health care delivery.

Parenthetically, I had a letter here not too long ago that went to the governor from a 15-year-old person in one of our communities that could not for the life of them understand why we didn't just simply lock them up and give them nothing but bread and water. Maybe they'd be a little more appreciative of life in the free community. People who believe that way will believe that anything, outside of a Bandaid and an aspirin, is too much.

And in the absence of those kinds of health care cost containment procedures, there is always a chance that we'll deliver some health care services that maybe there's cause not to deliver. But my position is, most of the time, we deliver what we would be obligated to deliver, according to community standards on assuring the life and safety of the people charged to our care. And it's what keeps us out of court.

Do you ever see treatment becoming part of the D.O.C. policy again?

I don't think we've ever not advocated treatment. I think some of the things that might suggest to some that we don't is one, there aren't a whole lot of penalties for not participating in treatment. It's become more of an individual choice, offender choice, about whether they will participate in programs. Another piece of it is we're not able to provide 100% programming opportunity for 100% of the inmates. And that's not a case of not wanting to or not believing in it. It's a case of there are only so many dollars to go around, and we stretch things as far as we can.

It was stated to me, and I believe I can quote, "It is not the mission of the Department of Corrections to provide treatment. It is the mission of the Department of Corrections to incarcerate."

That's true, and probably the one public policy that embodies that perspective more than anything is our sentencing statutes. We went from an indeterminate sentencing statute to a determinate sentencing in 1984.

What an indeterminate sentencing said to most people was if you get into some form of treatment and respond to that treatment, then you'll be rewarded by an earlier release. And so there was some marriage of reward and opportunity.

Then determinate sentencing came along, and to many it says, "You'll get three years for doing this offense, and you can go to school every day, and improve yourself, and you'll do three years; or you can sit in your cell every day, and you'll do three years." It's really not as clear as that because actually inmates can earn time off of their sentence, called earned early release; and they get earned early release credits for not getting any rule violations in the institutions and for participating in the program. And if they get into trouble or don't participate in the program, or both, then they'll do a little bit more time than that other person.

So there is still some semblance of that notion of reward and participation, which suggests some support of the treatment module. But our sentencing policy does send the message that what's important here is punishment and incarceration. But I don't believe you can walk into one of our institutions, and walk through any of our vocational shops or any our academic classes or any of our work programs, and not get some sense that treatment is an effective model for changing people's behavior.

Is there anything that you would like to speak about? Perhaps a personal anecdote?

I used to wonder an awful lot how I ended up in this kind of career. My father operated a business. He was kind of a scientist. He was educated to be an entomologist, which is a bug man, and ended up with a very successful business, responding to the needs of orchardists and packers for fruit.

And, for all intents and purposes, if I had wanted to, I could have easily ended up in the same business he did and followed in his footsteps. And I wondered for an awful long time why I didn't because it was a good business, and as a teenager and young man, I worked there every summer and enjoyed the people and enjoyed what I did. But, for reasons that were hard for me understand, I didn't feel led to do that.

It's only been in more recent years that I've come to understand that better, that, I think, we're each called to do whatever we do, and I've become more convinced in more recent years that I was called to do exactly what I'm doing. Irrespective of whether some people think I'm doing a great job, and others may think I don't do so great a job, I feel very comfortable in what I've been doing for the last ... nearly 29 years, looking forward for whatever time I have remaining to do this kind of work.

I think I respond fairly well to troubled and troublesome people, and I think I have demonstrated some sensitivity and caring for the people I work with, whether it's staff or inmates. I just feel very satisfied and comfortable with my career choice. And, all that does is just reaffirm, even more, my feeling that I was called to do this. Call it whatever you want, but divinely called to do it is as good a calling as one could ever want.

I appreciate your time. And, again, I'd like to ask you if you realize that you have been on a tape recorder and that this material is not going to be held in confidence. It will be shared with the public and with other people. Are you aware of all that?

I am aware of that, and the only proviso that I would attach to it is that you told me from the outset that what you're planning to do is write a book, and to the extent that you want to use this material as part of that book, you're welcome to do so. To the extent that you have any intent to release it to or share it with the press, I have a problem with that. If the news media wants to get information from me, then I expect them to come to me personally and do it, as opposed to sharing it secondhand. That would be the only restriction I would place on it.

Thank you.

My pleasure.

Reverend Jon Nelson

I'm in the office of the Reverend Jon Nelson. Reverend Nelson, are you aware that this conversation is being tape-recorded?

I see the tape recorder, and I am aware of it.

Reverend Nelson, perhaps we can start by talking a little bit about you?

Well, I grew up in a parsonage family, and my dad was a pastor at a couple of places in Minnesota. And then most of the time I was growing up in Washington, D.C.

It was always a part of my folks' lifestyle that they were deeply connected, and connected us as a family, to prisons in the area. And in our home, tracking through were people who would be coming out or friends that they had made in their prison association. So it was something that was just normal to our understanding of the way that we wanted to live our life.

Then, as I began to be a pastor, I started out working with parishes, and then I went from there to campus ministry for 19 of the 35 years of my ministry. All those years, I've continued that practice of whatever I was doing, as what you'd term as a regular parish pastor or a campus pastor, a part of that element would be my connection with the prisons in the area and an attempt to understand the life there and to be connected to it. In a sense, I could not only be present and might bring some resources, but also that I would find an inspiration and meaning in that relationship that would serve me and feed me.

We helped to originate the Prison Awareness Project at the Monroe Prison, where we would offer a ten-week course through the experimental college that would introduce people to the realities of prison life. The prisoners themselves would teach the prospectus, and in the process, we would gain some folks who wanted to stay on and work on a continuing project, so we had what we called class night and project night, that is two different nights with the Awareness Project. I was involved in that for 7-8 years. That project's still going, by the way. At one point, I became upset about it because it had become a white power crack in the prison. And so I resigned in distress at the fact that it had some racial overtones. And since that time, the Awareness Project has changed some of its operating premises, and so on, and so that has been bettered.

In the meantime, the Lifers contacted me after about a three or four month hiatus there and said, "Hey, Nelson, we'd like you to come over and help us rejuvenate the Lifers' group." The two principles that I had said were very important to me were one, it would be absolutely open to every racial segment in the population. And then secondly, we wouldn't carry tags on people. They wouldn't put down people that came in with a sex offender crime, or so on. I said in the kind of presence I want to be, we treat everyone the same. And so they agreed to those two premises in reorganizing the Lifers' group.

It was during these years I was involved in civil disobedience on the nuclear issue, on the South African issue, on the homeless issue, on the El Salvador issue. And so, from time to time, I was doing time in jail. And I'd very often see people that I knew from my acquaintance at the prison, and it was very helpful to have friends and acquaintances. Once thrown in the King County Jail, you're very susceptible to a lot of different pressures. But having some friends who could clue me in, and who also acted as a presence of support inside the jail, was real important. So that's just an aside, but it's worked out.

When I went back with Lifers, I knew that the Lifers represent the most stable and probably the best citizens in the Reformatory. They're going to be there the longest time; they want it to be their home; they want it to operate right; they don't want it trashed. They want the food to be decently delivered. They care about the ongoing programs; that's their lifeline to the outside.

We've worked on many, many different things. The Lifers' group, for instance, has amazingly adopted children through the Christian Children's Fund and provided regular monthly support for three or four children over the years since '79. And some kids have grown up, and then they've replaced them with others. And it's a wonderful way for them to be in contact with kids and to be doing something constructive with their monies.

They've used their monies or efforts in other constructive ways: giving to the Matthew House Program, which helps visitors and people with distress problems among the prisoners' families. Or they have given money to the Food Bank or to the United Fund Drive. Quite unusual for prisoner populations to be doing those kinds of constructive activities. And these energies, by the way, have come out of the group themselves; they've really done that on their own and shown the leadership for that. So it's been very, very positive.

May I ask you, Reverend Nelson, where do these people who are incarcerated get money?

The funds they have come from projects that they're able to undertake inside. Like the Lifers have gotten agreement from the prison that two or three times a year they should be able to offer for sale products--cheeses, sausages, spices, and so on--that are sold through a specialty shop here in town. Then they get a percentage of that. Those monies then are put in the Lifer program funds for them to disperse for these charitable purposes. And that's how they've supported their kids that they've adopted. Then other monies are inmate welfare funds. These are monies that are made off of the confections that are sold at visiting room or off the telephone system. The calls that people make inside to their families, there's a certain profit on that, and part of that profit is split with the inmate welfare fund.

How is there a profit made on phone calls?

Well, the phone company agrees to return a certain percent to the Inmate Welfare Fund for the privilege of serving the institution. It's a tremendous captive audience, and the calls are very expensive, and it's prisoner families that are taking the costs of those calls. They're collect calls. So any call that goes in, there's a certain percentage of it that goes to the Inmate Welfare Fund as specified by the contract.

I see. And speaking of adopting children, I understand you've adopted a few yourself.

Yes, my wife is an amazing woman, and over the years, we have a family of 14 children, 11 of whom are adoptive kids. And now they're getting pretty grown up, so we're down to just a couple left in the house.

Fourteen children?

Then we've had many other foster children. And she, as well, runs a daycare in our home to help support--so we've had a lot of little kids around here. She's a very gifted woman, both in that she's able to manage a daycare with such ease and a good spirit, and you never notice the kids whining, or fighting, or anything like that. It's an amazing process, and it kind of has its own life over the years. And then she's also taken in kids with special disabilities. We've often had kids that the state says, "We've got a Short Arm Chromosome No. 4 Deficiency child. Would you be willing to take this?" Well, until you see the kind of disability you're talking about ... It's amazing the kind of care they need. And she's gifted to do that. That was also part of my family growing up, so, I was used to that, but I didn't expect 14 myself.

Has that been difficult for you?

Well, yes. I say going to jail is nothing compared to trying to raise 14 kids. And yet, it's been a great richness in our lives, too. I mean, the more you risk, the more you open yourself up for the lavish experience of life.

And we've had our heartaches. It's certainly no great success story. I mean, we've got wonderful kids, but we've got some kids that have gone through real troubled times, and we have one in that situation right now, and it tears at our heart. We've had to learn to offer the love we could and then to be there when they come to themselves.

Could you speak a little bit more about your going to jail and what brought you to that point? That's a very strong conviction, to be able to offer yourself up to that.

Well, part of that is an understanding that Dr. King helped us with, you know? Gandhi was really lifting up some operative principles that are there in the life of Jesus: not to succumb to the powers that seem to be in charge of oppressing people in the world, but, with dignity and care, to stand up for justice.

And offering oneself rather than taking arms against it, or taking a violent revolution, to display that resistance in a way that is non-violent and takes the punishment on one's self. And as Gandhi said, "The power of that expression is directly proportionate to the jeopardy." Let's say if you can lose your life in the process, then the expression that you're offering is very powerful. And people, of course, found that out through the civil rights movement in this country. It had a major effect on changing public consciousness, I believe.

We've been working out here on nuclear issues, the Trident as a first-strike weapon and a weapon of death that would destroy not only an enemy that we would think of, but ourselves in the process. They say it would kill--one Trident submarine, for instance--would kill 60 to 80 million of the people we were targeting, and then 8 to 10 million of our own people through what they call "acceptable collateral damage." So we never really thought about that; it's a suicidal weapon that we've got cruising out there in the Pacific, and we're so proud of. Not only that, it totally bankrupts our literal economic future for our children when we're spending money for that and not for education, and the infrastructure, and the necessary environmental developments that we need to do for our sustainable future.

If we really could see what's happening--I say I belong in jail. I've felt more at home in my heart and my spirit there than in a society like this that has gone crazy after materialistic pleasures for the moment and isn't paying attention to the longer-range needs of people in our society.

Which leads me back to a whole notion about incarceration. We've got a very barbaric notion of criminal justice and dealing with social pathology. In the Jubilee Laws of the Scripture, there's a provision that every 50 years, every prisoner would be released--an amnesty. And the effect of that--if you can think of--what if that rule were in effect in our society? It would make us all rush to the prisons to befriend the prisoners because they're going to be coming out and realize that they're a part of our lives and what they represent to us. They had responsibility for their crimes, yes, and they need to own up to that.

But we, too, in our social life, helped to create the conditions that make those crimes happen. So we need to take some responsibility ourselves, and we say as a society, we've got to work on healing that. It would force us to a totally different attitude and response to crime than we now have, where we try to shove people away and get them out of sight, and throw away the key, and lock them up like animals, and then let them out after they've done a certain punishment time. It's a barbaric notion of criminal justice.

Are you recommending that? Is that a viable proposition?

In some form, yes, I do. There are ways that we can implement an amnesty by, first of all, changing our relationship to people who are in incarceration. Recognizing them as our fellow human beings. They're wonderful human beings. And the violence in them is the violence we know in ourselves, and we can't separate ourselves from that. And you'd see that they have tremendous gifts, that they need to be healed as well as their victim needs to be healed from the crime they perpetrated.

Okay, I just need to stop you here for a moment, Reverend Nelson. You just made a very strong statement. You said these people who are incarcerated are wonderful human beings?

Right.

How do you justify saying that after they've perpetrated such heinous crimes?

Jesus had a saying, "If you've called your brother a fool, you've committed murder against him" in the sense that you wish them dead. You've had a hate-filled, vengeful attitude toward them. We're all susceptible to them. I don't separate myself from those fellows inside at all. There's a saying again in our faith tradition that "at the foot of the Cross, the ground is level." We all need the same forgiveness. In my instance, it was thoughts, or bitterness, or resentments, or anger. It may have been neglect, or whatever. There isn't a scale of what's rank and so on. I say the experience of going out there and meeting folks and finding that, even the guys that have got the worst rap on them, have tremendously redemptive areas of their life. They may have some pathology that we need to help protect them from. I don't deny that. But, at the same time, they've got great gifts that need to be honored and shared in the human community, too.

You've made a statement a little while back and used a phrase, "public

consciousness." It seems like right now the public consciousness is very punitive, and there's a lot of fear and frustration. Can you speak to that question? What are some solutions? How can we calm our fears, and how do we forgive this?
Well, you know, a heightened public consciousness about the fact that we are living in a less secure society is right. It's misdirected, however, to put the blame on those bad guys there.

The seeds of our criminal threat in society are really diverse and many and have to do with the materialism that's caused us to neglect our families. It has to do with the breakdown of the home and the training for children; the kids are lashing out in violence against their lives and against the violent images they've seen around. We've idolized violence. As long as we depend on violence for our security as a nation, we set the condition for individuals using violence to create their own security. Why the handguns? Why the shootings? We need to deal with the roots of violence in our society that are economic, that are environmental, that are educational, that are spiritual.

I also agree, however, that we have not faced people quickly enough with the consequences of their actions. And so we've got young people who think they can get by with stuff too easily, and we haven't brought them together with the people they've victimized. We could do that earlier, so that they see we're paying attention, but it's a caring attention, not a punitive attention. Say, "You can't do this. And if you do, these will be the results." And that's the way I believe in raising children. If a child is acting out, they've got to be faced with the results of that. You can't let them get by with it.

My wife and I are kind of old-fashioned that way. Not that we use physical punishment at all, but that you have to act socially to gain the privilege of the group at our house. And if you're acting asocial, if you're on a temper tantrum, whining, or not sharing, then you say, "That's fine; you can do that, but you do that all by yourself for a bit. See how that feels. And we'll talk about it." It's amazing how quickly kids will change their tone. They have one tone for our daycare, by the way. Their parents show up and immediately they use the things that tyrannize their parents: the whining, the refusals, and all that. And you can see parents are getting oppressed by their children. I hope I give you the sense of direction. I think we've got to deal with base causes, the economic injustice in our society, the poverty in our inner cities, the lack of job opportunities, the lack of constructive educational programs--all these things are cleansing the river at its source, rather than just coming down with lock and key and clanging steel doors at the end of the road. Once we begin to deal with those fundamental things, we'll create a climate in society that will be quite different.

So, Reverend, do you hold hope at all?
Sure I do. Against every reality, I am hopeful that there is a new day coming. I believe that. That it will be a day for the people of this earth, that it will be a day of harmony and justice for the kids, with enough for everybody to go around, a use of the land that's sustainable. I absolutely believe that day is coming, against every indication to the contrary.
So my own sense is not a panic-stricken feeling, like there's no hope or what's the use, but it's to say that's the way I want to live, with that vision in mind. And that's the way I tie up to good living myself. I don't think people are happy just because they've got a nice new car, or they can rent a condo down in Mazatlan, or something like that. Doesn't make people happy. Happiness is being involved in vital things, and that has to do with healing the health of the community. And I've known that in my life from my parents and grandparents, and so there's a tradition in the community of faith that I belong. And I'm not trying to say that that's the only way of understanding God's work in the world, but it's been mediated to us in this understanding.
I've got a sister, for instance, who has been working in community development in Chicago for 34 years, who was beaten, raped, left for dead in her work. Hires 550 people, full time, in the ghetto there, in the worst kind of ghetto in the country. And some would say, "Well, I don't know why you sacrifice to be in that kind of city." She would say, "What do you mean sacrifice? This is really living. The people to feel sorry for are the ones living a sterile life out in the suburbs somewhere, where they think they might be safe, but they're afraid of every corner, and they got locks at the gates on their project developments, and so on. Those are the people that are living sterile lives."
I've heard this said, and I'm just wondering your feeling on this, that the people that we have incarcerated right now are lost. It's too late for them. There's no hope for them. If we were to find a hope for the future, we're going to have to start with our children, and it's almost a sense of we should just kill them all.
Given up on them, huh?
Yes, if we just bury them in some way, if we just annihilate, get rid of all the convicted felons because it's too late for them.
That's a terrible notion, and it's so far from what's real.
People from the community who are involved in volunteer prison programs say it's like finding a treasure of people and gifts of personality and competencies, artists, expressive people, loving people who want to do something with their lives.
And one of the things you can see is a person who comes in all hostile, and bitter and turned in on themselves; maybe in four or five years after that time, there's

some healing in spite of all the things that prison is about, or maybe because of some other fellows out there, or who knows what's happening in them. Suddenly, they begin to sprout a new life, a new shoot of life. It's like after winter a new blossom pokes its head through the surface.

And you can see that happening, new constructive energies happening in people's lives. And the sad thing is that we can't take advantage enough of that timing when a person is making that move. And it doesn't have to do with games they play for the parole board, but it has to do with the healing mechanism that's inside of them. If we were close enough as a community, we would understand, and we could see this happening and the fruits of it and the realities of it happening.

I can see it in the fellows I know. Some are at the point just where the old bitterness still has hold of them, or some are beginning to make a move, and they become perceptive and accept responsibility for what they did but also work on new development in their life. Then the sad thing is when they get denied. There's a kind of a--oh, what should I say? You can see the old cynicism taking over again, and there's a very sad process in that, where a person kind of gives up hope, lapses back into a--oh, a resignation, I guess, is the word I'd use.

So, anyway, I certainly would tell anybody that offered the solution that we could give up on them, "You're crazy. You ought to meet these people and then tell me what you think after a couple years of getting acquainted."

I guess I pick up a tone of real caring for these people who are incarcerated from you. Someone who's killed somebody or raped somebody: how can you care for that person? How can you say they're wonderful people?

Well, every one of us is a child of God, and it's very hard. Sometimes it's easier for someone else to say, "I care for your kid" when they're angry at their own. We need other people to help us sometimes when we're not capable of that at the moment. That's why I don't think the families of victims should be on the boards that determine what happens in our state with regard to corrections. It's not a healthy--we need to have the protection of our perspective. We need to listen to them, to what their feelings are, definitely. And the victims are taken seriously enough in our system. But at the same time, it's not healthy to have victims' families determining corrections policies.

There's a spark of God's life in every one of us, and sometimes that gets covered over with the wrong things, but it's there. I believe it, and I've seen it. I've read books on the stories of certain offenders, and then I've met them. And it's very hard, knowing all those scenes of the bad things he'd done, to be able to say, "Well, yes, I'll treat you as another human being, whom God loves and cares for, and whom I should love."

The promise is not that we'll bring God inside to folks like that, but that we'll find God there in their midst. We'll find Christ there.

So, you say, Reverend Nelson, that you've actually seen growth, or you've seen positive results, or you've seen men or women heal themselves to become capable citizens of society?

Mm-hmm.

So one of the questions I want to ask you is, can these people actually change?

Can a tiger change its stripes, huh?

Right.

Well, I do believe that there are certain disfigurements that will be like a disability all their lives. And in the case, for instance, of certain sexual--imprints, we understand that it's very difficult to change that, so that we need to be careful and subtle in our discerning about what constitutes a risk.

But that is not to exclude the rest of the person, that person who's there. I've got kids that have a polio disability, and all their life they'll be overcoming that. But there are other areas of gifts to life and to the community.

And so I look on that similarly, that it may be some people, maybe in terms of anger management, will always have a sector where that might explode. And so we need to protect them from that, and our society from that, in a setting where nonetheless their constructive gifts can be offered. Does that make any sense?

It does. It sounds like you've had quite a bit of experience going into institutions.

Right.

Could you tell me a little bit about the treatment of prisoners and what their life is like?

Well, one of the givens is that whenever you set up a power group on behalf of society to manage another group of human beings, you set up an explosive and demeaning situation.

I know a number of people are familiar with the Stanford films, where they took classes, and they organized some of them into the corrections people and others into the prisoners, and they weren't three days into the project, and the thing was just totally getting out of hand. There were the animosities that became real despite the fact they were supposed to be role-playing this. Under those conditions, you set up a "we and them" that's antagonistic and that looks at each other as the enemy.

And yet, you find people in the administration who can break through that given, who have a sense of humanity and civility, and very often it isn't the one that's smiling at you. It's the one who presents a dour face and a gruff demeanor. As a prisoner, I've noticed that. I have to be wary sometimes of the ones that seem to offer a friendship. It's like a rose with a hook underneath it. They're offering something to maybe trap you and make a fool out of you, and it's a power play. Whereas the people you can count on do their job and just back off of your space and let you do the time. There's a kind of understanding of the pathos of the scene in that we're all involved in it.

In my process of interviewing people, I've heard two really diverse pictures of the situation. One is the complaint that prisons are almost country clubs anymore. They're so lackadaisical, and prisoners have so many benefits. Then I've heard the other side of that coin, where people say there's abuse, and there's things going on that people in society don't know. What do you see?

In no way, in any prison that I've been to, has it resembled a kind of a recreational facility for people, or something that's easy to do time. And there are a number of factors. When you're locked up, first of all, there's a loss there that's irreparable. You can't imagine what it's like to have the doors locked on you and not to have your freedom as a human being.

Secondly, the major reality of prisons is they're very drab. The space is utterly confining, and if you have a seven-by-eight-foot space per person, you're very lucky. They want a two-person cell at Monroe. You'd have two people living in a seven-by eight-foot space. Unthinkable! And the reactive psychological formation is riot-producing because you're stressed beyond the capability even of your unconscious to handle to it.

I've been in situations, like in King County Jail, where there were 1,100 people, and there's only supposed to be 600. We were sleeping six in a seven-by-eight-foot cell. If you make a misstep in the chow line, just happen to touch somebody unconsciously, they turn around, and they'd be ... I had a guy fly at me, and if it weren't for the fact that I'm quick at ducking, I'd have been pasted. And I couldn't blame him. It was the conditions of overcrowding.

Other prisoners also become your hell. Here is everybody with these pathologies, and these psychological problems, and working out their own stresses and family disfigurements, and so on; and you have to live with the toughest bunch to live with, and if you can manage that and still stay sane, you've got to be amazingly put together inside. Because these are conditions that would drive the normal person to insanity: noise, threat, predation, extortion, lack of space, lack of dignity, and the numbing institutionalization.

I don't understand these people. They just show a naivete' that's unbelievable when they talk about them as country clubs. Those people have never obviously seen the institutions that I frequent in our state, and known the day-to-day life. I actually honor people for the fact that they're able to act like human beings to each other in the face of that.

I'm interested in your views on women getting involved with criminals.

My first feeling is people should know coming in that there's a tremendous attractive quotient that's set up. It's like bringing a pitcher of iced tea to a desert. And that is just in terms of the music of the feminine perception of life. It's what I call the erotic fluid--not the specific sexuality, but the larger question we're missing something when we're in an all-male society. It's a terrible loss.

And so we set up then the attraction. It's powerful, and then there are also--the fellows inside tend to be type A, you know, and decisive, strong qualities make them attractive as human beings. They aren't passive in the face of their troubles; it was their activity that got them into trouble in the first place. I like to warn folks that come in with me as volunteers, but I'm understanding of this developing, and I've seen some wonderful relationships develop.

The next thing is if you take on a marriage with a person in prison, you undergo a tremendous special challenge in your life. Now it may be just the marriage some women want. I had one woman, I think, that liked her time down in Palm Springs, and just about once every six weeks was enough to see a male. But, on the other hand, it's very stressful, and the woman really becomes in jail herself. She has to go through all the scanner procedures, and her privacy is invaded in what she can bring in or what can be exchanged, the kind of communication. It's difficult communicating in a big room full of other people. There are a lot of aspects about it.

Then, you know, just the whole thing she has to deal with on the outside, and the fellow is dealing with his inside life. It's very hard to exchange a total thoughtfulness or awareness of what's happening that way.

And then, when the person is getting out, the formula changes; the equation changes so much. There's a tremendous difficulty. It takes almost a year, at least, for every year you put in to shake it out of your system. I know that when I came out, I was tough to live with, and my wife told me so.

So, all that being said, you're undertaking a special challenge. But, then again, with challenges in life, sometimes special benefits are conferred. There's a deepness of relationship that you might not have in a drab marriage that was ready-made out in society, and people can respond and know that. There's a sense of meaning in the love that can overcome these obstacles, and that's beautiful.

So you hear me saying it's paradoxical that there are difficulties involved, but I've discovered people who surmounted them beautifully and whose lives are rich for it; other people, for whom it's been a difficulty, shed a lot of tears and face disappointment in it, and hurt. And that's what life's about, I guess.

You're a Lutheran minister; is that correct?

Right.

And that is a Christian ministry?

Right.

How do you hold the place of different belief systems within the system, the prisons?

I just say this is how God has been talking to me, through this tradition.

How has God been talking to you?

I feel that Christianity has often been taught with exclusivity and a triumphal notion, and that's wrong. You don't see that in Jesus. I don't know if I can say any more about that, but when I go with a prisoner, I don't have an agenda of wanting them to be converted to my point of view. I want to discover who they are. I don't want to bring them from A to B because I don't know what B should be for them. But I want to be who I can be, as best I can; then I want to discover the richness of life they can share with me.

There are number of people that look at our work in the world as this: to discover where Christ is, and what Christ is doing in the world, and then to be present there. I see that as not just blind optimism, but I think that if we have a spirit of life that commends itself, it's catchable. More than it is if you can convert somebody with a certain doctrinal presentation.

I appreciate you for everything you've done in the world. And I want to ask you if there's anything you would like to say in closing?

Well, I want to invite people to the experience of becoming volunteers. We have an amazing range of gifts that have showed up out there. We have a woman who leads a Tai Chi class, a woman who teaches handwriting analysis, people who teach Braille and signing. We have a woman who goes out as a registered public health nurse, who does quit-smoking classes. We have a professor from Seattle University who leads a class in journaling and creative expression. There are a lot of ways to get excited about living and to be involved in meaningful programs.

The other thing is we have to work at the same time on the constructive issues with both the Department of Corrections and the legislature. We need people who will work both on the projects, and on the lobbying in the legislative, and then on the personal, relational side of it. And I invite people to do that.

Juice

I'm here today at Washington State Reformatory speaking to Juice. What is your relationship with the Department of Corrections?

I'm locked up.

How long have you been locked up?

This is my thirteenth year.

Thirteen years?

Yeah.

And where have you done your time?

Here in Monroe, Washington.

Can you tell me what you were accused of doing? What are you doing time for?

I'm doing time for murder one.

Can you tell me what murder one is?

Murder one's when you kill somebody in the process of a felony.

Can you tell me something about your particular incident?

Well, I was 16 years old. I was with a friend of mine. We didn't have nothing to do, you know, and that was the one thing that we could think of to do.

And what was that?

Kill somebody.

Really? You just went out to do that, just for a fun thing to do?

Pretty much.

Were you on drugs at the time?

No, ma'am.

Why did that happen to cross your--you know, that's not a usual thing to cross someone's mind?

No, it's not. But from the environment that I was--I was kind of conditioned that death really wasn't perceived as a life, per se, but more a tool to an end. So it was a robbery, and, in the process of the robbery, came murder.

I see. So you didn't actually just go out to kill somebody? You went out to rob somebody and also kill them if that happened?

Yeah, you could say that.

You went out just to kill somebody?

Yeah.

Yeah. Okay.

Throw you for a loop?

Well, I understand that happens more and more these days, particularly with young people.

Exactly. And that's the thing. Because we have no sense of value, not only for money, but for life. Because our lives really don't mean nothing to us at that time because we haven't experienced anything. You know? So if you feel like don't no one love you, you really don't love anyone else, so it's easy for you to commit those type of heinous acts.

Okay. So you were 16 years old at the time?

Yes.

And you went out to rob somebody with a friend--

Right.

--and you killed somebody?

Right.

Then how were you caught?

He told on me.

Your friend told on you?

Yeah, he told on me.

I see. Okay. And then you were arrested, and you were accused of this crime?

Right.

And were you tried as an adult?

Yes.

So you were sent to Washington State Reformatory when you were 16?

Yeah, I was classified for Walla Walla, though. But at that time, I was one of the youngest people in the Department of Corrections, so they elected to send me to Monroe, versus Walla Walla.

Just because of your age?

I believe so. I believe so. That's what they said.

You came to Washington State Reformatory 13 years ago?

Right.

The atmosphere here was a little bit different than it is now?

Absolutely. Absolutely.

Could you talk a little bit about that?

Well, the same things that were reinforced on the street, the acts of violence and rage, were going on in here, you know? So it was like I really didn't leave the streets at that time. So it took a little longer for me to learn what I needed to learn to be a man.

It must have been complicated--very difficult to be a 16-year-old ...

The only 16-year-old.

The only 16-year-old. And coming to an adult male prison?

Absolutely.

Can you tell me how that was for you?

Well, when I look back, there were grown men being raped and stuff. So I felt like my level of violence would have to escalate in order for me to protect myself, so I more responded out of fear than anything else. So I survived off fear. People feared my fear.

I see. So you became such a dangerous person yourself that people wouldn't attack you.

Exactly. Exactly.

And were you ever attacked?

No. No.

So you established a reputation--

Absolutely.

--pretty quick?

From the first day.

From the first day?

From the first day.

How did you do that?

Well, when I went to the jail house, they told me, "Well, you go find the biggest person in there, and you go bring it to him." So, that's what I did. I--when I got off the chain, I had some brand new tennis shoes, and some guy said, "Oh, yeah, I be coming to take those."

So when I got in there, in the institution, I came in and I threw my tennis shoes on the table to the guy who said initially, when I was getting off the chain, that he wanted to take them. I put them on the table, and I told him, "Take them," and I had a knife in my hand. And he said he didn't want them. So ...

And that established your reputation?

I believe so.

I see. So you never really had to hurt him?

No. I didn't, no.

Has there ever been an occasion, while you've been incarcerated, where you've been in a fight?
Yeah, I've been in quite a few fights. I had to keep that bravado up. They knew that I was capable of violence at that point, but then I had to kind of like show them, or allow them to understand, what type of violence that I was capable of. So, yes, I've been in violent confrontations.
How old are you now, Juice?
I'm 30.
And as time has gone by, have you changed?
Oh, absolutely. Time brings about a change. I've grown up, and I've been responsible, and I do all the things that a normal 30-year-old responsible man of two children and a wife does. I go to work; I participate in Bible studies and keep away from the negative influences around the institution. Because they still exist.
Are you still capable of violence?
Anyone is capable of violence. But like before--violent acts, never again. But I think anyone's capable of violence. And no, I would never commit another crime again.
So that's a big change?
Exactly.
That's a big shift from who you were when you were 16 years old?
Exactly.
And what would you attribute that change to?
Jesus is the reason. That's one of the things that I have embraced. By putting Christ first, it makes everything else smaller, you know, including myself. And that's one of the biggest things that me as an adolescent had to overcome was my pride because it got me in a lot of confrontations, amongst other things. So I just continue to put Christ first.

And I have a loving wife, someone who's finally loved me, and it's not a mother who puts you out in the middle of the street in the middle of the night. It's not a father who's never around. It's somebody who's always there, no matter how good, or no matter how bad you are. And they accept you and embrace you for who you are, in spite of what you do.

So I have a tendency to gravitate to the more positive things and respond to those.
You said you credit a lot of this to Jesus?
Right.
Did you find the Lord while you were in prison?
Yeah. I don't think I would have found Him outside, either. The environment that I was raised up, I don't even think there was enough time for Him at that point. But, this allowed me the time to not only grow but to slow down and really pursue my own

happiness, and not at the sacrifice of someone else's.

How can you find Jesus in a prison?

Well, they have quite a few people who love God more than they love themselves, who find God more real than they find the next man to them. When you see those people, those people affect you--you know what I'm saying? They leave a lasting impression.

Are those people other prisoners?

No. No.

Volunteers?

Yeah, those are normally volunteers. There is a body of prisoners here, a handful I might say, far and few between, but there's a handful of people who love Christ just as much, or as equally, as I do. Those are the people that I do my time with.

I see. I'd like to, if you wouldn't mind, Juice, talk a little bit about your early background years because you seem to have experience in the same area that a lot of young people are having trouble with these days.

Right. Peer pressure, you name it.

Yes. You were very young. You were a child.

Right. Absolutely.

Could you talk a little bit about your mother and father and your background when you were a child growing up?

Well, my father was incarcerated. I didn't really meet him until I was 13 years old. I think that's when you hit your puberty, and you're going through your identity crisis. You want to know who you are. You're looking for your independence. And it really flustered me because I thought for the first 13 years that someone else was my father. So to find out someone else is your dad, and--and your mother always knew it, then you believe that the rest of your life, those past years, were a lie. Therefore, you go to see who you are.

I was trying to find out who I was, and unfortunately it led me to prison and taking a life.

Your father was incarcerated? What was he incarcerated for?

Bank robbery. I believe mostly bank robberies.

And then when you were 13, you finally got a chance to meet him. Did you meet him in prison?

No.

No?

I met him on the streets. I never knew him until 13.

And how did you find out this was your father?

My mother told me one day, "There's somebody I want you to meet." Took me up there and introduced me. "This is your dad." "Boy, this can't be my dad. I just left my dad."

It was a big shock for you?

Oh, absolutely. Absolutely. Yeah, absolutely.

You mean a turning point in your life?

Yeah, because at that point I thought everything else that she had told me could have been a lie. It put doubt in my mind about everything else she said, that breach of trust. Ultimately the decision comes back to me. What I did was all me, not on my mom and dad.

So the man that you thought was your father, he was not your blood father? Was he good to you? What was he like as a dad?

A drunk. He was a drunk. He was all right when he wasn't drunk, but when he was under the influence, I didn't like him. I remember times we were supposed to go places, and I would just walk out of his house and just start leaving, and he'd be all mad, drunk, wondering, "Hey, where you going? Where you going?" "Man, I'm going home. I ain't going with you while you drunk." So, I would be leaving. What really severed our relationship was his drinking because I wasn't into drugs or anything. I was just a kid. I wasn't into nothing but baseballs and girls, like everybody else.

And how was your mother as a parent?

She worked hard. She worked hard, and I think that she used the tools that she knew at that time to be a parent. Unfortunately, it wasn't as effective as it could have been because her mother taught her about abuse, so when it came time for discipline, I was abused. And, unfortunately, there was time where the Department of Child Protection took me away. So I stayed with somebody I didn't even know, who really didn't know me or didn't even care about me. And I stayed with them, so I was almost worse off than even being at home in the abuse environment.

How old were you when they took you away?

Had to be about 12.

Can you describe some of the abuse you went through?

I remember the one incidence, the reason that they took me away. I was supposed to stay home. She kept me home from school because she had to work, but we needed the telephone cut back on. So I was supposed to stay home and let the telephone man in to service the phone. And I went to school. I went to school. So in the process of me getting to school, the telephone man came and left a note on the door, saying that he'd been there. When she got home, she got the note. I was at track practice at that time. She just sent my sister up there to go get me, so my sister got up there and told me, "Look, Mama's mad at you." So when I went in the house, I had shorts on. I used to always get whippings with either extension cords, or Hot Wheel tracks, or something like that.

So she took the phone cord and, you know, I had welts and stuff all on my legs, and it was bleeding and stuff. So I jumped out the window. I was running down the street, and then the fire company stopped me because they seen my legs bleeding. And then they told me, "Hey, what happened?" I told them I was in a fight. And they said, "Well, you know, we're going to take you home" after they patched me up. I said, "No, no. Can't go home." So at that point, I believe that they figured out what had happened, and they put me in the juvenile, somewhere I'd never been. So I think that was the starting point.

They put you in a juvenile detention center?

Absolutely. Before I went to the foster home.

What was the juvenile detention center like?

I mean for a kid who's never been in trouble, never. I was pulling A's and B's, you know? I think that was in sixth grade, or something like that, when you're 12. I mean it was just a whole new world. It was scary, and I had to go alone. 'Cause not only did I not have a father to go with me, but I then didn't have a mother because she was the abuser.

So I just did the best I could. Scared, and all that. The whole nine yards, by myself.

By yourself?

Yeah.

So then they placed you in a foster home?

Yeah.

And were you taken good care of in the foster home?

No, not at all. Foster homes aren't the way I perceive foster homes. It was no more than food and shelter, and I didn't know anything about hustling, or anything, at that time. They kept the cupboards locked. No trust. It wasn't a family atmosphere.

I used to smile a lot, and I used to laugh. The lady called my counselor at the juvenile and told them that because I was laughing a lot, I had to have been under the influence of drugs. I didn't even know what drugs were.

So, anyway, they sent me to my grandmother's house, and her boyfriend came into town one day, and she brought me back to my mother's, and I was at my mother's ever since.

Was there any more abuse after that from your mother?

Oh, absolutely. Oh, absolutely. Didn't nothing change. It was still my mother, and it was still my mother's house, and my mother's rules, and my mother's dictatorship, and everything else.

You have a large scar on your arm.

Mm-hmm.

How did you get that scar?

At the age of three, I reached over the stove, and my sleeve caught on fire.
Where was your mother then?
Outside. I think she was on the porch, smoking a joint; she didn't smoke cigarettes, and she was smoking something.
So you're about 12 years old. You're in the juvenile facility, and then you go to a foster home?
Right.
And then, in a roundabout way, you get back to your mother's house?
Mm-hmm.
So when you're 16 years old, are you living with your mother at this time?
I'm on my own by this time.
Oh, when did you leave your mother's house?
I left my mother's house, off and on. I would leave for maybe six months, come back for six months, or two months, or whatever, then leave again. So I left there around 13 or 14. We agree upon 13, me and my mother do. So, I left there then, and I was trying to do my own thing at that point.
Where would you go? A 13-year-old child, where do you go?
Same place every other 13-year-old child goes when they don't have nowhere else to go--on the streets.
So you lived in the streets?
Yeah, I lived on the streets.
What's living on the street like?
Well, it was like living in prison. When I said it didn't change anything about me coming from the streets to prison, exactly like it was. There was a bunch of wolves on the streets looking for kids, and there was a bunch of wolves in here. But I survived in here, and I survived on the streets.
Where would you sleep at night when you lived on the streets?
Hotels, friend's house, cousin's house, whatever, wherever I had to sleep. I've even slept on the back of a Greyhound bus before.
So you would try to find a shelter?
Right. Right.
And how would you get along? How would you eat? How would you have money?
Robbing, stealing, whatever I had to do. I was selling drugs, whatever you gotta do, you know? Pimp, whatever. Whatever. Whatever you have to do.
I see. So, you learned to survive ...
Absolutely.
... with street skills?
Right.

Did you ever get involved with a gang?
Oh, yeah. That was my family. That's where I was when my mom wasn't there, or my grandmother, or Dad, who was never there. My family. My gang members was always my family.
Can you help us understand? How can a gang make you feel like that's a family?
Let's use the most primitive example, a mother and a son's relationship. A mother takes care, nurtures, provides, protects, and guides. And that's what the gang was. That's what they did. They nurtured me when I didn't have no one else to nurture me. They guided me. Whether it was good or bad, that was my guide. They protected me, and I protected them, with our lives.
And that's how it was. That's the family that they talk about.
I see. Did you stay with one gang?
Just one gang.
One gang?
One gang.
And that gang had a territory?
Yeah.
A neighborhood or something?
Yeah. Yeah.
Did you wear certain clothing to indicate you were in that gang?
Well, back then you'd wear one earring. I still have the hole. You'd wear a blue rag, you know, but more than anything else, you know, it was about where you lived. You know what I'm saying? I didn't need to wear a blue rag because they knew where I lived at. You know what I'm saying? And that was blue rag enough. I didn't have to get tattoos because they knew where I lived, and you never venture too far away from home anyway.
You were a very young person belonging to this gang.
Right.
We're talking before 16 years old?
Yeah, 13. I wasn't a hardened criminal until like maybe 14--15. When I realized that there was nobody but me to look out for me. When that point in my life came about, I had to make a decision to either live or die.
And that's how I felt at my mother's house, that either I was going to live in there, or I was going to die in there. And that's why I got out, and from then on, it was Crip or die.
Okay. So were there adults in the gang?
Oh, absolutely. Absolutely. Just like you have a mother and father, we had big home boys and big home girls that was like mothers and fathers.

Were there initiations? Did you have to do certain things to in order to be members of this gang?

Then you didn't have to go shoot nobody or sleep with nobody, how they do it nowadays. You just had to fight your way in. I think they call it "get jumped in," but in my neighborhood, it was called being "C'd in."

C'd?

C'd in 'cause I was the Crip.

Uh-huh.

So instead of being jumped in, I was C'd in. You know, used to check your heart and make sure that if something came down, you wouldn't run if there was ten on two, you wouldn't go nowhere, you'd be there to the end.

Okay. So they might have ten people jump you?

Whatever.

Whatever. And then they wanted to see how you'd react to that?

No. Not how you react, but how you survived that. Because they're fighting. They're fighting. The same way they would fight on the street, they fight you.

They could kill you?

They could kill the next man. They couldn't kill me. See, the street taught me too much to die like that.

So you were a Crip?

Yeah.

Are you still a Crip?

No, ma'am. Remember? I told you, I love Jesus now.

And Crips don't love Jesus?

How can they?

I don't know.

I mean, when you think about it. If you know anything about the Bible, the Bible says that darkness can't occupy light. So I can't say that I love God and then be a gang member or a gangster or do anything that is contrary to the Word of God.

Well, I've heard that once you belong to a gang, you never get to leave it?

Well, I been here 13 years, so that says something. I left. One way or the other, you leave.

I see.

You know? Either you grow up and get out, or you die and you're out. You go to the prison, and you're out.

Oh.

And those shouldn't be options. Those shouldn't be options, especially for children.

I agree. But, I also see that it's a complicated problem because a child who doesn't

have a family is going to try and create a family.
Absolutely.
So do you see any alternatives to this problem?
Well, I mean, if you think back to early civilization, they say it takes a whole village to raise a child, and that's what we have to go back to. Because it's not your child doesn't mean that it won't affect your life, one way or the other, in the future. So help that child as much as possible, so when it comes time, it ain't going to be nothing but positive. You know what I'm saying?
We got doctors and lawyers that are now gang members, or dead in the grave. You know what I'm saying? They could have been doctors, attorneys. Lot of potential. It's getting worse. It's not getting better.
Was it another gang member and yourself who decided to go out and kill somebody?
Yeah.
Okay. So, two of you, you're just sitting around talking one day?
Yeah. Yeah, just nothing to do, just walking around, kind of a new city, nothing really to get into. Because the atmosphere in Washington wasn't like it was in Los Angeles.
You're in the state of Washington when this happened?
Right.
How did you happened to move to Washington from Los Angeles?
Mother running from a boyfriend. Mom running from a boyfriend.
You came up here with your mom?
Yeah.
Okay. And then immediately you went out to find your gang member friends--family?
Yes, I mean I had to have some type of family, you know.
And did you find each other by wearing your colors?
No, because they weren't wearing colors then. We found each other by the same things that we did. I mean, when you go to school, you're around students. When you're a gangster, you're around gang members. You know, pimps are around ho's. Same thing applies.
Pimps are around what?
Ho's.
What are ho's?
Ho's are prostitutes.
Oh. Okay. So you're sitting around talking, and you just decide, well, it might be fun to go out and kill somebody?
No, it wasn't necessarily that. We just didn't have nothing to do. When we located the person, it was really just up in the air. It wasn't a robbery; it wasn't no murder, initially. When I pulled out the gun, it was just--it turned into a murder at that point.

Wasn't any big thing planned about we were going to go find somebody to go kill, or nothing like that. It was just--in the process of the robbery, you know, the gun came out, and--

So now you've shot someone? Is that what happened? You shot someone?

Right.

How did you feel after that?

Well, to be honest, I don't think I felt anything because that's how I was conditioned; I was conditioned by violence. There was violence in my home. My mother didn't feel anything when she did stuff to me.

And that same attitude was the same attitude that I took and raised myself in the street and then, inevitably, got myself locked up with. Violence wasn't nothing. I didn't see him then as a human being because I thought as a child. I thought as a child. So his life didn't mean anything to me, or mine to him. If he would have killed me, I probably would have been none the wiser.

So you're saying that if he killed you, and you could have still been standing there, looking upon the situation, you probably wouldn't have blamed him, or anything?

No, wouldn't even have flinched. I mean, it wouldn't have made me a difference if it was me on the ground.

I think a lot of children these days feel like that, too.

We feel invincible.

Invincible?

Yeah. Yeah, we feel invincible. I mean, you know, if you think about it, you look at all the stuff that TV shows us. TV shows us people hang gliding, you know, jumping out of planes, and parachuting, and bungee jumping. I mean, all those things are exciting. You know, we see cop movies every day of the week on TV. You know what I'm saying?

You want to be like everybody else. You want to be accepted; you want to be embraced; you want to be like everyone else. And, unfortunately, the everyone else that you see is those people on TV Because doctors aren't accessible. Doctors aren't in your neighborhood. Politicians aren't in your neighborhood. You know what I'm saying? Dr. J, or Magic Johnson, or any of them guys aren't in your neighborhood. So you want to be like the people you see. You know? And, unfortunately, kids are around a lot more stuff than an adult would be.

Because an adult has made up in their mind where they're going to go and what they're going to see whereas a child is taking it all in. You know what I'm saying? So he may see what an adult won't see.

So sometime here at Washington State Reformatory, you met your wife?

Right. Right.

And you have attributed a lot of the changes you've gone through to her?
And my kids.
And your children?
Yeah.
How is it? What did they contribute to your life that would create that sort of change in you?
Well, anytime you can find someone who loves you unconditionally, even if it's going to be a friend, then you would hold that friend dearly. You know what I'm saying? We were friends first. No matter what I did, she was my friend. And I didn't have to go rob nobody; I didn't have to have a pocketful of money. I didn't have to be a rocket scientist. I didn't have to do anything to earn her friendship. There was nothing I could do to earn her friendship.
That gives you an affinity for that person. That's my belief about that.
So you learned from her that you had intrinsic value?
I did. I have value. I have worth. You know, and it was something that was already there, and it was something that money couldn't buy. It was a nice change from always being around somebody who always wants something. Even in prison. I think especially in prison because this is where they send all society's rejects. They send them here, and then I have to deal with them.
Or youngsters, and it's getting younger and younger. They just passed them laws for 12 and 13 year-olds, 14-year-olds to go to prison. This is no place for a child. This is no place for our men and women either.
You're African-American?
Yes.
Can you give me some insight into what it's like to be an African-American in prison? Is it any different, do you think, than being Caucasian or any other nationality?
Absolutely. The prime example that I can think of, the most recent issue of racism that I've been made aware of, was on the Rush Limbaugh show, unfortunately, of all people, because I really like him.
But he was talking about a black guy who is in the Senate. He was on the floor addressing the senators, telling about our history, about coming over from Africa, how they brought us in their ships, and how, when we died under in the bowels of the ships, they would throw us overboard, and the sharks would follow us. You know, follow the ships all the way to wherever the ship went. So he went on and on and elaborated on the history.
After the history unfolded, Rush came to a place and was laughing. They panned the audience, and the audience were all white people, laughing at what happened.
So my thought was first I was--I was upset. Then it came upon me that it was

ignorance, and ignorance should not be spited, but embraced.

And I was thinking, well, gee, he just really needs to know. But when they panned the audience, all the audience members were white. Would they have laughed about the Holocaust? Did they laugh at the Chinese when they came over? Did they laugh at the Irish? You know what I'm saying? Because that's what America was made of. But they laugh at the sharks following the blacks when they're getting thrown off the boat. And that's just crazy.

How did you interpret that laughter? I don't see anything in that to laugh about.

And I didn't see anything to laugh about. But the way the audience was panned, it was like, "Oh, ha, ha, ha, we got it over on the niggers."

I see. Do you feel like that sort of prejudice exists inside prison?

Oh, absolutely.

Do you feel you're discriminated against by officers?

I believe so. The way I see it, when you're mean to somebody, or you're aggressive toward someone who's already in a position where you can do just about anything you want to do them anyway, that's bad. That's like kicking a dog when he's down.

So when you read about violence in prisons, you can definitely contribute to not only how prisoners think but also to the conditions. Conditions have a large part to play in it. And it's getting worse.

They got bills on the floor right now making it more and more difficult for a man to be productive when he gets out here, or even productive while he's here. It ain't doing nothing but getting worse.

Juice, I appreciate your coming here and sharing these insights.

It's been a pleasure.

And I wonder is there anything that you'd like to say?

Well, I think that we shouldn't give up on our kids because our kids are our future. And if we learn to embrace our kids and give our kids what we desire, the more desirable attributes, then I think America would be better off. Because not only would we have senators, congressmen, lawyers, doctors, and priests who care about us, but our kids would begin to care about themselves. And when they find value in themselves and worth in themselves, then they won't be so fast to respond in a negative manner because they'll have a lot of positive influences to act from.

And I think that whoever is in charge should really think about the things that they're doing. It's a sad state of affairs here in the United States. If we structure our lives according to God's plan for our lives, God's purpose for our lives, then I think the world would be a whole lot better.

Look at David in the Bible. David was a murderer. In the days prior to his death, he was a great man. If you think about Solomon and Bathsheba ... I mean, you could think of anybody. You can think of Juice, you know. Who Juice was at the age of 16, at the age of 13, or at the age of 12. And who Juice is at the age of 30. You know what I'm saying? I mean, I'm no saint, but I'm definitely no criminal. I'm definitely no murderer, and that's only because I've had a opportunity to recondition, to learn love, to learn how to love, to know that it does exist, and it's not just a fallacy of someone's mind, or a fantasy. But it's real, you know, and God loves us.

We gotta keep God first in the United States because that's what our founding fathers put forth. I don't know how much credence is put into the Declaration of Independence anymore, but let's return back to how it was supposed to be.

Section Five

Are There Solutions to the Problems We Are Facing Today?

Mike Williams

I'm in the office of Mr. Mike Williams at Washington State Reformatory. The first thing I'd like to ask you, Mr. Williams, is what is your position with the Department of Corrections, and how did you came to that position?

Long story. Twenty-three years ago.

Right now, I'm the Acting Associate Superintendent of Custody for the Washington State Reformatory.

I went through the normal process of education for somebody in my position: high school, college; I graduated from the University of Washington with a B.A. in Psychology and an M.A. in Sociology from PLU in 1976. And part of my bachelor's degree was doing a quarter's experience in a social welfare organization.

For the last two years, a little over two years, I've been Associate Superintendent in three different institutions, in four different positions: at the Corrections Center for Women, at the Twin Rivers Corrections Center, and here at the Reformatory in both programs, and now, in custody.

So I've probably moved around more than most, both physically and, I think, positionally. I've really enjoyed myself, and it's been a good experience.

Mr. Williams, you spent a period of time in charge of an area of the institution called protective custody?

Yes.

Could you tell me what protective custody is and what your duties were as the person in charge of that unit?

Well, it was interesting for several reasons. One, I was new to the Reformatory. This was my first position at the Reformatory, certainly in a supervisory capacity. Also it was unique in the sense that there had not, before my coming to the Reformatory, been a unit supervisor.

There hadn't been any unit supervisors at the Reformatory. The Reformatory was one of the last major institutions to establish unit management. Unit management is simply a better way to manage smaller units of the institution. The rest of the institution was not used to having a unit supervisor.

And then, thirdly, protective custody was unique in itself. Oftentimes institutions have places where they send inmates who need protection from the rest of the general population inmates. They move them to different institutions, or they move them to different units in an institution.

But I think it was a sign of the times when they actually made a unit entirely composed of people who needed protection. It wasn't just one, or two, or ten, or twenty. We had several hundred inmates that were in a unit.

There was an actual wall put up in the middle of A unit. Half of the inmates were in general population; half of them were in protective custody. Initially, it was just a rope across the middle of the unit. Then it progressed to a fence, and then to a wall. And the protective custody unit was completely shut off from the rest of the institution. We had to feed them at different times, recreate at different times, etc.

And then you'd have to kind of ferret out the pecking order. The ones at the bottom are usually the ones that end up in protective custody--to protect themselves from the general population inmates.

This kind of natural phenomenon of the pecking order reared its ugly head in protective custody as well, so we had a protective custody pecking order. And you had to protect people in protective custody from other people in protective custody.

There were so many inmates at that time, most of the cells were double-bunked. So you had to be careful about putting a predator in with the prey. The predator might, in general population, be picked on, but he was a big man on campus in the protective custody unit.

People would check into PC for a variety of reasons.

You're saying that people go to protective custody voluntarily?

There's two ways: voluntarily and involuntarily. Most of them went voluntarily. Inmates would have drug debts that they couldn't pay, and so they were getting pressure from other inmates for different things, and they decided that it would be better to put themselves in protective custody than to subject themselves to physical abuse, or intimidation, or extortion.

So they would check into protective custody for a certain length of time. Then we would try to work with them in getting their debts paid off, or send them to another institution, or what have you.

And how long would someone stay in protective custody?

I don't know. I was only there six months. But the majority of the people that were there to begin with, when I arrived, were there when I left.

Still in there?

Oh, yeah. There were people who had been there for years.

Years?

Years.

In protective custody?

In protective custody, yeah. And there were some that we had to put in PC against their wills. We got information that a particular inmate needed protection. And we would call him in and ask him, and he would say, "No." And we'd ask certain people that we knew we could trust, and they'd say, "If he doesn't check into protective custody, or you don't check him in, he's going to get hurt. We can guarantee it." And we would move him into protective custody involuntarily.

But the majority checked in by themselves. They just decided it was safer for them. And, of course, we're trying to run a safe institution.

But, again, that was in the early '80s. The institution is much different now than it was then. And right now, we don't have a protective custody unit. We did away with that. We just have other options besides making a whole unit.

When you make a unit protective custody, you actually create a city within a city. It's almost too convenient for inmates to check into PC You want it to be a little tougher for people. You know? Maybe they shouldn't get into gambling or drugs.

You said now there are other options? Could you expand on that a little bit?

I think most of it has to do with the way that we manage our prisons. We have geared it up to a higher level. We have better supervision. We have the institution physically laid out, so there's better supervision and security.

We call the shots now. The institution is under staff control. We have more staff, better-trained, and we have positions for staff, like investigators, who actually will talk to the inmates, keep their ear to the ground, know what's going on, know before others do that an inmate is vulnerable.

And the other thing I think that's significant is the fact that back then, we had only three major male prisons. Now we have eight. We have more places to put individuals who need protection. We can move them to another institution; we can move them to a minimum institution or close custody. We have more secure spaces to put people. There's just more options.

Mr. Williams, one thing that you had mentioned was one of the reasons an inmate might bring themselves into protective custody was they were in trouble with debts and that you would work with that inmate to help them relieve that situation. Would you speak a bit more on that subject?

It's against the rules of the institution to gamble or to buy and sell drugs. But it did go on then. It goes on occasionally now too and we're aware of that.

We do the best we can to keep the drugs out of the institution. We try to do the best we can to keep people from gambling. But when you have gambling addicts or drug addicts, where there's a will, there's a way.

And so you do find individuals who will come to you saying, "I'm in trouble." And we start talking to them, and what it comes down to is, "I can't pay off the debt" for whatever reason. "I don't have the money." So we can say, "Well, too bad, you know. You're going to have to just live with it, and whatever comes, comes."

But the state is charged with protection of the inmates here, providing a safe, environment, so we have to protect them.

If somebody has a debt, they ought to pay it off. The inmates feel that way, too. They don't say, "I don't owe it." They say, "I owe it, and I can't pay it. And this person I owe, he's got his strongman coming up to me saying, 'Now that you haven't paid it, it's double.' So now it's really bad. I can't pay what I owe, and I certainly can't pay twice as much."

So we would say, "How can we work this out?" There would be ways to talk to the person who it's owed to or just to say to the inmate who's in protective custody, "You talk to the person you owe it to, and you make an arrangement to get that paid off. What will it take to get you out of protective custody?" And he says, "Paying it." "Okay. So, make an arrangement. How can you get that done?" And he says "Well, okay, so, I've talked to this inmate who I owe it to. He understands."

So we've talked this victim into how to pay off the debt in a way where the institution doesn't get involved in collecting the debt or paying the debt.

Another thing that you mentioned is you worked for a while at a correctional center for women?

Yes.

Can you talk about that a little bit? Are there differences working in an institution that incarcerates women from working in one that incarcerates men?

Well, I was only there for four months, so I was just getting my feet wet when I moved back here to the Reformatory.

I had heard a lot about the Corrections Center for Women. Most of it had been that there was in-fighting with the staff. I didn't hear too much about the female prisoners. What I found was there were a lot of competent staff who wanted to do a good job and needed direction.

But there were a number of ways, too, that it felt strange to me. I think more often it had to do with the fact that the female inmates somehow behave differently in a group than male inmates.

I think that certainly their medical needs are different. They have a tendency, and I am speaking generally, to be more dependent: on staff and on drugs. I thought, at the time, that there was an overuse of medication to "solve" women's problems rather than dealing with the problem.

The large majority of the women, as I recall, were in for drugs or drug-related offenses. And to continue this notion that pills will cure your ills had a strong influence on me in the way I did business. I wanted to get away from that, and I feel I made some inroads there.

I think there is this kind of victim role that a lot of the women have played, both to men and in their crimes. A lot of the crimes had to do with pleasing men or doing things for men, with getting caught up in drugs, in prostitution, in stealing things for the man in their life, in being co-defendants, co-conspirators in crimes the male counterpart was involved in.

I really felt that what was needed was a program that taught women self-esteem, independence, critical thinking skills, how to make decisions for themselves. I really felt that they needed some volunteer programs, like Toastmasters, Breaking Barriers, Alternatives to Violence, etc.

I've got to say that different male institutions feel different ways, too. And it sometimes has to do with the clientele. At Twin Rivers, I didn't see much of the inmates.

I'm used to the Reformatory, where the inmates will come up to you on a regular basis. They'll assert themselves. They're out there, they're up front, they're talking to you, they're dealing with their issues, and they feel like they can connect when you're walking around in the big yard or on the inside. Whereas at Twin Rivers, it was like the inmates kind of went from one place to another, and you'd walk through the middle of them, and nobody would approach you; nobody would talk to you. And you'd talk to them, and they'd act surprised.

And, of course, S.O.C.--Special Offenders Center--is different, too. It's locked down a lot tighter, and there are more inmates on medications that affect the way that they behave. They have more violent offenders who continue to be violent in prisons there. Every institution has a different kind of milieu.

Can you speak a little bit about the milieu at Washington State Reformatory?

You're going to have inmates who don't talk to you and then inmates who talk to you all the time, write to you, talk to you every day, and think that you're bosom buddies. Then you've got this large group of guys that, by and large, were high on drugs when they did what they did. Or they had some emotional catastrophe occur prior to the offense. There were things that happened over time that they've worked out. They're not on drugs or alcohol now. They don't have serious mental health problems. They have behaved violently but oftentimes under the influence, and/or it was a particular individual to whom they were violent, like a wife or a loved one, or a significant other, or the drug dealer, or what have you. But now that they're in the institution and have a regular routine, they're working, and they're normal folks. You know? They come and talk to you, and they can carry on a decent conversation. They show you respect, and they certainly show you more respect if you show them respect and courtesies.

I think part of the reason why the atmosphere at W.S.R. is that way isn't just the inmates, but the staff and the administration and the way that we treat them. You give respect, you get respect. I think the Reformatory is unique because over the years we've built up a group of inmates, a core group of inmates, that would like the operation of the institution to run smoothly because they're going to be here for a while.

And so it's in their best interests to keep the place running smoothly. And that means playing ball with the staff and the administration and asking for things that they think are legitimate.

The administration here is open to listening to ideas from inmates. It's not like, "Well, they're just inmates."

And, of course, we have the grievance process like any other institution. The staff take it seriously, and we try to nip problems in the bud.

I think also the fact that the inmates over the years have developed, along with staff, volunteer programs. They're very solid, legitimate, tested programs that help inmates get their lives together. I think the inmates really appreciate that, and the staff appreciate these volunteers coming in.

Having had a great deal of experience in a variety of institutions, do you have a preference of how things work? Do you see any one system more effective than another one?

I think it's important that the administration have certain values and that they influence the staff and pick staff who share those values.

I think institutions that are value-driven are probably better off, by and large, than those that are rule-driven.

And what do you mean by "better off"? How are they better off?

When you have administration who believe in honesty and open communication, in trust, and in keeping commitments, when you show respect for each other, people to people, not just staff, but inmate-to-staff, and inmate-to-inmate. When we start putting decisions through a filter of values, then we're starting to come up with some consistencies about how we relate. Inmates respect consistency. They don't like consistency when it's not reasonable, but when it's reasonable and consistent, they appreciate that. They like knowing what to expect, that you're not going to change day to day. Day in and day out, they know what to expect. That's the same with staff, too. That's one reason this place is unique. A system of values makes a big difference to the way that they live their lives and the way that the staff interact with each other and with them.

You're always going to have staff who get through the interview process saying the right things. But after a while, what we find is those people who don't do the job, who come in with a chip on their shoulder, or they're power-tripping, they start rising to the surface. You find that they stick out. And then you deal with those individually.

How can you deal with them?

Oh, you deal with them in a variety of ways. They themselves may figure it out and say, "This isn't the place for me."

It may be that a simple conversation with them, sorting things out, saying, "This is what the administration wants to have happen. This is the way we want people to interact with people. I've noticed, or I've heard, that you interact differently. You interact this way, and I want you to know that that's not the way that we want you to interact. We want you to interact this way. We want you to come around, and we're not going to give you a lot of time to do that. We'll help you to do that if you want to. But if you choose to continue this way, this is where it's heading. You're going to be heading out the door. So you can either change and be part of this team, or you can choose another place to work with our help or--or voluntarily. I'm quite willing to talk to you about how to make those decisions and how the kinds of decisions you're making now are not consistent with what we want at this institution."

You spoke about something called a grievance. Could you tell me what the grievance process is and what it does?

The grievance process is a formal method to resolve conflicts. There's a grievance process for staff to do that, and there's a grievance process for inmates, as well.

If inmates believe that we are violating our policies, or the practice isn't fair, or that staff members are behaving contrary to the rules, then they can file a grievance, which basically is a sheet of paper that says, "Here's the problem. This is how I'd like it resolved."

It has several steps. If the inmate doesn't like the first response by a neutral party who has investigated the situation, then he can bump it up to the next level. Some of them can go all the way to headquarters to be resolved. But usually they're resolved at the first or second level.

The grievance process is a kind of a safety net when one can't get the problem resolved informally. Or if it's important enough that they want to bring it to the attention of the higher authorities, rather than have it resolved at a lower level, where there may be some retaliation involved, and that type of thing.

There's not to be any retaliation in the resolution of a grievance. If there is, then that's a grievance in itself.

Retaliation by staff?

By staff, yes.

Is a grievance put in a staff's record? Or once it's resolved, then that's it?

It depends. If we find in the investigation the staff has violated policy, or violated the rules to the degree that a written corrective action needs to be taken, then that could go in the staff member's supervisory file or personnel file.

Usually, by the way, staff who don't learn the first or second time with a verbal reprimand from their supervisors and continue doing it, and we find a pattern developing; then that's the time where usually some paperwork addresses the issue and states that further behavior like this will result in more severe corrective or disciplinary action.

You said that you were an associate superintendent in charge of programs, and then you went from there to being associate superintendent in charge of custody. Can you tell me how those two departments differed, and did you find a change in your attitude or change in the way you had to conduct business when you moved from department to department?

Yes. I certainly have had no misconceptions that custody is the backbone of the institution, that security and custody provides an orderly, safe, rule-oriented institution, and that the primary reason for prisons is to incarcerate and incapacitate inmates, people who have been sent to prison, oftentimes for some very violent acts.

The primary mission of the division and the department is the protection of the public. Certainly the public is protected while the inmates are incarcerated. The other half of that is that the large majority of the inmates are going to be getting out, and that's where programs and the program department steps in. Because I think it's important that we create a climate inside the institution where inmates learn to behave responsibly and be prepared for their eventual release, so that when they get out, they are less violent.

That's the second half of protection of the public. And that's the one that's often missed, both in an institution and by the public. John Q. Citizen thinks that an inmate goes to prison and now they're safe. Then they get out, and why aren't they rehabilitated? But they don't even think about what happens in prisons.

In terms of the difference, what I've found by moving to custody is I've have a lot less contact with inmates and a lot more contact with staff. Security and custody is keeping the inmates inside the prison, keeping them safe, keeping the place secure, and making sure the rules are enforced, etc. That has a lot to do with the staff and the physical layout of the place. It has little to do with the inmates themselves although it does because obviously we wouldn't exist if it wasn't for the inmates.

The other point I wanted to make about the transition is I had less than sixty staff under my supervision as acting associate of programs. I have about 260 staff under my supervision now. So I really need to be more staff-oriented at this point.

We have over 214 correctional officers, 23 sergeants, 6 lieutenants, and a captain.

I have a lot more to do with training than before. I have much more to do with emergency response issues. What happens if there's a disturbance in here? Are staff well prepared? What do they have to do in case of an emergency of any kind: if an inmate gets sick or dies, if an inmate escapes, if there's a natural disaster, if there's a fire? A whole myriad of things. What if a helicopter lands in the big yard? What's the established plan here?

In terms of dealing in programs and treatment with inmates, do you believe that change is actually possible; do you think that these people can change?

I wouldn't be here if I didn't. I would be totally frustrated. I've seen people change. I know people who agree with me, and I know a lot of people who don't.

There are people who believe that inmates are in prison "*as punishment,*" and there are people who believe that inmates are in prison "*for punishment*". A real clear distinction.

There are staff members who think that inmates are slime, that they're the lowest of the low, that they've committed crimes, and they ought to be punished in here, and they should be not given any respect at all because of what they did.

But the law is quite clear that they are in prison as punishment. That's the punishment, being in prison. The law doesn't say we have to punish them while they're in here unless, of course, they commit rule violations. And even then, the rule violation sanctions are clear. Certain things we can do; certain things we can't do. We can't take them out back and beat them up. That's not in the rules. If we do that, we're violating rights, human rights, and we're in violation of our own policies.

And then there are people who probably would do fine without going to prison to begin with, but they're in prison because they didn't have enough money for a good attorney, their race, it was a bad day for the judge, the victim was too influential, it was on the front page of the paper rather than on the back, etc.

Do I think that inmates can change? The question really is, "Who changes them?"

You've got this group of people who won't change regardless. Then there's this group of people who probably could survive in prison and get out of prison and not ever come back again, with or without your help. They don't have a habit pattern of illegal behavior.

Then there's this large group of people I really think we ought to be concentrating on in the gray area, the people that are on the fence, the people that are looking at the people who are playing the game on one end, and looking at the people who seem to be doing just fine without hardly any effort on the other, and wishing they were like them, and kind of wondering what to do. They range everywhere from telling themselves, "I'm here because I didn't commit this crime, but I committed other crimes." Or, "Well, if it wasn't for my crime partner ratting me off, I wouldn't be here." Or, "The only thing I did wrong was get caught. Next time I won't get caught." You've got everything from that to "boy, I really screwed up, and now I'm in prison, and I don't like it. But, you know, I don't ever want to come back. And what do I need to do to not return? And what do I need to do when I get out so I don't come back?" This gray area group, that's the one we ought to be concentrating on. Those are the people that can make the changes.

We've got to create a climate in here where they can start changing. I think people are pretty much the same all around. They have needs. They've got the need to belong, to love people, to be loved, to have some freedom in their lives, to have some fun in their lives, to be goal-directed. Those, I think, are very human needs. And they're the needs of staff, the needs of inmates, the needs of people on the street, the needs of the President of the United States, the needs of you and me.

I think the majority of the guys are in here for trying to get their needs met in illegal ways. All we have to do is help them learn how to get those legitimate needs met in a legitimate way. If they can get in the habit pattern of figuring out how to get their needs met in legitimate ways here and then carry that habit pattern out there with some coaching in the transition, then I think we've got a way to reduce recidivism, lower the possibilities of future victims for generations to come. Because victims aren't just victims in one generation. They pass on their victimization to others as they go. Inmates families would like nothing more than to have somebody come out of prison and succeed and to be proud of them.

I have heard you refer to yourself as a visionary. How do you see institutions in your vision?

Well, I'd say my vision is fairly radical. I may not even see this in my lifetime.

Prisons were established initially in this country by the Quakers. We call it a "penitentiary" for a reason. The Quakers thought that if they were just quiet and left to themselves, they would become penitent.

Then we had the era of the "reformatory." It was time to reform them. Then we had "corrections." So inmates' behavior could be corrected. Before that, we had "treatment" because we needed to treat them like a medical model. They were the patients and we were the suppliers of the remedies. They would be treated and, "go sin no more."

I think the pendulum has shifted quite radically over the years to "lock them up, and throw away the key."

All this has shifted the attention of politics, the public, and the legislature to think of prisons as warehouses. That's very shortsighted. I don't think that the community really wants "Three Strikes, You're Out." When somebody robs a person three times with a toy gun and gets $50 to $60 in cash each time, and he's 18 years old and he gets convicted for the third time, he's looking at life without parole. And the taxpayers have to pay for this person in prison until he's 70 or 80 or until he dies. Do taxpayers really want to do that, at the cost of incarceration each year? I don't think so.

There needs to be people looking at the "long range" plan. All I see in the future, with the way we're going right now, is building more prisons and incarcerating more people. I think we'll end up sending more people to prison than keeping people out of prison. I'm trying to look to the future and say, "What can we do up front? How can we educate the youth? How can we make the family stronger? How can we keep people from going to prison who don't really need to be in prison? Why can't we send people who are first-time or property offenders or low-risk offenders to institutions that help them sort out the problems, so they can get back out and learn how to make responsible decisions, so they stay out and be not only responsible but also contributing members of the community?"

I would like to be able to use prisons in a variety of ways. Those people who wouldn't need prison anyway, put them all together. People who aren't going to make any changes anyway, they're a bad seed, and they're damaged goods, and no way is anybody going to ever rehabilitate them--warehouse them.

Then take the salvageable group and help them learn how to make responsible decisions, get their lives together, how to interact with people, how to live successful lives and get their needs met in legitimate ways. Then transition them out, and have the community help out in this.

They came from the community, and they'll go back into the community. The community needs to take responsibility for helping them make the readjustment, make them part of the strong, positive culture back with families and social services and community groups that say, "You're back with us. You committed the crime. That's in your past, but you've got your future to look forward to. You can actually be a model for people who are on the edge in the community, almost ready to go to prison." What's wrong with that?

That's the vision I'm looking at. Now, I don't know if that's ever going to happen, but I really believe that it's possible. And I'm willing to live my life committed to that vision.

Halisi

I'm speaking with Halisi at Washington State Reformatory. Halisi, are you aware that this conversation is being tape-recorded?

Yes, I am very much aware this conversation is being tape-recorded.

Is that all right with you?

Yes.

Halisi, can you please tell me what your relationship is with the Department of Corrections?

Yes, I can. I've been a prisoner for approximately 29 years. I've been incarcerated since 1966, continuously.

And what are you incarcerated for?

I was convicted for the alleged crimes of homicide--two counts--four robberies and one assault, first degree.

And how much time were you given?

I was given a staggering amount of time, and when I say staggering, I mean I was initially sentenced to death and spent approximately seven years on death row. From there to five 20's running consecutively.

You spent seven years on death row?

Yes, I did.

What was that like?

It's a gruesome situation, really. I mean it was a very ugly situation.

We was in our cells for approximately 24 hours a day, and on a good day, we was allowed an hour out. About every other day, we was allowed out for a shower, the yard, and all that within one-hour period of time. And that was it. Your meals were brought to you in the cell.

I spent a lot of time reading and studying. About 16 hours a day, I would spend in that state of mind. About four hours of sleep I averaged a night, and the rest of the time I was studying.

You say you only slept four hours a night?

Yeah.

Is that typical for you, or is it just it was very difficult to sleep there?

I think it was a choice for me because a lot of guys did sleep a lot. I wanted to do a lot of reading, a lot of studying. It was a personal choice on my part.

Did you believe that you were going to be executed?

No, I didn't.

You never believed it?

I never believed it for one moment. I know it might sound strange, but not for one second, not for one moment, did I ever think that I would be executed.

Why?

One, because I wasn't guilty, and two, because I knew that I shouldn't be. And it might have been blind faith or ignorance or whatever, but that just was my attitude. Looking back, I count my blessings in the sense that it could have happened, easily. Whether I was innocent or not, it could have happened. Especially looking at the situation today, where innocent people are being executed knowingly. Looking back in retrospect at that, I truly count my blessings. Seriously.

You said you were innocent?

Right.

You did not commit the crime?

I did not commit the crime. That's a known fact and it's been documented. But what can you say? What can you do?

You've done 29 years for a crime you did not commit?

Yeah.

How does that affect your mind?

Well, I identify with, in a spiritual type of way, Dred Scott. He was a slave that had left one of the states that practiced slavery, and he went to a free state. Well, the slavemaster wanted him back.

Anyway, while he was in the free state he petitioned the court, saying that slavery wasn't legal there, so therefore he shouldn't be forced to go back to his slavemaster. But the court said, "No, since you was property of this guy, even though you're in a free state, you're still his property. Therefore, you have to go back into bondage, into slavery."

So, that's kind of how I feel about this situation. Even though I'm innocent, even though I shouldn't be subjected to this, I am. So the best thing that anyone can do is just survive, and pray, and do the best that he can.

Where have you done your time?

I've been fortunate in some cases, in the sense that I've been allowed to go to various institutions.

You've moved around a lot?

Moved around a lot. A heck of a lot. I've been--for instance, I've been here at this institution three times. I've been to Walla Walla three times. I've been to McNeil twice. I've been to Clallam Bay. So that kind of broke up the monotony. Sometimes it was by choice. Other times it was by the fact that "We're tired of you. Get out of here, and we'll see you later." I've been in IMU also, so I've had a little taste of it all.

Can you tell me what IMU is and what that's like?

It's Intensive Management Unit. That's a place where one is sent to when he has bottomed out on points, and he's considered a danger to the orderly operation of the institution. Sent there for a period of time from a matter of days, up to X amount of years.

Fortunately, I was only in there for approximately 65 days. I should not even have been there. I hadn't been classified for IMU. It was just, "Go."

Seriously. I wasn't classified for IMU or anything of that nature, and they put me there for approximately sixty days. In fact, I had to file a lawsuit. Fortunately, I won.

Why did they put you there?

I haven't found out to this day. Seriously. I have not found out to this day.

They didn't charge you with anything?

They didn't charge me with anything.

You called being on death row "gruesome." Could you elaborate a little bit about what you mean by that word?

In my mind, "gruesome" was a state of despair, a state of loneliness, a state of where you're isolated. And gruesome in the sense that the people, those so-called caretakers, treated you less than human. Degraded every day, harassed. You couldn't talk.

You had to shave. I was just a youngster, wasn't shaving or anything. But they made me shave. If you didn't, you was subject to go to the hole--isolation, segregation for X amount of days.

You couldn't think for yourself, and you wasn't allowed to think for yourself, anyway. You was told what to do, when to do it. You were in the cell 24 hours a day, but you was still controlled.

You said you weren't allowed to talk?

Right. Right. Like sometimes, when you were going to the yard, you can't talk. You just wait until you get to the yard. You're not supposed to say anything.

You go to this little--strip you down, every time you go to the yard. You got to go to the front of the cage, and then they'll strip you down, bend over, and all--you know, go through the routine and everything. And you're not supposed to say anything during that period. And when you get to the yard, then you can talk.

I thought it was just a form of total control, you know.

When you talked earlier about being degraded and harassed, that being "stripped" process was part of what you were talking about?

Right. Right.

Was there anything else?

You had some officers that was very red-neckish.

At that time there was about nine of us on the row, and five of us was African-Americans. And this one particular officer used to come by and make these little old remarks about, "They want to string you niggers up," and stuff like that.

When you're taken to the hole off of death row, how much worse can they make it for you than death row? What's the difference between death row and the hole?

They used to have a process; it's called "blackout." You don't have any lights--completely black in there. The only time that you would have the lights on is when they bring the food around so that you can see your tray to eat. And when they pick up the trays, you go back on blackout. You couldn't read; you couldn't do anything. And that was a matter of days. You know? It depends on your attitude, how long they kept you on blackout. Several times, I was on blackout the entire time that I was over there.

Were you ever physically abused?

In the county jail I was, but not on death row.

We went on a couple of strikes, when we refused to come out of our cells. They'll bring in the goon squad, and they'll goon us. Only in those situations, when we felt that it was time to stand up and be counted as human beings, we would put ourselves in a position to sacrifice our body in order to make a change, and whatever else that went with it.

Refusing to go along with the rules, you knew what the consequences were going to be, and you say, "Okay, I'll suffer through that."

What's the goon squad?

Goon squad is a group of guards; the biggest, fattest, and so-called meanest, that would come and get you and would man-handle you. Use whatever physical force was necessary in order to subdue you and to carry you to the hole or to the destination that they wanted to carry you to. There was about six or seven of them, big officers, big guards, you know?

How did you get off of death row?

In 1972, the U.S. Supreme Court ruled that capital punishment in its present form was unconstitutional.

Most of the guys that was on death row at that particular time had been convicted by a jury or juries that believed in capital punishment. The jury was stacked.

Individuals who had scruples against capital punishment wasn't allowed to sit on the jury, even though they might be able to find the individual guilty. The process was totally biased. That was a decision that came from Foreman vs. Georgia and Stewart vs. Massachusetts in 1972.

That applied to everybody that was on the row in the country. And, at that time, I think there was approximately 500 individuals that was on death row.

In 1987, I was granted a rehearing after 21 years. My attorney failed to call alibi witnesses at my initial trial although he had been told that those individuals would definitely testify on my behalf as to my whereabouts and what I was doing at the time that the alleged crime took place. But those witnesses were never contacted.

The Court ruled that my rights had been violated, that the attorney was incompetent, and that he didn't do an efficient job as far as representation was concerned.

But, when I got back to court, it was ruled that after 21 years, somehow the witnesses wasn't credible.

Do you believe that you were prejudiced against in some way?

Very much so. When I was convicted, all the juries were white.

Twenty-nine years incarcerated? There would be those who would say, even if you were innocent, after 29 years of being in a prison--innocent or not--by now you must be a criminal. How would you comment to that?

My response to that would be that no, I'm not a criminal. Because you're in a criminal environment, that don't mean that you have to adopt those attitudes or those characteristics.

In fact, speaking for myself, I've done everything within my power to move away, not to be associated with that environment.

I've tried to instill within myself some moral character and spiritual enlightenment. People are going to think what they want to think anyway, and there isn't anything that you can do about that, other than to walk the walk and let the proof be in the pudding. How can you prove that when the opportunities haven't been given?

Being in a criminal environment don't mean that you have to be a criminal. And, not to sound flippant, but I think that real criminals are not locked up anyway.

What do you mean?

I think that the people who are able to abscond with billions of dollars, people who are in a position of power, who are denying or depriving people an equitable opportunity in life, people who are denying other people the opportunity of justice--to me, those are the criminals.

People who are greedy, not allowing people to even get an education, to economic opportunities. Those are the criminals, and the residue from that is ....

If there's anything you'd like to say, go right ahead.

The thing that I want to say is we're all fallible. We make mistakes. And because people make mistakes, that don't mean that they're totally bad. It means that they made a mistake. And that means that they have an opportunity to correct that.

I think that people have become so dogmatic. I believe individuals ought to seriously do some studying, and have more compassion, and look at the situation more than just from an emotional level, try to see it in its totality. I would like to also say I think that we have more in common between each other than we have not in common. That we tend to put more emphasis on the differences, rather than emphasis on the commonality.

If we could become more bonded, a lot of the problems that exist today could be eliminated, just by the fact that we look at each other as human beings.

I would like to say that it's the small things that count. It's the little things that count. A smile, hello, how are you doing, just an expression of gratitude towards one another in sincerity and honesty, being able to open yourself up to the next person: I think that would make a difference. I'd just like to say that.

Nancy San Carlos

Your name is...?

Nancy D, as in David, San Carlos.

The reason I became involved in prisoner's rights and prisoner's programs, and that whole field, was because I lived in upstate New York, in a town called Middletown in Orange County. And I was the elected chair of the two-chapter county of the New York Civil Liberties Union.

We had a lot of attorneys and even some judges who were members, so I always felt that was a real privilege that they voted for me.

It didn't take long to find that many people whose civil rights had been violated ended up being in jail, and they were poor.

And when I was visiting them quite often it turned out that their arrest was not technically a civil rights violation, but they had so many other problems, not being educated, not having any job market skills, and maybe no place to go when they got out.

And I started to become aware of it through that.

So I had about four years of doing that. But after my divorce, I went to college full time, and I intended to be a high school English teacher.

Unfortunately, people were voting down all the school bond issues in the area. And one wonderful job that I had been offered had to be retracted. Not only could they not hire anyone new, but also they had to let several people go.

I went up to the job placement office in the college that I attended, the State University of New York, and the woman told me that there was a position opening up that she thought I would be ideal to do. This was a little less than two years after Attica.

The position was Coordinator of Volunteer Programs, and the whole concept was the results of the Commission's report on Attica. It ended up that I scored second highest in the state. I knew so little about civil service regulations, I did not know that, except for the person who scored one in the state, I had my choice of any prison in the entire state that I wanted to work in, but I found that out a long time later.

So when I started the job, right from the very beginning, I was harassed because I was the first woman. I found out the day I was hired that I was the first woman administrator in a male prison.

In the entire country?

No, in that state.

New York?

Yeah.

When I was there about three months, a very ugly situation developed which could have easily turned into a riot. I wrote up two guards for racism and incompetence. I knew enough, even in those three months, not to use humanitarian reasons. I used security reasons. These people were so prejudiced that they couldn't tell the difference between one African-American prisoner and another, and they didn't understand that the people they were offending were the leaders of all the subgroups in the entire population.

That's the point that I took with that. That my life was endangered, and so were all the prisoners, and so were all the other people that were in prison, because of their bias and race hatred.

I tried to talk to somebody on the prison level, but no one would talk to me about it. They wanted to ignore it. Anyway, I sent it out of the institution to the commissioner directly, which was a major mistake.

One of the young guards came and told me that, as far as they could tell, I was the first civilian employee in the history of the New York State Department of Corrections who ever wrote up a guard. And I had written up two them, and they took action on it. So I was on their list, you know?

May I ask you at this point what they had done?

Yes. We were having a program for a Black Solidarity Day. And we were having two groups. Each one was going to be putting on about an hour performance.

But even in those three months, I had come to see in the beginning of any program it was a restless time, like about 15 minutes, where younger prisoners in particular would be wandering around and saying, "Oh, this is crock" and other terminology. And to get everybody settled down was a little bit difficult. Once they settled down, they were a wonderful audience, a fantastic audience.

So I had suggested to the guys on the committee that they come up with something that would be the first part of the program. And from my little suggestion, they came up with this fantastic thing where they were doing dramatic interpretation of poetry, and in the background there was a guy that was tapping on the bongos and someone else playing the flute. And then two other guys were doing some modern interpretive dance. And it was fabulous. They were just as good as the professional people who came up.

But we were having terrible problems in getting rehearsal time in. They never were able to get a full two hours of rehearsal. So the last week before the show, I asked them to have a morning and an afternoon rehearsal time. And then I found out that the guards would pretend that they lost the key, and they would lose pretty close to an hour every single time just because of this kind of harassment.

So I went to the Captain, and I insisted that they had continuity. That they would have the same person there in the morning and in the afternoon, to try to cut this out.

The day that all this happened, I received a phone call from the Deputy Superintendent in Charge of Security's secretary, saying there was a big thing going on with some of the guards, and I had to go to the auditorium. I came into a room that they called the chart office, and it's where the guards hung out before they got their job assignments. This one was saying, "They're saying things like brotherhood!" If you could distance yourself from it, it would be funny. But it wasn't. They were in a rage.

They said that the dancers were doing martial arts, but they weren't. It's stretching exercises, which is very much like modern interpretive dance, and that's all they were doing.

So this one guy ran into the office, and he said, "You can't have that as part of the program." So, I said, "Guess what? It's going to be back in at tomorrow's rehearsal, and it's going to be in the show on Monday afternoon." I said, "You've already wasted enough time. Let's go right now."

So when we got in there, he was afraid of the men that were there. And they were angry. They were furious at him, these musicians with big bass fiddles, and guitars, and all their equipment, and everything. And they were all milling around and angry. They were so mad at him. Meanwhile, there was a guy who was harassing a prisoner who was about something. I said, "I already told you before, we cannot discuss this now." I said, "You seem to be in so much of your own world, you don't see there's a real major problem happening here around us. I will see you tomorrow morning; we'll talk about it then."

I could see that some of the guards were asking for their passes. In that prison, they had to have a written pass that was signed to go to anything. And the guys were throwing them at him, crumpling them up, and then elbowing him out of the way. I knew that I was not in any danger because I knew all of these men.

The leader was out in the hall, and he said, "Nancy, why are some of these pigs treating us like this?" The guards were calling them niggers and saying, "These niggers think they're going to have another rehearsal this afternoon. They certainly aren't." I mean, they were saying things like that right in front of them.

So when I was leaving, this guard started yelling at me, and his face was all red, and he said, "I want you to write Noah up." I said, "For what?" He said, "He called me a pig." So, I said, "First of all, I was the person having the conversation with him, and I did not feel that anything he said was inappropriate or offensive." I said, "He was using a general term." He said, "Why are some of these pigs treating us like this?" I said, "By the way, just so you don't have any misunderstanding, you are a pig."

He screamed and yelled and argued with me all the way until we got back to the guard room. And several other people saw him, and they were kind of shocked. I made them all write statements and had them notarized.

And he was screaming at me, "You're the supervisor. You have to do this. You have to do that." I said, "I don't have to do anything." And I said, "And nothing happened. It's all in your mind and from your bigoted, narrow-minded attitude that has caused the whole problem. I am not writing anything." And I said, "And I do not want to see anything happening to that man."

So my secretary was really upset. She said, "I'm afraid for you to go back there tonight. There's nobody there for you. It's so dark up there." I had to go down into dark corridors and everything to get to the auditorium.

So, anyway, when I came I went right into the chart office. And there was only one guy in there. He said, "Well, I see your boyfriend got himself locked up." I said, "What are you talking about?" Noah had been locked up in his cell, which usually happened before you got thrown into segregation.

And I said, "I want to see the report that authorized this." And he said, "We don't have that here." So someone else, of course, escorted me inside.

As soon as I got there, I found out that the guy who played the drums and two other very important people in that program, who all lived in the same housing area, were not there. So I just waited, kept calling; finally there was a free line. I said, "Are you so and so?" He said, "Yes." I said, "Well, I want to tell you something. I want all three of them released from that tier immediately and over here in two minutes." And I said, "If they are not, I'm telling you right now, and I don't make threats, I'm going to walk right out of this prison. I'm going to walk all the way over to the Superintendent's house, and I'm going to report you, and you're not going to have a job tomorrow morning. Do you understand that? Two minutes." And I slammed the phone down. Well, they came running over there.

So the next morning I went in, and I talked to the Lieutenant, and I was able to refute the whole report.

The prisoners said, "You don't know what the guard's union is going to do to us about this and you." And I said, "Well, I don't really care because they are acting unprofessionally, and they are also creating a situation where this prison could blow up, and it's only two years after Attica. I don't think anybody wants that to happen again. This is a very major security problem that those two men caused."

So I went to the 1:00 o'clock rehearsal on Friday afternoon, and about 15 minutes after it ended, all of a sudden Noah came walking in and just shook my hand. That was a major accomplishment to them--Noah's release and writing up two guards.

So you did turn this report into the Commissioner?

The Commissioner of Corrections.

And what happened then?

They checked it all out, and both guards transferred to other jobs.

And what happened to you?

Well, my superintendent put me on an illegal six-month extension of my probation period and put me under the supervision of a new person who was the Deputy Superintendent of Programs. From that, then all the other kinds of harassments started. The next summer, I was warned by someone who had overheard a conversation where members of the Ku Klux Klan had identified me as their number one enemy because I didn't hate prisoners who weren't white, and I treated everybody the same way. I said to this person, "Well, you have to tell me who these people are. I have to know who these people are." And she said, "I can't because they would know that I told you." I said, "What do you mean?" "These people are all high-ranking officers who treat you very nicely. They're very pleasant and courteous to you. And they would know immediately that you knew. And I'm afraid. I'm afraid." So, I said, "Okay. I can understand." Later, the Education Director told me that when he was hired, the Superintendent showed him a list of all the people that were in the Klan that worked there.

The superintendent had a list of all the employees who were members of the Ku Klux Klan. And so I said, "I'm going to try to make them give me a copy of that list." Well, a couple of months went by, and then on the day after Labor Day, my secretary was not there, and I came in. I could see that somebody had been in my office and had moved things around, and drawers were open and files were out.

A letter had come in internally, you know through the internal mail, and it was something that was cut out from a the Klan magazine called *White Lightning*. It was all very bad racial, anti-black stuff that was signed, "The Ku Klux Klan."

So I told this to my boss, and he was going up to Albany for something the next day, so I called the state police in. And somebody made an appointment to come out and interview me.

And then I found out a couple of days later from my boss that there had been two investigators from the department's internal security down there about something else, and they never even did anything. So I called up there, and I said, "Are you one of the two investigators who were here on Thursday and Friday?" And he said, "Yes." So, I said, "Would you please tell me why you didn't do anything about this?" And he said, they had orders not to.

I said, "Well, I know that there is a list here of the staff who belong to the Ku Klux Klan.

Since they're declaring war on me, I want to know who they are." And he said, "They'll never let you have a copy of that list. I'm telling you this, this is really serious. You better call the F.B.I."

So I had an F.B.I. agent and a B.C.I. (Bureau of Criminal Investigation) agent, and it was a wild thing. But, finally, this superintendent was sort of harassed into an early retirement, and then they got another one there, and I knew his job was to get rid of me. They don't like whistleblowers. I knew my rights. And so this was in the *New York Times* and the *Daily News* and all kinds of newspapers, and television stations, and radio stations, and we got really good coverage.

All my friends were worried sick about me, and they wanted me to have a press conference in the beginning. And I said, "No. We can't do it now because I will just say that I have this letter and that I'm accusing them of having this knowledge, and they'll deny it. And that will be the end of it. We'll just wait. We have to have something to show that it exists in other prisons in the state, too. So that we can show that there's a conspiracy, a silence in the departments."

So what happened was on the day after Thanksgiving, I read that there was to be a big Klan rally, and the property was owned by a guard at another prison about 12 miles away. I called the F.B.I. agent up, and I said, "Listen, I just read that they're going to have this state rally." He said, "What do you mean?" I said, "Oh, for God's sakes, you know damn well you're going to have F.B.I. agents there. I just want to make sure that they listen very carefully in case they hear plans made for my demise." And I said, "I was planning to go myself when I read it." And it was so funny because F.B.I. agents are so cool and laid back. And he started yelling, "No! No!" My secretary could hear him across the room.

So that's when I called my boss up, and I said, "I have to tell you my friends are going to go the press because they're worried sick about me."

I got a phone call from the wife of one of the guards but she didn't tell me her name. She said, "You know, I have to tell you I don't agree with hardly anything that you believe in, but I've always respected you because you're a very courageous woman." And she said, "It didn't bother me when they were harassing you because they were trying to get you to quit. And even the threatening letters." "But," she said, "now they want to plant explosives in your car. And they know where you have to park your car."

I called my boss up, and I said, "I want to park my car right up in the front, right in front of the prison, next to the Superintendent's car."

Early on in your story you were telling me that someone had said to you, "Do you have any idea what the guard's union will do to you?" Do you feel there's an association between the Klan and the union?

Oh, yes. Yes, in that prison.

That Monday, the only people who spoke to me were my secretary and the prisoners. No one else spoke to me. They were all afraid. They wouldn't even make eye contact with me.

I had 17 offers from prisoners to kill those people. All I had to do was tell them who they were. I said, "No. What do you think? There's a scarcity of racists out in the community to replace people who would be killed?" And I said, "And it's not worth you spending another five minutes in here." The prisoners were very afraid because they felt that the guards would kill me in the plant and that they would accuse the prisoners of it. So, from that time on, we had a plan. Any time I had to go on the inside, I would call a guard and say, "Would you please send so-and-so down to the guard room floor; I need to talk to him about something?" Then the prisoner I called for would escort me out there. Any time I went on the inside, the prisoners always rushed up to me, and the guards would sort of be pushed out of the way. I had somebody in front of me, behind me, and on both sides of me.

So I was leaving, like 25 after 3:00 just before a shift change, and as I went into the chart office, I saw the whole room was filled with these men who all hated me. I mean, it was the most frightening thing. So I went and got my gun out of the arsenal. I just prayed, "Please, don't let the bullets fall out." And I walked out.

I want to ask you, all the threats and trials and tribulations you went through with this KKK problem, how did you survive? Why didn't they kill you?

Well, I think, for one thing, I was smart. And I'm a fighter. I mean, they knew that I was a fighter. I went up to Albany a few days after that incident with the guards, and I said to the administrator, "Are you trying to say that they think that I was castrating them because I loaded my gun up in front of them?" And he said, "Yes, that's right." "Well," I said, "you can't castrate people who are already missing two of their parts."

You bring up Attica quite often in this interview. Would you like to express your opinion about Attica?

It was something that had been developing over a period of time. To over-simplify things, you cannot treat people like animals and show no respect to them about anything and expect that they're going to take it forever. I've always felt that people can handle a major deprivation, as long as it's fairly administered, better than they can the constant, daily harassment, where the guards who work the day shift will let the prisoners do something; then the guard who comes in on the swing shift will write them up for the same thing.

The prison system is run in a quasi-military basis. You have sergeants who are over the officers, and the sergeants are under the lieutenants, and the lieutenants are under a captain. In most prisons, they only have one captain, but very big ones like they have in New York, say some of them with 3,000 prisoners, I guess they might have two captains. But no one ever seems to hold anybody accountable. They say, "Gee, John Jones is certainly sending a lot of people to segregation this month." Like maybe they might figure out the guy has a problem and try to see what it is. But it doesn't seem that ever happens. Prisoners were not allowed to get mail because there was nobody who could censor the mail. They couldn't write letters out or receive them. And there are just so many things, you know?

And they were warned. They knew ahead of time that all these things were festering and brewing. And then it just broke out. It was so horrible to see that they lied and said that the prisoners had stabbed and killed hostages, and all this other--castrated them--and, I mean, all these wild things. None of it was true. Every person who died was shot by state police or corrections people. Every single one of them.

I remember the first article that came out about the Klan in the Friday paper. When I came into work on Monday, a lot of prisoners were all out there, and they had to see me right away. Apparently, over the weekend the guards went crazy. They started locking up white prisoners and accusing them of being in the Klan. There were three main leaders: the leader of the blacks, of the Hispanics, and the whites. And they were there. And before the white prisoner could say anything, the black prisoner said, "You gotta help the white prisoners, Miss Nancy." And the white guy looked at him, and the black guy said, "Hey, man, were we all in Attica together, or weren't we?"

Winston Eagle

I am interviewing Mr. Winston Eagle. Mr. Eagle, are you aware that our conversation is being tape-recorded?

Yes, I am.

Are you further aware that I'm going to transcribe this conversation, that I'm going to print it in a book, and it's going to read by the public?

Yes.

And is that all right with you?

Yes.

All right. Mr. Eagle, can you tell me what your relationship is with the Department of Corrections?

Yes. I'm a correctional officer and President of the WPEA, and I've been employed there for ten years.

You've been a correctional officer for ten years?

Yes.

And when you say you're the President of the WPEA, what is that?

Washington State Employees Association.

Is that a union?

Yes, it's the union. It's a labor union for the state workers at the institutions.

How long have you been the president?

I've been in office now for a year.

Can you tell me a little bit about the union? What does it do?

It's a bargaining unit that we utilize for labor management, correctional officers and other staff, the nursing staff, maintenance--any employee affiliated with the institution. We mediate grievances and different labor disputes between management and the laborer itself.

You represent labor?

Yes.

And labor would be correctional officers?
Correctional officers, AC cooks, nurses, some of your office staff.
And management, that would be administration?
It's the people in Olympia, the people in administration, all the way down to our sergeants, that work on line with us. You have your department heads, supervisors and superintendents.
Okay. So, not all correctional officers are in the union?
No.
And that's by rank?
Yes. Lieutenants and CUS's are considered management, and they're not union. The sergeants on down to the officers are protected by the union.
Okay, so a sergeant down is union?
Yes.
Is there more than one union?
Currently there's another union that would like to represent us. The Teamsters solicited signatures for that purpose. Eventually, between the unions, they'll vote for a closed shop. That would determine whether or not an employee would have to enroll in the union upon taking employment there at the institution.
Is that what a closed shop means?
Yes.
It means you're required to belong to the union?
Yes.
I see. It's not a closed shop right now?
No.
Do you think it will become a closed shop?
I think so because the negative side of not having a closed shop is you get so many that's anti-union. When the union strikes for a particular goal, it's a hinder.
You said that another union is attempting to represent the workers at W.S.R. Do you have any preference yourself how things go with that?
No. I'm for whichever group comes out to be the strongest because that's what we need, the strength. I'm mainly looking at if the majority goes with a certain union, then I would definitely have to follow that majority.
At this point, we have a bunch of small groups with different beliefs and different theories on how unions should be run and what laborers need. And you got a lot of pulling the opposite way instead of all together. I believe management is pretty happy--divide and conquer. It's critical at this point. Until we become one, I don't see any fair bargaining agreement. We're 30% underpaid as it is.
When you say you're 30% underpaid, where do you get that number?

Thirty percent underpaid as opposed to the other correction officers throughout the state.
Why do they make sergeants and below union, and any rank above that not? It seems like that alone would divide you?
Well, the union saw that it would be a conflict of interest. When I first started working there, everybody was a part of the same union. If you were reprimanded by one of your supervisors, it was a big conflict of interest. It was proposed in the bargaining agreement last year that CUS's and lieutenants be excluded.
The administration, let's face it, they're human just like we are. They make mistakes. Yet and still, when they make mistakes, they'll always interpret the policies of the institution the way they want to interpret it. They tend to twist it around to the point where it best represents or serves them. And that's not good for the employees because so many of them are unjustly being accused of certain things and being reprimanded for these things at the same time.
Can you just give me an example of what they might be accused of?
It ranges from deserting your post, to excessive amount of days off, to disorderly conduct. There's a number of things--sexual harassment too. It goes on and on. If you happen not to be one of the good old boys, you're guilty, you know? And that's just the way it is. That stuff has been going on, and on, and on, and on. If you're not a good old boy, you're guilty, or if you happen to be the wrong color, you're guilty.
I've seen it many times. One time a individual left his weapon, supposedly, on the outside of the gate. And another individual left his weapon inside a vehicle that came inside the walls. These people got light sanctions. As opposed to, I've seen some people actually lose their job on something less than that. Those are very, very serious charges.
So, like I said, it all depends on who you are. If you're not one of the good old boys or if you got the wrong paint job, or if you happened at some time to piss off the superintendent or one of his relatives, you've had it. Simple as that. You're guilty.
There are officers prejudiced against because of who they happen to be, or if they've upset someone in power, or maybe the color of their skin? Is that true?
That's true, yes.
Can you address that a little bit more?
Well, as in a white officer making a request for a particular job assignment being granted the position. And a particular black officer requesting the position, before and after the white officer, being denied.
A lot of people want to close their eyes to it, but it exists, you know. I see it every day. Maybe I'm to the point where I'm used to it.
Does this prejudice also exists against inmates?
Yes.
So, if you're a black prisoner, you're not treated the same as if you're a white

prisoner?
No.
Can you tell me what some of those differences might be?
I've seen certain inmates get infracted, and when they go to the hearing, it's heard by the unit sergeant. You white, "Fine, not guilty." You black, "Guilty," or Hispanic, "Guilty," Asian, "Guilty." I've seen it.
What about female employees? Do they get prejudiced against?
One hundred percent.
A hundred percent? Could you speak to that a little more? That's a lot of prejudice.
One of my best friends ... they almost ran this lady crazy. She used to carpool with me. And you know how people talk.
She was a Caucasian?
Yes. She rode with me at least three times a week. There was two sergeants that was hitting on her. One of them even wrote letters on state memo paper. I seen it. Wanting her to leave her husband that she'd been married to for 29 years and come with him. And another one, he touched her, he grabbed her from behind.
When she reported it, right away administration built up this defense that she's imagining things.
The whole syndrome in the institution is this. You can advance quickly if you participate. If you don't participate, you're put on a shit list. And in time, they'll have you out.
My friend that rode with me, they thought we were intimate friends. But as a matter of fact, her husband was my true friend. I dropped her off and continued on home, and he'd pick her up at that spot. Worse came to worse, and they made up some story about how she was fooling around with an inmate. That was one of the biggest lies I've ever heard. The lady was very competent on the job, very smart, sharp, ready to take on any task. The lady wound up going to a mental facility for a month or so and was forced to resign. There's a lot of that that goes on in there. You have to be a strong individual, being a female, to work in an institution like that.
You have already said that it's a man's world in there. Can women legitimately raise up in the ranks?
It would really take a special type of female to accomplish that. She'd have to be smart. Her social skills would have to really be sharp because they're always laying to get you, especially if she happens to be picked out as a target.
There's a few that have, but I've found most of those have relationships within the institution.
You've been a correctional officer for ten years?
Yes, and I'm telling you, the administration puts us last on the totem pole. They are so relaxed in there. The Japanese didn't believe in Godzilla till it tore up Tokyo. And that's

just what's going to happen, and it's unfortunate that some of us will lose our lives behind it, whether it be inmate or correctional officer.

You got people dictating different rules, different ideas on how and what should take place inside an institution, or what sanctions, or what kind of punishment. I've even heard ... as far as the food that the prisoners eat ... I saw a film clipping on the news say, "They're eating gourmet salmon." The salmon that I've seen come through that institution, I don't even think your cat would eat it. But they give that to these guys. I've seen certain products come in through those doors; you look at the dates on them, and I've seen them three to six months back-dated. This is old food. But they tell us taxpayers, "This is where your taxpayer's money goes."

Even down to the construction that we get there. They'll make a mistake and say, "Oh, yeah, we forgot to put air conditioning in it." And then have to tear the whole thing down, and it costs the taxpayers lots and lots of money.

Here's a real good for instance. W.S.R. put in a proposal to go close custody. It would take $3.6 million to convert W.S.R. into a close-custody facility. In order to turn that institution into a close-custody facility, alls you'd have to do is put razor wire in between the fences. I've seen warehouses full of this razor wire they already have. Who's getting this money? That's what I want to know.

I would call it misappropriating funds if you really look at it as a taxpayer. And I'm kind of angry about it because there are so many things that come on the news--all swept under the carpet.

Because the inmates are hurting, the public's hurting; myself, as a correctional officer, I'm hurting.

You sound like a reasonable person to me, Mr. Eagle. I've spoken to several people who would categorize correctional officers as not very reasonable people. Can you speak to me a little bit about correctional officers?

Some are good, and some are bad. Some correctional officers don't know how, or don't have the social skills, to deal in that particular area. I've seen many officers that appear to be good officers. Most of them under pressure usually break.

I'll tell you something about two correctional officers I really admire. There was an inmate that had been contemplating suicide. The shift lieutenant had gotten information about it and sent two officers down to pick him up to take him to the suicide unit.

The inmate was kind of calm, and he cooperated with the officers. As they left the area, heading toward fourth floor hospital, this inmate broke and ran all the way up to the top. When he got up to the top, he went to leap over the banister. And when he went to leap over the banister, the two officers just barely caught him by his ankles before he went over. And these two officers were very, very shook up.

These two officers focused on one thing. It wasn't about being an inmate. It wasn't about being a correctional officer. It was about saving a life. After the whole incident was over, you'd think the administration would say, "Hey, good job, go ahead and take a couple days off administrative leave." Because these two guys were really shook. But nobody patted them on the head. Nobody said, "Good job."

But I admire those two. I congratulated them because I could see the fear in their eyes and the effort at saving that kid's life. Wasn't about what color he was or he was a convict. It was about a life. And nobody cared.

But I can truly say this: I'm one of the few correctional officers that can walk through that institution and not worry about getting stuck in his back. You got some correctional officers, they come there and they belittle these people. They look down on them; they push them around; they call them names; they send them through a lot of emotional trips. If they know anything about this inmate's family, they use these things against these people. I hate working with an individual like that. If an individual don't have enough compassion in his heart to....

As a matter of fact, it's sad to say, if my life was on the line, if anything was to occur, I don't think I could depend on another officer to save my life. But I could depend on that inmate, and they get the worse end of the stick all the time. And I'm not just saying that to be saying it. I'm telling you the truth. These people are human, too. But they really get the shit end of the stick. It's all about people: people needing help, people wanting help. A lot of people think that some of these people don't have any remorse for what they did. They have remorse, but they don't know how to express it.

I remember a scripture about "the keeper of the key" and often wonder how far would I go before I give up being the keeper of the key? Because, scripturally, incarceration is not of the law of God. And this country, you know, bases its foundation on God.

Why do you say that incarceration is not of the law of God?

The way I see incarceration in this country, in the way they do it, couldn't be of God, to treat another human being in that manner.

If that's, in fact, justice, then I won't be a keeper of the key very long. At the same time, I think I was brought to this place because I placed it in the Man's hand Upstairs, and that's what He gave me.

And when they threaten me about being fired, I don't have no fear because I came here with nothing, and I'll leave with nothing.

There's nothing that those people could ever do for me. They couldn't pay me enough to mistreat those individuals or another employee. I would never bear false witness against him to see that man or that woman lose their job. I've seen this type of activity going on.

In conclusion, Mr. Eagle, is there anything that you'd like to say?

I just wish the public would take responsibility in really wanting to know what goes on in an institution. To bring about this change, it's going to take all of us. Not just for the criminals to stop committing crimes, but even for us, the ones that are supposed to be there to help them. But now they got it to the point where everyone believes we're against each other.

And that's not the way it's supposed to be. There's nobody that's not capable of committing a crime. We all commit them. And until we stop pointing fingers and start dealing with ourselves, this vicious circle will continue to roll on and on.

And Corrections--that's a big title, a real big title.

Epilogue

Those who run prisons, work in them, and live in them are the minority of people affected by our American correctional system. Also affected are the families of these people, their families' families, their loved ones, their children, and you and me. No one in our society is immune.

I wrote this book to help give insight to those involved in the system. I now see that this is just the beginning of the impact this book could have. In addition to the 21 interviews printed in THE KEEPERS AND THE CAGED, I have also interviewed children of prisoners, wives of prisoners, prison therapists, and victims of crime. Those interviews will be printed in my next book, FAMILIES: DOING TIME IN AMERICA.

When I started this book, it was not my intention to come from any particular position; rather, I preferred that the readers come to their own conclusions. However, as I spoke with the people I interviewed, it occurred to me that however diverse each person's interview was, they all had one thing in common. Each made an impassioned plea to bring an end to hatred. I don't think I could put it any better than Officer Winston Eagle when he said, "To bring about this change, it's going to take all of us. Until we stop pointing fingers, and start dealing with ourselves, this vicious circle will continue to roll on and on."

I cannot thank enough all of those who risked and gave so much to see this book published. I believe that kind of commitment genuinely shows that we are more than our color, we are more than our gender, and we are more than our career choices. To paraphrase Nancy San Carlos, are we all in this together, or aren't we?

Book Order Form

To order additional copies of THE KEEPERS AND THE CAGED call our toll free number: 1-800-228-0810. You may also order by faxing this order form to our service representative at 1-800-772-9165.

Please fill out this page, remove, and fax or mail to:

Kendall/Hunt Publishing Company
4050 Westmark Drive P.O. Box 1840
Dubuque, Iowa 52004-1840

Please include a check for $16.95 per copy, plus $4.00 shipping and handling for the first book and $0.50 for each additional book. 5 books or more will be sent UPS.
Number of Copies____________@ **$16.95 Ea.................................Total** ______
Shipping Fee.................**$4.00 for first book+$0.50 for each Additional Book** ______
Total ______

Check Enclosed ( ) Please make checks payable to: Kendall/Hunt Publishing Co.

Please Charge My Account: Visa ( ) Master Charge ( ) American Express ( )

Account No...Exp. Date.................Signature............................

Name____

Address ______________________________________

City, State__________________________Zip__________

Phone Number ( )______________________________

Clarity Training

Clarity Training is a charitable, non-profit corporation that helps prisoners become responsible citizens. Clarity Training supports educational programs and projects (such as this book) that help bring awareness to the public.

If you would like to make a tax deductible donation, please fill out the information below and mail to:

Clarity Training
P.O. Box 5451
Wenatchee, Washington 98807-5451

....*cut-along-this-line.*...

Name____

Address____

City___________________________State__________Zip___________

Telephone Number (optional)
Home: (   )____________________ Work: (   )____________________

I am making a donation of:

$10.00 ( ) $20.00 ( ) $50.00 ( ) $100.00 ( ) Other: $__________

Please make your check payable to: Clarity Training.

Please add my name to the mailing list to receive information regarding:
Workshops ( ) Events ( ) Volunteering ( ) Future Books ( )

How do you want us to come out of prison? As a part
of the community, working to help it grow and become
a place anyone would want to live, with skills to hold
a real job, education so we can communicate with others
in a positive way; or broken, as we came in, with the
same issues running the monster within each of us?

Michael Spencer
Prisoner # 628598